Collision

MARYANN KELLER

Collision

GM, Toyota, Volkswagen and the Race to Own the 21st Century

CURRENCY

New York   London   Toronto   Sydney   Auckland

DOUBLEDAY

A Currency Book
PUBLISHED BY DOUBLEDAY
a division of Bantam Doubleday Dell Publishing Group, Inc.
1540 Broadway, New York, New York 10036

Currency and Doubleday are trademarks of Doubleday,
a division of Bantam Doubleday Dell Publishing Group, Inc.

Library of Congress Cataloging-in-Publication Data

Keller, Maryann.
Collision : GM, Toyota, Volkswagen and the race to own the 21st century/
Maryann Keller.
   p.   cm.
Includes bibliographical references and index.
1. Automobile industry and trade. 2. General Motors Corporation. 3. Toyota
Jidōsha Kōgyō Kabushiki Kaisha. 4. Volkswagenwerk. 5. Automobile industry and
trade—United States. 6. Automobile industry and trade—Japan. 7. Automobile
industry and trade—Germany. 8. Competition, International. I. Title.
HD9710.A2K45   1993
338.4'76292—dc20   93-11071
CIP

ISBN 0-385-46777-x

10   9   8   7   6   5   4   3   2

To

Eleanor and Andrew,
Nelson and Jung,
Julius and Engred

Acknowledgments

I HAVE LEARNED over the years that my best ideas and insights usually come in collaboration with other people, and this is certainly true when writing a book about three of the largest global auto companies. First, as an American woman, I could never have gained a full "inside" understanding of Japanese and German business and culture without the help of two people to whom I am very close.

The first is my husband, Jay Chai, a Korean-born American citizen who has become the top-ranked American executive in a major Japanese company. Jay's fluency in Japanese and his thirty-year association with one of Japan's largest trading companies have given him a unique range of perspectives on Japanese business—the way it operates at home and the way it relates to the West. I have accompanied Jay to Japan on many occasions, and there are always new things to learn.

The second person is Christiane Oppermann, an economics and business writer in Hamburg, Germany. Christiane and I met and became friends because of our common ties to the auto industry. She has considerable inside knowledge of German industry, and brings refreshing humor and personal detail to her observations. Her collaboration in this project provides both her knowledge of German industry and her perspective as a German citizen watching her country adapt to new challenges.

I had been interested in the dynamics of General Motors,

Toyota, and Volkswagen and their global impact for some time, but it was my agent, Jane Dystel, who urged me to begin putting words on paper. Jane's dedication and advice, through all the cycles of completing this book, gave me added confidence, and her judgments are always on target.

I am also grateful to Joel E. Fishman, the editor at Doubleday who understood my vision for the book and was its enthusiastic advocate, and to Bill Thomas, the editor who helped me refine my vision and philosophy.

Catherine Whitney worked closely with me to help me articulate my thoughts clearly and in an accessible fashion. She knows how to take what otherwise might sound like inside-the-business discussions and give them a human angle.

I am deeply appreciative to the many people within the industry who gave their time and input to the writing of this book. In particular, I'd like to thank Jack Smith, Carl Hahn, Dr. Shoichiro Toyoda, Tatsuro Toyoda, Hiroshi Imai, Inaki Lopez, Lou Hughes, Ira Millstein, Harry Pearce, Bill Hoglund, Jim Womack, David Brown, Yuki Togo, Hiroshi Okuda, Akira Takahashi, Dr. H. Shimohawa, Bob Lutz, Peter Frerk, Bob Eaton, George Eads, and Dr. U. Seiffert. Special thanks to Mary Anne Maskery, Japan correspondent for *Automotive News,* and Miyako Yoda of Toyota, who endured my endless questions and patiently provided answers.

Contents

xii   Contents

Collision

INTRODUCTION

The New Global Big Three

A fine wind is blowing a new direction in time.

—D. H. Lawrence

MOST PEOPLE remember their first car. What it was like to get behind the wheel for the first time. The virgin smell of the leather. The feeling of satisfaction and ownership. The thrill of taking it out on the road. It's a universal experience, whether you live in Chicago or Tokyo or Berlin. Arthur C. Clarke once wrote, "Technology is indistinguishable from magic," and that's the way it's been with the automobile. Its invention changed millions of lives, injecting them with the magic of speed, freedom, and opportunity. Beyond that, the business of building and selling cars, which is the subject of this book, has changed the way the world works.

The cars that sit in our driveways have become one of the most predictable facts of our existence. Barely a century old, their absence today would be inconceivable, since most people now alive couldn't fathom a world without cars. They have become a simple fact of life.

But cars are more than the sum of their parts. And although they have become so ordinary that we rarely contemplate it, their influence is massive and far-reaching.

Consider the business of building and selling cars. There is no other product on earth whose existence incorporates so many materials, processes, and technologies, and so complex an intelligence system—in the creation of the car and throughout its useful life. No other product has such a dramatic impact on the world economy. Most people can grasp this in a personal way because a car is the second most expensive purchase (next to a home) they will ever make. It is essential—both a pragmatic and an emotional choice. They might not know who made their home appliances, but everyone knows who made their cars. Furthermore, unlike appliances, which silently perform their functions until they conk out and have to be replaced, people are constantly intrigued by what's new in cars. They regularly replace perfectly functional models so that they can participate in technological upgrades.

On the scale of global business, carmaking is so vast an enterprise that it requires its own infrastructure, which includes energy, technology, electronics, computer programming and engineering, as well as every kind of science, and a wide variety of systems and materials—plastics, rubber, petrochemicals, machine tools, metal stamping and castings, conveyors, and painting systems. In order to build a car, massive resources and talents must come together, comprising a substantial percentage of a nation's economy. Without the car, many industries could not survive. It is commonly understood in developing nations, such as China, Mexico, India, and Brazil, that one of the first steps to economic maturity is the establishment of a car industry—starting perhaps with transplant facilities from established companies, but ultimately leading to local control of the entire process.

The auto industry stands alone in its ability to affect the economic fate of nations, just as it is unparalleled in its effect on the lives of individual consumers. It is a powerful force. In the pages of this book, I want to take you inside its core and show you something of its drama—which is, like everything else we experience in this life, a very human drama.

Often, when I tell people that I am a financial analyst for the automobile industry, their first response is one of surprise because I am a woman in a "man's field." But after the surprise fades, their eyes begin to glaze over. They assume that my occupation has nothing to do with them—that it exists on a remote plain where people study stock prices and chart the rise and fall of corporate earnings.

Yet the car business is only tangentially about finance, in the sense that all businesses are a part of the economy. In order to perform my job, I must do more than study trends and numbers. I must immerse myself in the life of the business. I have learned that in its essence, this industry is about men (and occasionally women) who grapple with issues that sometimes overwhelm them and at other times inspire them to rise above their own limitations. The story of the automotive industry is about that familiar mix of human characters—from the blind company loyalist, to the narrow-minded autocrat, to the fervent "car guy" whose eyes sparkle when he talks about twelve-cylinder engines, active suspensions, and antilock brakes; it's about the political insider, the unconventional outsider, the quiet workman, and the rare visionary; it's about people who love the car business because they've grown up in it, because fathers and grandfathers have passed the passion down to them—three generations in a factory town—and sometimes it's about people who don't know much about cars, couldn't tell you how they are built, but who understand what people want and help to shape that desire into reality.

All these players, and many others, fill the ranks of the world's great auto companies, each leaving his mark in large or small ways. Fifty years ago, their faces were mostly American. Today, they bear the diverse imprints of many cultures, and struggle to understand one another and to learn from each other's experiences as they share a world stage well beyond the cozy confines of their home cultures. They are competitors, but not in the way we have come to understand that term. The competitive movements now seem more like a chess game than a war.

In this new environment the decisions the great auto companies make today will affect entire nations for many years to come.

The new Global Big Three, as I call them, are General Motors, Toyota, and Volkswagen. Many people have expressed surprise at my choices. In particular, they wondered how I could exclude

Ford and Chrysler from the list. After all, the term "Big Three" has long been synonymous with the three American carmakers. Ford, especially, has been a staple of auto manufacturing ever since Henry Ford invented mass production. To some extent, every carmaker in this century has borrowed from Ford's genius. Ford also pioneered the "living wage," then five dollars a day, so that workers who produced cars would also be able to afford to purchase them. But while Henry Ford's company has remained a strong carmaker, it has not been an innovator in this industry since the 1920s. And it is not number one in any market.

Chrysler has sometimes seemed like an innovator, especially in the full flush of Iacoccaism. Today, having risen from the ashes several times, it is one of the best-run auto companies. But it does not have the global presence to match those I have selected.

Neither Chrysler nor, for that matter, other contenders like Honda or Nissan has anything approaching the size, wealth, and global scope of General Motors, Toyota, and Volkswagen. Even though the many problems of these three companies are frequently aired in the press, their problems do not disqualify them from positions in the Global Big Three. We must examine a variety of factors.

First, each of these three companies is the largest in its home market, a factor that cannot be ignored. We're talking about massive enterprises whose influence spans whole continents—companies that earn and dispense many billions of dollars a year and have a direct impact on the survival of related industries.

Second, each of these companies has been, at various points in time, the driving innovator in the automobile industry. Among them, they have defined management principles, organizational strategies, and product and marketing concepts that have created new paradigms for their own and other industries. For most of this century, GM has been the personification of the car industry. It was Alfred Sloan, the automotive genius of the 1920s, who devised the concept of carmaking for every class and purpose. Volkswagen rose from the shambles of post–World War II Germany to become the first foreign car company to make a meaningful dent in the American market. Beyond that, VW was the first to truly market a reliable, inexpensive small car for the masses. Toyota, tenacious beyond our Western power to imagine, invented a production system that was so brilliantly efficient that every other auto company has borrowed from its model.

The contributions of these three companies have been so fundamental to carmaking that it is fair to say other successful companies owe them credit for their pioneering efforts.

Today, these companies are distinguished not only by their size, wealth, and past achievements but also by the fact that they all face major challenges that are forcing sea changes in their corporate cultures. Still large and influential, they are nevertheless being forced to confront the emerging realities of a new era. These crises are not unique to the auto industry, but our three companies are in a special position to take the lead in resolving them. Because of their visibility and their influence over other industries, GM, Toyota, and Volkswagen will be carefully watched, and any one of them might serve as a model for other companies.

These challenges demand answers to questions that have seldom been raised before in such an urgent way. They include:

- How do companies shake their entrenched nationalistic positions to participate fully in a global economic process—where the methods that made them formidable might have to be adjusted to meet the needs of other cultures?
- How do successful corporations, which by their very natures grow rigid and cautious, free themselves to learn, experiment, and adapt to the changing world around them?
- How do corporations govern themselves to ensure, not just survival, but the prosperity of all stakeholders (not just stockholders) and the integrity of their long-term missions?
- How do auto companies remain conscious of the impact their product has on society, and dare to limit the ways in which it is destructive to the environment and the infrastructure?
- How do conventional companies grow unconventional leaders who can see the future while struggling with the immediacies of the present?

These are the broad questions that will be explored in the pages of this book. Together, we will search for the ways that GM, Toyota, and Volkswagen are being forced to address them at the same time they struggle to stay alive. Of course, one might ask, if GM, Toyota, and Volkswagen have so many problems, how on earth can they be expected to take the lead in resolving such universal issues?

I have learned, by observing this industry and others, that severe blows can sometimes provide a catharsis that leads to transformation. Especially in big business, where attitudes and structures become entrenched, it is often the case that only the most severe crisis provides the window for change. We will see many examples of this dynamic at work among the new Global Big Three, because each of them is standing at a critical moment—a crossroads between the past and future where daring actions will be required.

I have also selected these three because we live in a different kind of environment than we did twenty-five years ago, when American auto companies thought they could ignore their offshore competitors. My Global Big Three represent the triangle of international leadership: America, Europe, and Japan. All three deeply reflect their national heritage and social culture, providing a look into the soul of their countries.

Because the issues these companies must address are so universal, this book isn't just about cars and carmakers. I hope it will serve as a cautionary tale for all businesses, especially those that have grown fat and complacent with their past successes.

In particular, all companies are challenged to become openminded—to learn from others and to observe the competition, regardless of where it is located. The greatest risk comes from not understanding the global nature of industry. As much as many people (including corporate and government leaders) might clamor for a return to nationalistic ways, the fact is, we have moved far beyond the time when any country or business can be isolated from others. Again, the auto industry has served as the primary example of this reality. Since the 1970s, carmakers in the United States have seen their greatest rivalry, not among U.S. companies, but with the Japanese. Likewise, Europe's industry has been challenged. Traditionally, it was closed and protected from the outside. Now, suddenly, with a movement toward a true common market without internal borders, it must anticipate more foreign competition.

The world has become smaller. Companies headquartered thousands of miles away are effectively right next door. Businesses no longer own their home turfs, but neither can they afford to be reckless in their international pursuits. Furthermore, as you will learn from the experiences of these companies, there is no such thing as a final victor. At the peak of its success, each of these companies grew fat and rich and complacent. They became vulnerable.

The title of this book is *Collision*. At first glance, one might infer that the collision is expected to take place among the companies themselves—resulting in a final victory for one or the other. But the reality is much more profound. I believe that we are seeing a collision, not between competitors, but with the future. The twenty-first century challenges the tried-and-true ways of the twentieth century and presents a new world scenario that is unfamiliar to everyone. The central question of this book is: Will these three companies, representing the cultures and economies of America, Europe, and Japan, survive the sea change or flounder? Will the actions of the men who are standing at the helms be wise and visionary, or will they revert to fatally anachronistic courses?

These are fundamentally important questions. They are relevant to every individual, to every company, and to every nation. Let's watch how the new Global Big Three struggle with their challenges, and learn from them who will win or lose in the next century.

—Maryann Keller
March 1993

ONE

Breathless in Tokyo

Knowing others is intelligence; knowing yourself is true wisdom. Mastering others is strength; mastering yourself is true power.

—Tao

Tokyo—October 1991

IT WAS A FINE DAY for a pilgrimage. The sun was high and warm, and the early autumn winds had blown away much of the smog that normally colors the air in Tokyo. Thousands of cars crawled along the Shuto Expressway toward Makuhari, passing through the gray industrial/commercial area surrounding the city. Logjams were a daily event on this heavily trafficked road, but on a normal day this would be a forty-five-minute trip. It had already been more than two hours since these travelers left the plush lobbies of their Tokyo hotels.

It was press day at the Tokyo Motor Show and everyone was headed, as one body, to the new Makuhari Messe (exhibition center), a sprawling two-year-old hotel-office complex built to accommodate large exhibitions and trade shows. Makuhari was within view of Japan's Disneyland, and passengers could see the spires of Fantasyland Castle from the highway as the cars and buses crept toward their destination.

An American veteran of auto shows back home—say, at New York City's Jacob Javits Center or Detroit's Cobo Hall—would be astonished by the traffic, crowds, and sense of expectation surrounding this event, which topped even the premier auto shows in Geneva, Frankfurt, and Paris in attendance and in attracting the world's automotive press and industry leaders. Although America has been, for nearly a century, the fatherland of the auto industry, its car shows have been small, local exhibitions, often no more inspiring than an afternoon in a large auto showroom. Recently, Detroit had tried to change that, but it still hadn't generated the drama and combined sense of expectation and dread that the Westerners felt at the Tokyo show.

In Tokyo it was different, not only in style but also in substance. The Tokyo Motor Show, held every two years, was an important business event, attended by foreign automotive executives, car dealers from around the world, and car-crazy Japanese consumers, who came to see the latest models that would make their nearly new cars obsolete. It was not merely a showcase of new products. The industry counted on the event to boost domestic sales. Later that week, the public would arrive some 2 million strong. Most of them would travel not by car, but by train—a quick thirty-minute trip from the center of Tokyo.

As evidence of the seriousness with which Japan viewed its industry, and the auto industry in particular, Crown Prince Naruhito himself was on hand to open the show—just as his father, Emperor Akihito, had done for years before him. Although his presence was ceremonial in nature (one could hardly imagine the future emperor driving a car), it was a testament to the cordial relationship between industry and the state in Japan. The executives of each Japanese company lined up at attention, and a flurry of bowing accompanied the prince's rounds to each exhibit. At the Toyota stand, Eiji Toyoda, the venerable board chairman, Dr. Shoichiro Toyoda, his nephew and company president, and every other key executive formed a receiving line according to rank to greet the thirty-one-year-old prince. They each bowed stiffly, with the reserve prescribed by Naruhito's exalted status as heir to the Chrysanthemum Throne.

In spite of the ceremony and glitter, the gaiety was somewhat artificial. The Japanese were deadly serious about the show, and everything operated with well-timed precision. Security on press days was tight, which was typical of events in Japan. Credentials were studiously checked by uniformed entrance guards who were polite but rigorous in their duties.

This, the twenty-ninth such exhibition, would be the largest ever, attracting thousands of foreign visitors, press, and industry insiders, in addition to the citizenry. Everything within ten square miles of Makuhari was bristling with the energy of the event. Hotels in Tokyo and those around the convention center were packed, and there were many meetings, press conferences, luncheons, and parties hosted by each of the world's automakers.

The show's futuristic theme, "Discovering a New Relationship: Man, Car and Earth as One," was soothing in its suggestion of harmony among clashing forces—a hint of "green" consciousness, a high-tech vision, and regard for the human spirit that was the real driving force for all.

The show was designed to bedazzle as well as to inform—with the clear emphasis on bedazzlement. Noise and color assaulted the senses. Beautiful cars rotated on platforms, and young Japanese women, dressed in bright suits and perky hats, stood everywhere, an integral if nonfunctional part of the displays. Each company competed to show the most attractive or unusual cars and the most beautiful girls, thus grabbing the attention of TV crews who would carry the first visuals that night to Japanese consumers. Press and invited guests crowded into glittering exhibits that seemed less of the earth than of space—silver, gold, and electric blue being the dominant colors. Everywhere there were cars—new models introduced in conjunction with the show to maximize visibility, some only in the concept stage. These "concept cars" provided a glimpse of the future, and although some were too bizarre ever to be produced, they were clever enough to draw the photographers. There were cars with cute names like the Cappuccino; tiny, lightweight vehicles constructed from aluminum, titanium, and composite plastics; cars using alternate fuels like hydrogen, methanol, and electricity; and "intelligent" systems that enhanced night vision, navigated a car through traffic, or sounded a warning if the car drifted toward a ditch.

Mazda displayed its bubble-body HR-X, a silver space-capsule-style car, hydrogen-fueled and ready for takeoff. Nissan's Cocoon, a product of the company's California design studio, clearly had California dreamers in mind, with a thickly padded womblike interior, a cat door in the tailgate, and a drowsiness monitor that sounded a warning buzzer and sprayed a wake-up scent if the car detected that the driver was getting sleepy. Honda showed the FS-X all-aluminum sedan and the ERX, a two-seater that placed the passenger behind the driver, jet-fighter style.

There were outlandish vehicles, too, impractical but crowd pleasers. The Isuzu Nagisa was hyped as the first amphibious car; it literally doubled as a boat. Suzuki's "Ugly Duck" all-terrain bike was bright yellow with balloon tires, duck-eye headlamps, and a duck-beak-shaped front mud guard.

Toyota, whose inexpensive compact cars had taken America by storm for years, used the show to tread deeper into traditional American terrain, displaying vehicles like the Fun Runner, a roomy four-seater with a sunroof and a rear sun deck; and the luxurious Aristo, which would sell in the United States as the GS 300. Also on display was the Avalon, a concept car unlike any other. A convertible "designed to feel like a Batmobile," it was fitted with oval sliding panels that closed flat across the top when the car wasn't in use. Unlike a standard convertible, there was no accommodation for protection from the elements, which made it impractical for anything but the mildest weather. Nevertheless, the car was so original it attracted large crowds to Toyota's stand.

Off to the side in a tented area were the electric car prototypes. They drew less attention than the main exhibits but were nevertheless interesting for their futuristic promise. Daihatsu's Rugger could travel at speeds of twenty-five miles per hour, and Nissan's Electric President twelve miles per hour. They were not commercially viable, but there were enough of them to suggest that Japan was prepared to provide electric-powered models if that was what the regulators demanded.

The German automakers were sprinkled among their Japanese

competitors. Most of their new cars had already been presented six weeks earlier at the Frankfurt Auto Show. There Volkswagen had shown its new Golf, making a big splash with the announcement that the car would be fully recyclable; the company would take it back at the end of its useful life.

When Volkswagen unveiled the Audi Avus Quattro, it quickly became one of the biggest hits of the Tokyo show. At 4:00 P.M. on press day, VW chairman Carl Hahn, assisted by actress Mariel Hemingway, whose provocative body-hugging outfit was an eye-popping contrast to the primly dressed Japanese models, presented the car to a near stampede of reporters. The celebrity spectacle no doubt enhanced the crowds, but the car itself was worth the attention. With its sleek, all-aluminum body and oversize wheels, the Avus was reminiscent of the Auto Union Grand Prix and the record-breaking racing cars of the 1930s. This model was built to travel at speeds of 212 miles per hour.

Never mind that the world's modern highways were so car-glutted that such speeds belonged more in the realm of fantasy than reality. The Japanese were enamored of the high-tech gadgets, sleek style, and the fact that the Avus was a German-built car. They revered German engineering, and even bought enough cars to run an automotive trade deficit with Germany. They were delighted that Audi was displaying this important car at Makuhari. It was like the "mountain" coming to them.

Noticeably missing from the presentation was Ferdinand Piech, chairman and CEO of Audi, VW's luxury car subsidiary. Officially, he was said to have kidney problems, but there were rumors that Hahn had asked him not to come. Hahn enjoyed having the spotlight to himself and he might have resented the fact that VW's big hit at the show was a creation of Audi.

Piech might not have minded staying home. Although he was considered a brilliant engineer, his social skills were hardly on a par with Hahn's. Japanese car company executives still talked about an earlier trip Piech had made to their country. One day, he had been taken to visit the Yasukuni Memorial Shrine, where the Shinto priest showed him a treasured collection of old samurai swords. Piech took the most beautiful of the collection in his hands and examined it carefully before returning it with a bow and a tight smile. He told the priest, "This one is a fake." There was a stunned silence. Japanese protocol forbade this type of directness, and Piech's hosts were deeply embarrassed by the comment, even though he was later proved to be right. The incident spoke volumes about Piech's unwillingness to abide by the standard courtesies if they stood in the way of truth. Hahn, on the other hand, was an expert people pleaser. At the Tokyo Motor Show, with Mariel Hemingway at his side, he glowed. Of course, his hosts were happy to treat him with all the deference custom allowed. The fact is, there's no place like Japan if you're a Western dignitary or industrialist. You're made to feel important, and reporters cling to your words as if they are spoken by a god. The deference may be more facade than reality, but it can be ego-boosting.

Hahn was in his element at the show, although he appeared tired and jet-lagged. He loved to be on center stage and, unlike the Americans who came grudgingly and full of complaints about the Japanese, he had long professed that Germany had to be an open market. German auto companies depended on exports just as the Japanese did, and Hahn didn't want to appear to be hypocritical by attacking the Japanese while his professed strategy was to expand VW's reaches to new territories, including Japan.

Hahn's reputation in Japan was that of a friend, not an enemy, and he was treated as such. Volkswagen was the best-selling import brand in Japan. For years, Nissan had assembled the Passat there. Although its success was limited, it had the distinction of being the only foreign car actually produced on Japanese soil. Volkswagen also had a special relationship with Toyota, since Toyota's pickup trucks were built by VW in Europe. Back home, Hahn proudly showed visitors at the Rötehof, VW's guesthouse in Wolfsburg, a huge vase sent to him by Dr. Shoichiro Toyoda to commemorate the reunification of Germany. He felt the gift was proof of his special relationship with the Japanese.

Fantasy was certainly a heady presence at the Tokyo show—be it the promise of space age technology or the pretty young women who were everywhere, holding open car doors, serving refreshments, or twirling in tandem to music, on platforms surrounding the highly polished cars.

Many displays were larger than life, stunning and seductive feasts for the eyes and imaginations. Sushi, beer, and even champagne flowed during press days, a real change for the Japanese, who in leaner economic times ran these affairs strictly "BYO," unlike the culinary extravaganzas at European shows. The extra flourishes were one more sign of the way Japan had come of age in the world vehicle market. Their new status required that guests be treated like royalty.

Casual outsiders (and even some more knowledgable insiders) would never guess that the glitzy displays masked an uncomfortable sense that the dream was about to end. Under the bright lights of Makuhari, there was deep anxiety among Japanese automobile executives. Even as they smiled and boasted and bowed, the Japanese stock market was hitting new lows every day. The confidence on display at the Tokyo Motor Show was hardly more real than the multicolored perfection of Fantasyland just a few miles away.

Still, the fears remained well hidden, and even the most seasoned industry watchers, whose cynical eyes were accustomed to cutting through curtains of hype with sharp, ready blades, were heralding the show as one of the most important in history.

A few notable exceptions were found among the American executives. Although their presence was stronger than it had been in the past, there was little in their exhibits that anyone would find unique or tantalizing. The one car Japanese consumers were eager to see—GM's Saturn—hadn't made the trip. While the German exhibits were crowded with journalists, the U.S. stands remained quite empty. Even if American carmakers had tried to make more of a splash, it was unlikely their stands would have attracted much attention. The Japanese assigned little status to American cars. The attitude was: Why own a Cadillac when you can drive a Mercedes or a BMW? The fact that American cars did not have right-hand drive made them even less appealing. The frequent complaints that the Japanese were unfairly excluding American cars from their market ignored the reality that the vehicles had not been able to create an image and identity to go along with the high prices.

Now Lloyd Reuss, GM's president, wandered the aisles, expressionless but for the slight salesman's smile and petulant downturn of his lip as he toured the competition's exhibits and took a cursory look at the new array of cars designed to knock his company further into the ditch. Members of the press followed in his wake, angling for a comment from the president of the world's largest, but somewhat tarnished, car company. "Not much to see here," he shrugged finally, dismissing the show as a nonevent on the world automotive scene. He was unable or simply refused to give the Japanese their due, even in the face of such overwhelming evidence.

American carmakers were still waiting for Japan's prowess to vanish in a burst of smoke. Their lackluster presence at the show seemed to announce: "We don't acknowledge the threat. Therefore, it does not exist." Lloyd Reuss and others like him had still not figured out that, after more than twenty years, Japan's carmaking success was not a fluke.

Tokyo—January 1992

A SECOND PILGRIMAGE. The president of the United States, George Bush, alit from the ramp of the blue and white Air Force 747 into the tacky, overcrowded Narita Airport—about forty miles from the center of Tokyo. The airport was chaotic. Inside, the shabby ticket and waiting areas were perpetually filled with crowds of people, who clouded the air with cigarette smoke. The airport, with its single runway, was surrounded by a high fence topped with coils of barbed wire, put in place to hold back the small group of farmers and their left-wing allies who occasionally gathered to protest further expansion of the airport. It stood on land that had been taken from farmers, and a few of them continued to stoke the flames of outrage. Some years ago, the group took over the airport's control tower and destroyed part of it. The memory of that incident was strong enough for officials to fear this group, as ragtag as it might appear.

Bush was in Japan in the role of "CEO of America," and he

had two agendas. The first was to urge the Japanese to open their market to more American products. Japan's trade surplus had reached huge proportions, with three-fourths of it accounted for by automobiles and auto parts. In 1991 American companies sold only 32,000 cars in Japan, most of them manufactured in Japanese-owned plants in the United States. By contrast, Japanese carmakers sold more than 2.5 million cars in America that same year. Despite repeated reassurances that the deficit would eventually narrow, it showed every evidence of widening. Bush hoped to address what Senator Donald Riegle of Michigan had termed "an economic Pearl Harbor."

The second part of Bush's agenda was to encourage Japan to be a better citizen in the United States, and again the focus was on carmakers. Although every Japanese auto company except Daihatsu now had North American assembly plants that employed American workers, it was just the tip of the iceberg. Assembly plants were not full-fledged manufacturing facilities. They still depended on parts and components imported from Japan. The so-called transplant factories revealed the importance of parts producers in the wealth creation of the industry. American parts producers complained that they couldn't break down the *keirutsu* structure that bound Japanese automakers to specific groups of suppliers as though they were part of a single family. This had recently become an issue in Europe as well.

Bush was counting on this trip to make some election-year hay back home by showing Americans he cared about jobs and was prepared to make their interests the focus of his globe-hopping excursions. Bush had often been criticized for spending too much time abroad, even as conditions in the States worsened. He had, in fact, postponed this trip from its originally scheduled date in November to show that he was concentrating on domestic issues. When he finally decided to make the trip, he tried to demonstrate by the makeup of his entourage that his agenda was to win jobs. America was still deep in recession, and auto production had just recorded its worst results since the recession of 1982. Unemployment was high and Bush needed help. He hoped the trip would accomplish what he had been unable to do by staying home.

Bush was joined by a group of more than twenty American

businessmen, but most of them were ignored as public attention focused on the powerful chairmen of Detroit's Big Three: Bob Stempel of General Motors, tall with sloping shoulders, looking grim and exhausted; Chrysler's Lee Iacocca, vigorous and arrogant, a longtime Japan-basher (he was heard on the Nixon Watergate tapes using the pejorative "Japs"); and Harold (Red) Poling, the quiet, fiery-haired chairman of Ford. Their presence was not a last-minute decision. At the Tokyo Motor Show in October, representatives of the U.S. Department of Commerce were poking around, trying to lay the groundwork for a series of meetings between American and Japanese auto executives. When Bush rescheduled his trip, the three chairmen became the featured players. Their presence was meant to demonstrate that the Americans were "armed for bear," but instead the visit had the eerie feel of a conquered nation groveling before the victors. One observer noted that it reminded him of 1962 when the Japanese prime minister went to Paris to see Charles de Gaulle, who dismissed him as a "transistor salesman."

Japan's prime minister, Kiichi Miyazawa, was eager to meet with Bush and his emissaries, although his remarks prior to the meeting betrayed that he was not altogether displeased with the state of things. "General Motors is like the Stars and Stripes to the U.S.," he said slyly. "I can imagine how shocking it might be when that company is beaten by the Japanese."

Atsushi Otomo, director of the Japanese Automobile Dealers Association, was equally blunt and more pragmatic. "If American cars were attractive to Japanese customers, we could sell them," he said. "But American cars are not tailored to Japanese needs. They are too big and they have the steering wheel on the left side." Otomo asked why, if Japan had built a fortress against imports, were the Europeans doing so well there? BMW alone sold more cars in Japan in 1991 than all of Detroit combined. In fact, while Detroit's car sales had declined in Japan, Germany's sales had increased fivefold in the past fifteen years. Even though this surge gave them only 2 percent of the Japanese market, the message was clear: The Germans were welcome because their cars held appeal, but nobody wanted America's left-side-drive cars, which now seemed to need the help of a president-turned-salesman to unload them on reluctant Japanese consumers.

Although the trip had been in the works for months, it was sloppily planned. Informed of the intended visit of Bush and his entourage, the Japanese were given little indication of what the group hoped to accomplish. In light of the coming U.S. elections, the Japanese wanted to make Bush look good, since they preferred the predictability of his reelection to the uncertainty of a Democratic administration. On the campaign trail Democrats had been talking loudly about the need for tighter trade restrictions. But even though the Japanese wanted to help Bush, the trip's planners made it hard by failing to articulate concrete goals.

The American auto executives were scheduled to participate in a hastily organized series of meetings with leaders of Japanese industry, to be held at the Hotel Okura, which was located across from the American Embassy. Representing the Japanese auto industry would be executives from Toyota, Nissan, Honda, Mazda, and Mitsubishi. The Americans planned to present "the Poling Plan," a proposal for managed trade authored by the Ford chairman, who was emerging as the successor to the combative Iacocca as the number one trade-basher. His plan was agreed to by the others. According to the Americans, Japanese car companies were not behaving like good global citizens. They were flooding the U.S. market with cars but their own market was closed tight as a drum. For their part, the Japanese carmakers appreciated the need to heal some of the hostility between the two nations and correct some of the trade imbalance. But they firmly believed that America's car industry was suffering at its own hands, not at Japan's. Why, they wondered among themselves, didn't America focus on making itself more competitive, rather than trying to solve its problems through trade barriers?

The meetings yielded little and Iacocca did not disguise his anger. "They say all the problems are our fault," he complained. "That's like blaming our Army and Navy for Pearl Harbor because we weren't ready."

Bob Stempel took aim at Toyota in particular. "Toyota is a

fierce competitor. Just put them in the warrior category," he said bitterly. "To hell with fence and parry. It's slash and kill."

Later, Stempel complained, "I didn't want to go. I told my board of directors, 'This trip is going to generate more bad publicity than we can handle.' The good news is, I was right. The bad news is, I was right."

Honda's CEO Nobuhiko Kawamoto countered, perhaps tongue in cheek, "The Americans say that their automobiles are as competitive as other makes. This message has not been properly transmitted to the Japanese customer."

What began as a scheme to "get tough with the Japanese" ended badly for Bush and his Detroit-based traveling companions. To be sure, vague promises were made, there were smiles all around, and the ever-gracious Japanese even looked politely away when the American president ended the trip by vomiting on the prime minister during a state dinner. But the men returned to the United States with little to show for their visit except a loose agreement for Japanese auto companies to buy more American parts and components and to try and encourage import of American cars. Actually, Bush did sell a few cars on the trip. In its wake, a handful of Japanese executives rushed to buy Cadillacs and Lincolns as their chauffeur-driven vehicles. It was a public way of offering a small gesture to the Americans, but it held no real meaning.

Bush and his entourage knew it wasn't much of a victory, and Kenichi Ohmae, chairman of the McKinsey Consulting firm in Tokyo, confirmed it. He admitted freely that Japanese companies could easily fulfill some of their promises without exactly "buying American."

"We will buy tires," he said. "Bridgestone owns Firestone. Sumitomo Rubber owns Dunlop. Yokahama Rubber owns Mohawk. Thank you very much." Ohmae's comments demonstrated a new but barely appreciated fact: One could purchase materials from a Japanese-owned entity and still "buy American."

Barely a week had passed after Bush's return to the United States before insults began to fly back and forth across the ocean. Japan started it with an ill-considered remark by a member of the Diet, calling American workers lazy and illiterate. Americans responded with a massive display of hurt feelings, culminating in Buy America campaigns. It wasn't the first time a Japanese official had suffered public foot-in-mouth disease. Periodically, America-bashing and even racist words slipped from the lips of Japanese officials. In 1987 similar remarks by Makoto Kuroda, vice-minister for international affairs with the Ministry of International Trade and Industry (MITI), were said to be partially responsible for Congress's decision to impose a tariff on Japanese semiconductor products. Ironically, the recent incident could not have come at a worse time for the Japanese, since Americans were already becoming concerned about Japan's rampant land grab of trophy U.S. properties and landmarks like the Pebble Beach Golf Course, Columbia Pictures, and Rockefeller Center. The trip, although widely ridiculed in the press as a poor way to pursue American access to the Japanese market, did begin to awaken feelings of insecurity in the American public, who were already frightened by rising unemployment and a recession. Lee Iacocca, with his customary bluster, jumped feetfirst into the fight. "I, for one, am fed up hearing from the Japanese that all our problems in this country are our own damn fault," he raved. "We don't have idiots running General Motors, Ford and Chrysler or our suppliers. Our workers are not lazy and stupid."

The insult fest merely highlighted negative perceptions that had been slowly brewing in America. According to a 1992 study released by the Pacific Institute, American opinions about Japan for the past twenty years had generally been mixed, with an overall positive sense of Japan's status as a friend and ally. But, the report stated, "During the last two years, polling evidence begins to mirror what one discussant called 'startling change.' An ongoing Gallup study reports that there is a 33 percent drop in American opinion rating Japan in 'very' or 'mostly favorable' categories." The report speculated that with the demise of the Soviet military threat, the Japanese economic threat was foremost in American minds.

Americans had good reason to be angered by the Japanese attitude of superiority, and business leaders had even better reason to be worried about the increasing influence of Japanese companies. But on a more fundamental level, the rift was caused by the frustration of trying to understand a culture and people whose actions consistently defied Western rationality. The differences between America and Japan involved a complex combination of geography, ethnic makeup, and religious heritage. It was difficult for Americans to grasp the fact that in Japan 123 million people (about half the population of the United States) lived in an area roughly the size of Montana. They lived in a monolithic, homogeneous society, without a strong religion shaping their values and moral behavior. Rather, elements of Buddhism, Confucianism, and Shinto, the "official" religion—created a highly conformist, rigid society where everyone had a place and accepted the rules that governed one's position. Shinto, which mixed ancestor worship with the deification of the emperor, was used more as a political ideology than as a force for moral and ethical behavior. The origins of racial superiority rested in the Shinto teaching that the Japanese emanated from the sun-goddess, giving them a special position in the world. The home of the sun-goddess was the Isuzu River (Isuzu Motor Company was named for it), from which it spawned all other gods.

The Japanese were so encased in the myths of their seamless tradition that before the late nineteenth century, Japan was a completely closed agrarian country, under imperial shogun rule. Contact with the Western world was virtually forbidden. Even after the doors opened under the Meiji Empire, Japan remained culturally chauvinistic and frozen in a mentality of cultural superiority.

Although they claimed to feel constantly threatened by the West, there was little acknowledgment of their own cultural failings. Ethnocentric ideals were taught in the schools and demonstrated in the marketplace. One example: The government claimed that Japanese blood was so different from Western blood that drugs approved in Europe and the United States were required to go through five additional years of testing before they were approved in Japan. But while the Japanese seemed blind to their own racism, they were fond of ascribing racist motivations to the West—especially America. In his controversial book *The Japan That Can Say No,* Shintaro Ishihara, an outspoken member of the Diet, wrote bluntly, "In World War II . . . the United

States bombed German cities and killed many civilians but did not use atomic bombs on the Germans. U.S. planes dropped them on us because we were Japanese. Every American I mention this to denies that race was the reason, but the fact remains that nuclear bombs were dropped on Hiroshima and Nagasaki. We should never forget this. The same virulent racism underlies trade friction with the United States."

Americans might counter that they should never forget that the Japanese bombed Pearl Harbor without being provoked. But the Japanese had a ready excuse for that, too. The attack was justified by America's refusal to sell them steel and oil. What could they do, poor resourceless nation that they were? On and on, the debate raged back and forth, with even the most logical words masking the deeply felt hostility between the two nations.

William Holstein, writing in *The Japanese Power Game,* placed the issue of Japan's craving for economic strength in perspective, noting that "Japan is a society where the struggle for economic power is paramount. . . . Any tactic is acceptable. It's revealing that there is no precise equivalent in Japanese for the Western concept of 'fair.' There are conflicting interpretations. One is that if I have power over you, you submit on the surface while struggling to overturn me by stealth."

Not that the Americans and Germans were outstanding world citizens. America also had a superiority complex, and it resented not being given the deference it felt was its due. The perceived threat from Japan was bringing some ugly behavior to the forefront, even from the nation's leaders. For their part, the Germans had their own problems with ethnocentricity. In many ways, they were very similar to the Japanese. They were rigidly tied to the German way of doing things.

The clash of the world's economic superpowers was inevitable as the world economy approached a period of interdependence unforeseen only a generation ago. But the hostility and cries for protectionism ignored the nature of 1990s global business. In reality, it wasn't so easy to tell anymore exactly what constituted a Japanese, American, or German product. If the issue was jobs, it had to be acknowledged that more than forty thousand Americans worked in Japanese-owned auto plants. However, probably twice that number had lost their jobs under the onslaught of imports and transplants—which, being more efficient, needed fewer people. Joint ventures and collaborations further blurred the lines.

But no one seemed interested in discussing the fine points, or in acknowledging that the head-in-the-sand mode of old-fashioned protectionism was no longer viable in this more complex, interrelated world.

The European Community had its own concerns about the threat of a "Japanese invasion." Although Germany's carmakers had been more successful than Americans in selling cars to the Japanese market, and although Japanese imports accounted for only 11.6 percent of the European market (as opposed to 30 percent in America), the protectionist debate was heated in Europe, especially since both Toyota and Honda were gearing up to open assembly plants in Great Britain. Nissan already had a plant there and was preparing to open a second. In 1992 Europeans would begin a quota system for all Japanese cars, scheduled to last until 1999, that they hoped would give industry some breathing time before a Japanese assault was waged on western Europe and the new markets opening in eastern Europe. Europeans were determined that Japan would not have free access to their markets as they had in the United States. There was no welcome mat being laid out, and Japanese carmakers who pressed for joint ventures were rebuffed. There would be no partnerships such as those developed in the United States. When Fuji Heavy Industries, maker of Subaru, offered to set up an assembly plant in France, it was told bluntly by business and government, "Go away. We don't want you here."

In Germany there was a fiercely nationalistic spirit when it came to cars. Germans believed their own makes were the best in the world. They viewed the German car buyer as the most sophisticated and demanding. In many places a consumer would have to defend the choice of a Japanese or American car.

While the Europeans were certain that they didn't want the Japanese invading their markets, their own situation was very fragile, complicated by the new world they had only just entered with the collapse of the Wall. The initial exhilaration was being replaced by a host of brutal economic realities. European carmakers had no way to predict the long-term sales potential of this new reality or whether the former East Bloc countries held promise or peril.

Carmaking in the final decade of the twentieth century was sometimes about style and sometimes about substance, and the trick was knowing how to have facility at both. The irony of the 1991 Tokyo Motor Show was that even as visiting auto executives cringed before visions of a new Japanese onslaught, even as the show presented Japan's carmakers as the new world leaders of whom every nation, especially America, was in fear, Japan's carmakers already knew that their own domestic market was beginning to crater, and they were desperately hoping the show would inspire a big turnaround. Because of the recession, demand for cars was softening in Japan. During the boom from 1986 to 1990, Japanese consumers had cash and an insatiable appetite for new cars. Now demand was slacking off and cash was getting tight as prospective buyers saw their stock-portfolio values dwindle each day. The population emerged from its spending spree with a bellyache of debts and little interest in the latest auto gadgetry. Seventy percent of consumers who did purchase new cars used financing, almost unheard-of only a few years earlier.

In the urban centers car purchases were inhibited by strict enforcement of a new law that prohibited anyone from keeping a car who could not prove entitlement to a legal parking space. Streets, especially in Tokyo, had become almost impassable due to the illegal cars parked in every spare inch, including on the sidewalks and in front of driveways. In the past the parking-space law was easy to maneuver around. Car dealers commonly rented one or two spots that they would offer to customers to use for a brief time. But carmakers feared that the renewed fervor of the police department in enforcing the law would cut into their already fragile business.

Japanese cars may have been the best in the world, but the robust real estate market, cheap money, and soaring stock market that had contributed to their success had reversed. The crisis was due to more than the recession. During the boom years of the

1980s many Japanese companies had abandoned their original principles, and their vast stock market and real estate assets had masked the fact that they had ceased to be the lean producers of old. Japanese car companies went on an expansion binge, wildly introducing new cars without regard to their sales potential—a strategy that would have been unthinkable in leaner years. Toyota blundered in featuring upscale, higher priced cars even as Japanese consumers were awakening to the harsh reality that they could not afford luxury. The new Corolla broke the 2-million-yen barrier and left buyers cold, as did the Aristo. Toyota's product strategy did not foresee the economic decline ahead— only more and larger cars. But deep within corporate Japan, the truth was becoming painfully clear: The party was over. Even so, automakers hoped that the Tokyo Motor Show would reinspire consumers to buy. They knew just how crucial this show was.

The massive gears of the largest car companies were shifting, throwing each of them into a state of flux that had become the uneasy status quo of the 1990s. The collapse of old dynasties, the fragmentation of cultures, the unforgiving squeeze of troubled economies, reverberated along the corridors of power within General Motors, Toyota, and Volkswagen. Each was effectively a global empire with financial resources that dwarfed other carmakers. Each would exert an extraordinary influence over the future of entire industries. And each contained potentially devastating flaws, largely unexplored, that could lead to a nuclear-strength explosion in the decade ahead.

It was an unsettling time to be a leader. Within the executive offices of each company there were certainly many men (for all of these companies were dominated by men) who looked back longingly to a time when every endeavor had been a guaranteed success, when the laurels had piled high from grand achievements and savvy strategies. After all, companies do not become great by accident or error. But the winning strategies of the past—even the recent past—were suddenly anachronistic in this dramatically different world. Now each company faced, in its own way, a cosmic battle between old ways and new, between isolation and globalization, between stagnation and risk. And each had to combat economic forces beyond its control.

The leaders of each company—Robert Stempel in Detroit, Shoichiro Toyoda in Nagoya, and Carl Hahn in Wolfsburg—had more in common than they might have acknowledged openly. Each was the leader in his respective market, yet needed international markets for continued growth. Each was saddled by an ingrown corporate culture that was resistant to change. And each was facing, around the bend of 1992, a jarring change of power that would create equal amounts of turmoil, danger, and opportunity.

Being in the driver's seat of a great car company in the 1990s meant traveling on the uncharted highway into the twenty-first century, charged with delivering cargo no less important than the economic futures of entire nations. The men who ran the auto industry during the 1980s, as visionary and successful as many of them were, had the dual benefits of surging growth in consumer demand and relatively stable economic conditions. The world had been more predictable, and so were the solutions to industry's problems. But in the 1990s problems would be more complex, solutions more elusive, and there would be less margin for error. It was an awesome burden, more so because the auto industry had always risen or fallen on the backs of individual men. That, at least, had not changed.

TWO

General Angst

If there were a self-help group called Corporations Anonymous, General Motors could be a charter member.

—Newsweek

Detroit—November 1991

IF LLOYD REUSS seemed distracted and a little churlish at the 1991 Tokyo Motor Show, he probably had good reason. By then, he and chairman Bob Stempel both knew that General Motors would have a record loss for the year, and once again the U.S. market share would drop in the face of strong competition. Meanwhile, neither man liked the way members of the board of directors were suddenly sniffing around, as though they had just emerged from a decades-long fog. While Reuss walked the aisles at Makuhari, Stempel remained in Detroit trying to put an end to the unraveling and ease the growing discontent of the board.

For some time, a number of board members had been educating themselves about the true state of General Motors and the individuals running it. A growing faction on the board was prepared to demand accountability for the progressively worsening state of the company and management's inability to meet their profit, cash flow, or market share projections. Not only was the board's new curiosity and diligence a radical break from tradition, getting tough was not a task any of them relished.

Stempel was well liked by many board members, who considered his tenure an improvement over the wild, destructive reign of Roger Smith during the 1980s. Stempel conferred a level of understanding of the dynamics of running a car company that his predecessor lacked. He had come to the chairmanship on a wave of hope, and his open-minded attitude seemed at first a refreshing contrast to Smith's iron-fisted rule. Personally, he was warm and thoughtful, preferring dialogue to edict. He seemed to be a good listener and he always asked for input, which he recorded in copious notes at meetings. Physically imposing, the six-foot-four former football player commanded respect. Better yet, he was, in Detroit parlance, a "car guy," an engineer rather than another in a series of finance men who had brought the company into this chaos in the first place. The board members desperately wanted him to succeed, but they could no longer tolerate the spiral of decline. Their own credibility was now coming into question. They were prepared to demand that Stempel depart from his tepid "evolutionary" course and take a more activist role in confronting GM's problems.

Stempel did not want to admit it, but the giant was on the ropes. He blamed factors outside of his control for the slide, and kept telling everyone that GM would come back as soon as the economy did. He might have differed in demeanor from Roger Smith, but in his heart he was every inch the loyal GM man who believed that all troubles were transitional, all losses were recoverable with time (once the recession ended or the Japanese stumbled or whatever was the excuse *du jour*), and nothing could bring down a company of General Motors' distinction, size, and financial resources. Even the board's new concern didn't worry him too much; he was skilled at setting people's fears to rest with his thoughtful, patient manner and voluminous knowledge of the business.

On the Fourteenth Floor of the General Motors building, where the executives resided in isolated and pampered surroundings, the mandate in late 1991 was bravado: *Things are looking up, we've got a handle on it, you're going to see a change, we're really on the right course now.* In fact, Stempel had begun to dismantle some of the structure and organization that he helped to create in 1984 when GM undertook an enormous (and ill-fated) reorganization. But this time Stempel was determined to go slowly. He didn't think the company could withstand a repeat of the chaos that ensued in 1984. It was this slow pace in light of GM's worsening troubles that made Stempel's promises seem hollow, especially in the boardroom, where the widening gap between fantasy and reality had begun to alarm anxious directors.

During the 1980s, when Roger Smith disguised his mistakes by claiming that he had made decisions and investments for the long term and needed more time to prove their potential, the board members usually acquiesced, with rare exceptions. One of these was John Smale, chairman and CEO of Procter & Gamble, who GM executives thought made a nuisance of himself asking why GM was a higher cost producer than Ford. Smale knew that the responses of the finance staff glossed over the truth, but he was virtually alone in even questioning management at that time. For the most part, board members never questioned Roger Smith's excuses for why sales and market share were declining, always accepting that the cars about to be introduced would restore GM's share to 40 percent. But how many predictions of a turnaround could go unmet before the time was finally up—especially when Ford and Chrysler, who had not spent so lavishly during the 1980s, were in better shape to face the recession? How long could a company tolerate a financial free-fall before it pulled the safety cord?

Perhaps the executives at General Motors had been isolated for too long in their secure corporate bunker. The Fourteenth Floor of the GM building was a place of legend. In Detroit and throughout the auto industry the words "The Fourteenth Floor says" were comparable to "The Vatican says." Everyone knew what they meant. The mystique of the Fourteenth Floor spoke volumes about the source of GM's problems. It was remote and protected from the gritty realities of everyday business; witness Michael Moore's futile attempts to get within an elevator ride of the place in his hit movie *Roger and Me.* Even had Moore or any other ordinary mortal managed to take the elevator ride up, it would be virtually impossible to get inside. An impenetrable security system secluded executives behind a bulletproof glass wall. In itself, this was not particularly revealing; tight security necessarily accompanied corporate executives in this grim era. But once inside, one could feel the sanitized dullness of the place. Beige walls and furniture, quiet empty hallways. There was no creative energy. Also telling were the many examples of executive privilege that seemed obscene in light of the company's burgeoning financial crisis. Free cars for most executives, an executive dining room, assorted perks, generous salaries and bonuses—all of these trappings of power were maintained in spite of the shambles below. This was not a management that would sacrifice anything to display a sense of urgency.

The GM building itself was from another time—a monument to the enormously wealthy company. It was quite beautiful, reflecting an era of design and craftsmanship often sadly lacking in the vehicles conceived by the men who worked there. As a company, GM reflected more the crumbling decay of Detroit's inner city than the durability of its granite and marble headquarters building.

The many privileges of its executives were not just a matter of symbolism, although clearly the image of the top people living high on the hog while thousands were losing their jobs left a sour taste. It was also reflective of what seemed to be the lack of awareness among the top people, starting with Stempel, that anything had changed. GM could no longer justify or afford extravagance, yet here it was. A visit to the Fourteenth Floor was like entering a time warp from GM's glory days. General Motors was a perfect example of the contemporary corporate malaise where income and privileges bore no relation to performance.

Stempel cultivated the appearance of being a regular guy, but his was a special brand of arrogance. He couldn't understand why the board and the press were on his case; he didn't believe things were really so bad. He was so out of touch with the true state of the company that he negotiated a labor contract in October 1990, two months after becoming chairman, that was the most expensive in the history of GM. It was an agreement that would have made sense only in a strong economy, with a superb sales environment and a strong product. As a "car guy," Stempel should have known that none of these conditions existed—least of all the product. But he thought GM's quality problems could be fully resolved through a cooperative work force that could be relieved from worry about the steady stream of factory closings and layoffs. Although he may have genuinely wanted to alleviate some of the anxiety of the workers, his contractual promise to pay three years' worth of wages to laid-off GM workers demonstrated his unrealistic expectations.

How this happened was anyone's guess. It's not as though Stempel wandered out of the woods to become chairman. He'd been president for two years prior to his appointment yet he didn't seem to grasp the fact that GM had big problems in the very operations he had run for years. Only later, when 21,000 laid-off workers were collecting their paychecks, would he be forced to confront the irrationality of this contract. GM's cash reserves, so desperately needed to pay for new products, were being depleted to compensate people for staying home.

The headlight glare of negative press and board frustration made Stempel defensive, and he relied more and more on the hope that time or an economic miracle would prove him right. Ironically, on the most basic level, GM's cars themselves were in a position to do better. A J. D. Powers survey of General Motors, Ford, and Chrysler cars showed that the average number of defects in the first three months of ownership was 1.5 per car, almost on a par with Japanese cars. But the competitive position of a car line depended on more than the number of defects per car. There was also style and engineering, not to mention the effectiveness of the entire organization. In this regard, GM didn't seem capable of getting its act together. Although there was talk about coordinating the work of designers, engineers, manufacturing people, and marketers to create new models in less time for less money (like the Japanese did it), management had no idea how to execute it. The reorganization of 1984 had left GM with a clumsy, unworkable structure that led to inefficiency and higher costs. The newly reorganized company was responsible for introducing some of the costliest flops ever, such as the GM-10 mid-size car, a $7-billion fiasco, and the 1991 Caprice, a car widely viewed as poorly designed and ugly—which consumers rejected out of hand.

There seemed to be no awareness that design and engineering decisions, not robots in an assembly plant, dictated costs. A belated effort begun in 1989, called Design for Manufacturing (DFM), began to address this issue, but like so many other initiatives in the past, it tackled only one aspect of a multifaceted problem. Unless the organization was choreographed to maximize the findings of DFM, it could not produce results.

Most disturbing of all, Stempel's public pronouncements that all was well may have eased the worries of dealers and outsiders, but inside the company they undermined any efforts to change by creating an attitude of business as usual. Stempel neglected the proactive measures that might have identified and solved the underlying organizational and product problems. Not all employees shared his optimism. Disappointed insiders, who had hoped Stempel's era would be a time of change and growth, privately admitted he was unable to pull it off. "Staying the course will eventually sink the company," said one discouraged executive. Another remarked, "It almost seems that Stempel has never really taken to the job he prepared most of his career to assume. He doesn't have the stomach for confrontations, and he hates the in-your-face behavior that the tough job demands. Denying there's a problem doesn't make it go away."

It was true that Stempel could be somewhat withdrawn. While he had admirers in the company, he had few, if any, real friends. Far from being the vigorous Pied Piper of change, he resisted bold actions. When things got bad, he fled into the tired old strategy of excuses and finger pointing—usually at the media and naysayers in the financial community.

To make matters worse, Stempel was weighed down by and loyal to an ineffective executive team cut from a worn corporate cloth—most prominent among them Lloyd Reuss and the chief financial officer, Robert O'Connell, both of whom had been rivals for Stempel's job. Even so, Stempel had to accept personal responsibility for much of what GM had become. He had, after all, been president for two years (1988–90) before becoming chairman in August 1990. And prior to that, he'd been a group executive in charge of one of GM's car groups, BOC (Buick-Oldsmobile-Cadillac), as well as head of the truck and bus division. He should have understood the depth of GM's problems far better than almost anyone, including Roger Smith, since Stempel came out of operations and had a firsthand knowledge of how the company functioned. He knew, or should have known, since the early 1980s that GM had a noncompetitive cost structure and inferior products, many of which were created during his stewardship in the vehicle divisions. Now GM was the industry's high-cost assembler and its six car divisions competed against each other with ineffective models.

Earlier, with his back to the wall, Stempel attributed much of the company's problems to poor vehicle quality in the past, yet he didn't seem to understand how to correct all of GM's problems simultaneously. The best that could be said about Stempel was that in 1990, when it was time to pick a new chairman, he was the lesser of two evils, the other being Reuss. Reuss's failures were renowned, and his ascension to the presidency was an example of the Peter Principle in action. One might think in a company of GM's size and stature there would be plenty of brilliant candidates. But as we know from watching presidential elections, the best and brightest are not always those who rise to the top. Both Stempel and Reuss were products of a lethargic GM culture that valued loyalty and longevity above all else.

Reuss was a slick bantamweight with the well-honed survival skills of a veteran politician, yet he was unpopular even inside the company. The day his appointment as president was announced, a chorus of jeers rose inside the auditorium at CPC (the Chevrolet-Pontiac-GM-Canada division Reuss created). For many, it was a confirmation of their worst fears. Reuss had nearly destroyed Buick by turning its image from a classic car into a muscle machine. He created the ineffective, bloated CPC. He built Buick City in a naive and futile attempt to duplicate Toyota's production miracle. He was rewarded for a string of failures with the presidency of General Motors. In that position he received little real respect; privately, Reuss's dictates were called LSDs, for "Lloyd Says Do It." And there was little question that the things Lloyd said to do were often ill conceived. By 1991 domestic market share was an anemic 34 percent and the North American operations were losing $600 million a month. The figures were so shocking that GM's stock fell and dealers clamored for better cars, wondering if they should abandon GM brands for other franchises. In November 1991 credit rating agencies warned that they would reduce the company's rating if they weren't given credible evidence of a turnaround.

But although he had never shown any talent for problem solving, Reuss was increasingly taking charge. As one insider observed, "The worse things got, the more Stempel backed into his office and let Reuss take the lead." This was futile because it seemed that Reuss's priority wasn't so much fixing things as making people believe they had been fixed. Like others on the Fourteenth Floor, Reuss refused to hear bad news, as though by denying the truth he could make it disappear. It was once said of him, "He surrounds himself with people who are not afraid to say, 'I was just going to agree with your next statement.' "

Stempel had also inherited Bob O'Connell, the portly, officious CFO who had been Roger Smith's loyal right arm during the 1980s. O'Connell had done his utmost to make GM's financial performance appear better than it was with a stream of accounting changes. He had also amassed power during that period through his cozy relationship with Smith. Before Smith became chairman in 1980, GM's financial strength was consistently underestimated by conservative accounting. By 1990 GM's liberal accounting policies were often the subject of ridicule in the financial community. Stempel, true to his nature, kept O'Connell on out of loyalty and because he, Stempel, knew little about finance.

Although some board members never quite trusted the slick CFO (unlike most CFOs, O'Connell wasn't offered a place on the board), years of service had made him seem like an indispensable fixture. O'Connell himself always believed that his workaholic devotion would earn him the chairmanship someday. In his early days, on the treasurer's staff in New York, he often stayed in the office for days at a time, chain-smoking cigarettes and consuming vast amounts of pizza and cola, never even changing his clothes. After he had moved to Detroit, his habit of enlisting his driver to haul boxes of papers and memos home each night was a subject of great mirth in the lower echelons of the company. No one believed a mere mortal could actually review so many cartons of paper each evening.

Stempel and Reuss had never been close, and by the mid-1980s, when they were the heads of GM's two newly reorganized divisions, they became competitors for the top job. Their management styles and philosophies had always differed—Stempel more team-spirited, Reuss more autocratic. In 1988 Stempel won the presidency over Reuss when Jim McDonald retired. There were rumors that Reuss would leave GM for greener pastures, but instead he stayed on, a loyal soldier in the company tradition. When Stempel became chairman in August 1990, he insisted on Reuss's appointment to president, in spite of some grumbling from board members. Stempel might not always have agreed with Reuss, but he admired his loyalty and service to the company. Reuss was named president but not chief operating officer, a tell-tale sign that the board questioned his ability.

Other contenders for the presidency didn't make it. Jack Smith (no relation to Roger) had returned to the United States from GM-Europe in 1988 as executive vice-president in charge of international operations, and he wasn't part of the inner circle. He was named vice-chairman, a position that was little more than a consolation prize. Bill Hoglund was a talented, popular executive who first came to the attention of those at the top with his "We build excitement, Pontiac" campaign in the early 1980s. He had been the first president of Saturn, then moved back to Detroit to replace Stempel as head of BOC when the latter became GM president, and was now executive vice-president of the components division. Hoglund was considered too outspoken for the top job, although he was the sentimental favorite of most insiders. A dark-horse candidate was F. Alan Smith (also no relation to Roger or to Jack), the smooth, silver-haired executive vice-president of corporate services, who later became an inside board member. But his chances for the presidency were doomed after his messy divorce became the whispered talk of Detroit inner circles.

In late 1991 Stempel faced a disgruntled board that, among other things, was questioning the effectiveness of Reuss and other executives. The GM board of directors had never taken a strong, independent position before, and Stempel could not have predicted how the board would show its dissatisfaction this time.

Like a slumbering giant slowly shaking itself awake, the General Motors board of directors was gradually coming to terms with some hard realities. Circumstances had forced the awakening and it had been a long time coming. The view of the board, like that of management, was a good twenty years out of date. During the 1980s the outside members, who collectively knew very little about the auto industry, were spoon-fed information by Roger Smith; it would have been unheard-of for board members to meet and discuss issues independently or to talk with other members of the GM staff or even the most senior executives. Ross Perot once derisively referred to GM board members as "Pet Rocks."

Smith totally controlled the flow of information to the board. He alone set the agenda for each meeting and avoided answering questions with any real depth. For example, when board members expressed concern about the quality of GM cars, Smith peppered them with magazine reviews and fragments of articles that showed individual vehicles in their best light. He was a master at providing selective information, and the deeper the company's troubles, the fewer details the board received. When O'Connell became CFO, he changed the content of the financial package given to board members at each meeting so they received less detailed information. When board members asked for a review of their concerns, Roger Smith conducted interviews with them individually and presented his report to the entire assembly. In this way, he always made it seem as though each member was alone in his or her concerns. So fearful was Roger Smith that the board might rebel at his choice of Stempel for the chairmanship that he remained in the room with the nominating committee until the deed was done.

Since Smith and then Stempel controlled information, as late as 1991 the board thought the money well would always be full. And they didn't work too hard to find out otherwise. Like boards in other American companies, they had an incestuous relationship with the chairman, primed by long-held personal relationships and a lavish system of perks. Board members received a specially prepped new GM car of their choice every three months and access to the company's jets for business travel, in addition to prestige, honor, and money. GM was adept at the care and feeding of board members. Everything was ritualized, and they obediently observed the protocol because that was the way things were done. Most of them were deeply honored to be members of such a prestigious group. Besides, they were generally very busy in their own careers and businesses. And because many of them were heads of companies themselves, they tended to side with the beleaguered chairman and to be suspicious of the media and Wall Street.

If one asked why it took so long for the board to act, the same question might have been directed at IBM, Sears, American Express, Westinghouse, and any number of other large American corporations. Like other boards, GM's was composed of conservative, very smart men and women who believed they were doing a good job. Without ready access to all the financial information, which both Roger Smith and Bob Stempel kept from them, there was little reason for them to believe otherwise—until things got so bad that they couldn't fail to see the truth.

Several outside board members had been losing confidence throughout 1991 as the situation grew graver, and they began to push for change. Four of the "activists"—Thomas Wyman, former CEO of CBS; Ann McLaughlin, former secretary of labor; J. Willard Marriott, Marriott CEO; and Dennis Weatherstone of J. P. Morgan—had been appointed to the board by Roger Smith himself. After years of double talk, they were becoming impatient with the excuses. They might not have been so suspicious had Ford and Chrysler shared GM's steady decline. If, as Stempel claimed, the sagging American economy and the fierce Japanese competition were at fault, surely the other two would be on the ropes as well. But while General Motors continued to experience huge losses, declining market share, and the threat of a credit downgrade, Ford was performing relatively better. Even Chrysler, which was in bad shape, had proposed a credible plan for a revival, and had impressive new vehicles scheduled for launch. Only in Europe was GM setting the right kind of records.

At its December meeting the board demanded that Stempel put forth a plan to stop the hemorrhaging. What followed was jokingly called the Nine Day Wonder, the number of days between Stempel's promise that he would have a plan and the announced "solution." During those nine days Stempel and his minions desperately cobbled together a vague plan out of a long laundry list of possible actions. One option—executive pay cuts—was instantly rejected, and the final product amounted to a Chinese menu of actions that lacked any underlying strategy.

On December 18 Stempel announced that GM would close six assembly plants and fifteen other factories, and would cut its work force, mostly by attrition. He made a vague outline of the plan, with the names of the plants to be filled in later. He was trying to show how serious he was about reining in costs, but even the number of plants he named was artificially inflated. At least one factory included in the count (the so-called Factory of the Future, in Saginaw) was already closed. Others were not factories at all, but sections of other operations that were being consolidated.

The specifics of Stempel's plan came as a surprise to board members, who were not consulted ahead of time. Obviously, he still believed he could keep them out of the loop. One board member spoke to this author the morning of Stempel's announcement, and wondered if I had any idea what he would say. I was astonished. "Don't you know?" I asked, only to be told, "I don't have a clue."

Although a General Motors press release later stated that the decision was made with the full concurrence of the board, it was apparent that while they agreed there needed to be a plan, they had not approved the specifics of it. Now they were displeased, to say the least. They found the measures completely inadequate. Most disturbing, the action seemed willy-nilly—there was still no comprehensive strategy for reducing costs and stabilizing market share. Rather than inspiring confidence that the company was reining in its excesses, the cuts looked like a Band-Aid solution. They only underscored Stempel's unwillingness to make tough decisions that would force him to repudiate what he and Roger Smith had created and then allowed to decay.

GM's old critics were sharpening their knives. In January David E. Davis, Jr., editor and publication director of *Automobile* magazine, gave a biting speech to the Washington Auto Press Association in which he blasted past and current management. "GM has been micro managed, planned, reorganized, analyzed and outside-consulted into second-rank status in the automobile world," Davis said. "Nobody set out to ruin GM, but ruination has been the bottom line."

In typical "kill the messenger style," Davis was punished for his harsh words by a temporary advertising boycott of his magazine, some say with a nod from Reuss. GM had often used this tactic with *Fortune* and *Automotive News,* among others, when they were displeased with articles.

In any event, it would be a futile gesture. The numbers on 1991 were in and they were devastating. The company had lost $7 billion for the year—a company record. Its share of the car market had shrunk to an all-time low of 34 percent. The erosion seemed unstoppable.

In late December the board hired John Smale, now retired from Procter & Gamble, on a per diem basis to interview GM's executives and ask them what they thought was wrong. Until now, the board had heard only what Stempel presented to them.

Stempel and his associates knew the board had become restive, but they couldn't imagine the consequences of Smale's efforts. He was deceptively low-key (he'd once referred to himself as "a dull guy"), but determined. While Stempel and Reuss were furiously trying to plug the leaking ship and present a picture of strength, Smale was rooting around in the dark corners learning the truth.

At the January board meeting the members were dispirited. They wanted to give Stempel a chance to turn things around, but they had little confidence that he could do it with his current staff. The board saw Reuss as a bigger impediment than Stempel. Touring the North American International Auto Show in New York after the meeting, they were asked by GM executives to say nothing to the press. As the board members rode around the floor in electric golf carts, they were joined by members of GM's public relations staff, who tried to keep reporters away. When one reporter slipped through the barriers and asked Ann McLaughlin her opinion of recent events, she replied cautiously, "It's just gossip about Stempel and Reuss being under fire." There was still hope, however faint, that they could pull it off and set things straight.

On February 24 Stempel added more specifics to his initial plan for a company turnaround. North American operations would be reorganized for the second time in eight years, under the direction of Lloyd Reuss. To get plants running at 100 percent capacity by 1995, GM would close twenty-one plants; now he began to announce which plants these would be. They included Willow Run in Michigan and Tarrytown in New York. These and other actions would eliminate 74,000 blue- and white-collar jobs by 1995.

The story of Willow Run's closing was one that had become increasingly familiar among GM plants. In December Stempel had announced that production for large rear-wheel-drive cars like the Chevrolet Caprice and the Buick Roadmaster would be consolidated from two plants to one because the cars weren't selling. (One factory worker at Willow Run said the workers knew it was coming the first time they laid eyes on the Caprice. "People looked at that car and said, 'Guess we're next. There go our jobs.' ") Willow Run and the GM plant in Arlington, Texas, which also built the cars, thus began a heated competition to stay open. There was no way to compare the impact of a closing on the towns. Willow Run employed 2,400 hourly workers (another 1,800 had been laid off eighteen months earlier) and supported the economy of the town, which was located only thirty miles from the GM headquarters in Detroit. Arlington faced the loss of 3,700 jobs in a town already hit hard by massive layoffs in other industries. Workers in both plants hated to be in the position of hoping the other would lose, but that was the standoff forced by GM. The unions bitterly referred to the practice as "whiplashing," and decried the callous methods GM used to close plants, even when they bent over backward to be cooperative and cost-effective.

Willow Run believed it had the edge. For one thing, its location gave it an immediate $325-per-car advantage over Arlington in freight costs. It had a reputation for high quality—although not significantly better than Arlington. And only a few years earlier, GM had invested $75 million in modernization. So confident was the plant management that Willow Run would stay open that on February 24, the day Stempel was to make the announcement, they prepared to host a party for the workers, ordering five thousand hot dogs. A stage was built for a victory presentation. When a GM manager stood on the stage and told them that they had lost to Arlington, there was a roar of disbelief, followed by sobbing, fainting, and general pandemonium. Nobody understood how Willow Run had lost. Neither Stempel nor anyone else was prepared to give a straight answer. (In documents filed related to a lawsuit by the town of Willow Run against GM, it appeared that Arlington's lower labor costs and willingness to consider three-shift assembly schedules were the important factors.)

Stempel's new plan was a case of too little too late, and his pledge that job reductions would be made through attrition was an impossible promise to keep. It now seemed painfully clear that the workers were paying for the obscenities of the eighties, including reckless capital spending and a lack of cohesive product vision. Stempel blamed the Japanese, the media, and even the Gulf War. He tried to defend GM's huge decline in market share, saying, "Our plan is based on being profitable at whatever share of market we get." But General Motors had closed eleven factories since 1987 in response to falling market share, and its domestic position was worse than ever. Loss of share—a decline in customers—shut factories. As a General Motors economist said wearily, "We couldn't close factories fast enough to keep up with our falling share. We need to stabilize the share in order to know how much assembly capacity we need." He was right. Stempel's random strike of factory closings was practically meaningless without a carefully orchestrated strategy that considered which factories were key to the company's revival and which could afford to be closed. And since no one seemed to know how many vehicles would be sold in the coming three to five years, all decisions were being made in a vacuum.

Stempel's announcement of plant closings sent waves of dread coursing through the country but caused cheers on Wall Street, where belt-tightening measures were met with approval. Newspapers headlined the story, giving ample space to the angry, frightened reactions of GM's workers. Even so, Stempel denied there was a morale problem inside the company. "The people on the factory floor understand if we're going to be in business, we've got to get our production up, we've got to get our productivity up, we've got to get our quality up," he said. It was a classic case of blaming the victim, and the unions bristled at the suggestion that GM's problems were the workers' fault. UAW president Owen Beiber laid the blame in the executive offices and criticized its haphazard and unfair policies, including the practice of whiplashing. Beiber had a point. It seemed that where workers cooperated with management, the factories were closed, so cooperation seemed to get them nowhere.

As Stempel and Reuss implemented their plan, leaking glowing stories about the new, streamlined organizational structure to the press, the board continued to assert itself. The sharper accountability troubled Stempel, but he never realized that the board was getting ready to revolt. The Band-Aid fixes and excuses had worked for too long, and this board of directors, as meddlesome and intrusive as they were becoming, had never "taken over" before. Why should they now? He virtually ignored the board's insistence that he start making management changes and firing members of the old guard. As the board began to press for Reuss's dismissal, Stempel got testy. "Lloyd's my man," he declared before a closed-circuit television audience in February. Later, he hinted that if Reuss was fired, he might resign.

Vice-chairman Jack Smith watched events unfold with a growing realization that circumstances were building to a critical point. By late winter he began to suspect that he might be called upon to take over the helm. The stocky, boyish former president of GM-Europe became a star during the 1980s, although he remained outside the Fourteenth Floor political clique. Smith's performance in Europe had been decisive and effective, in contrast to the muddling behavior of his colleagues back home. While General Motors posted losses year after year, the European operation was generating huge profits. By the time Smith returned to the United States as executive vice-president in charge of international operations, GM-Europe had become widely praised as the prototype for a well-run company. Before GM-Europe was created in the early 1980s, the company's European operations were appallingly noncompetitive. Viewed as irrelevant by the Detroit power brokers, they were deprived of capital and solid management. Traditionally, most people who went into GM's overseas operations (pronounced "G-moo") spent most of their careers moving from one foreign post to another, rarely making it back to Detroit.

The decision to place an umbrella organization over the group in the early 1980s was an attempt to make GM competitive with Ford-Europe, then the most profitable vehicle producer there. But it was Jack Smith's leadership in the mid to late eighties that really turned it around—especially his gift for managing people and his ability to challenge the system. He cut capital outlays, maintained a stable work force, sharply increased production, and mastered the chaotic and overpriced supplier network that previously formed a cartel around GM. His greatest achievement was finding the right people and getting them to work together. He managed the entire organization with only two hundred people, secretaries included, out of rather humble offices in Zurich.

Many of the measures Jack Smith employed were sorely needed back home, but during those years, Roger Smith was on a spending spree, investing more than $60 billion in plant automation and purchasing Ross Perot's Electronic Data Systems and Hughes Aircraft.

At fifty-four, Jack Smith was something of an enigma in the company. On one hand, he appeared to be born and bred in the classic Detroit mode; he spent his entire career at General Motors, rising up through the ranks like a good soldier. He began in the Framingham, Massachusetts, plant (now closed) rather than the more hallowed ground of Detroit, however, and he'd actually spent little time in the automotive heartland. As a result, there was an unusual quality about Smith. He was sharp but not overtly political, warm but not hail-fellow-well-met. He had a good sense of humor but could be bulldog-tough, too. It was an understatement to say that he was well liked. Everyone seemed to have a story to tell about how accessible and interested he was—

how he let people do their jobs independently while monitoring them in a respectful, unobtrusive way. Inaki Lopez, the man Smith enlisted to reform the supplier network of GM-Europe, used to say with absolute seriousness, "I'd cut off my right arm for my leader."

On the personal side, Smith was different from the average Detroit executive. He had raised his two sons alone, and his second wife, Lydia, a sophisticated Swiss woman, was determined to maintain a separation between their private and public lives. Professionally, Smith was a new breed. He enjoyed hearing diverse ideas, even when he disagreed, and was eager to get to the heart of problems and resolve them. Smith may have been born into the General Motors culture but the culture was not born in him. Roger Smith had liked him, but he never understood him. Stempel barely knew him at all, so he was not seriously considered for president during the change of regime in 1990. And now, as vice-chairman, he often felt that he was on the outside looking in at a terrible disaster, with little hope of making a difference. Even though Smith resided on the Fourteenth Floor and was credited by everyone for the financial success of GM-Europe (which was now pouring money into corporate coffers to offset losses in North America), Stempel never asked for his opinion or included him in most discussions of domestic issues.

Another man, an old colleague of Jack Smith's, knew for certain that drastic change was in the air at GM. Bob Eaton, a bright, talented executive, had replaced Smith as president of GM-Europe. But in March 1992 rumors circulated that Eaton would be leaving General Motors to join Chrysler as vice-chairman and heir apparent to Lee Iacocca. Shortly before Eaton made it official, he received an urgent call from John Smale. Smale wondered if Eaton would be willing to wait three weeks before making a final decision about going to Chrysler. "There might be a reason you'll want to stay," Smale said obliquely. Eaton had an idea what that meant, since he had been one of the executives interviewed by Smale in the board's information-gathering drive. Now he told Smale he would think it over and call him back.

Immediately, Eaton knew he wasn't being considered for a top job at GM—not the chairmanship or even the presidency. He and

Jack Smith were too close in age, and he knew that the next important opening would go to Smith. He couldn't guess what role he might be asked to play or the degree of turmoil that would await him should he decide to stay with General Motors. At least with Chrysler he had a pretty good idea where he stood —as long as Iacocca kept his word and retired on schedule. He was virtually assured the chairmanship after Iacocca's retirement. He called Smale back and told him his decision to move to Chrysler was firm. But the phone call had alerted him that something big was about to go down at General Motors. Sure enough, by mid-March, Stempel was quietly informed that a leadership change would be made in April. The board had finally become tired of waiting for Stempel to do it himself.

The shake-up would be major. Jack Smith was to be named president. Reuss would be demoted to executive vice-president of a hodgepodge of jobs that included responsibility for Saturn, electric cars, environmental issues, and the like. It was a humiliating comedown for Reuss, who, along with F. Alan Smith, would also lose his seat on the board. But it could have been worse. Several board members had lobbied feverishly to have him fired outright. "I look at Lloyd Reuss and I keep thinking about the 74,000 people who will be losing their jobs," one board member said. "Why should he get to keep his?" But in the end, Stempel's pleas that Reuss be allowed to stay and work until retirement won out.

The board also decided that O'Connell would be demoted to senior vice-president in charge of GMAC and GM's pension investments, and Bill Hoglund would be appointed chief financial officer. Many on the board were thoroughly disgusted with O'Connell's performance. They were especially galled by the way he ignored their demands for information, the legacy of his tenure under Roger Smith. For example, at the February board meeting, O'Connell reported that GM would take a huge loss for its investment in National Car Rental. Board members were surprised, since O'Connell had not forewarned them of continuing substantial losses at the company. Bill Marriott was visibly exasperated. "How many more financial surprises do you have in store for us?" he asked. O'Connell had no reply, and Marriott told him to prepare a report for the next board meeting outlining the issues that might bode ill for GM's financial future. O'Connell didn't miss a beat. With no awareness whatsoever that he was placing his own head on the block, he told Marriott that those issues would be impossible to predict. Marriott was furious. In a startling break with board meeting protocol, he said sternly, "Well, if you can't, maybe the company needs a new CFO."

That O'Connell survived at all was due to a handful of friends on the board—loyalists from the Roger Smith era. There was even a last-minute attempt by one of them to keep O'Connell as CFO. Such a heated discussion ensued that board member Ann Armstrong finally said, "We've already decided this. Let's get on with it." O'Connell's demotion would stand.

For Stempel, the final insult was that he was stripped of much of his authority and his chairmanship of the executive committee, even while retaining his title. There had been heated debate among board members about that, too, and they stopped short of replacing him—mostly because there was no logical candidate.

Stempel was informed by the board that the action would be made official at the April 6 meeting.

A few days before the meeting, Stempel called Jack Smith into his office and told him, in what Smith felt was a very cryptic way, what was expected to happen at the board meeting. Stempel then did the same for the others, trying, as was his nature, to soften the blow for each of the old team. Apparently, in O'Connell's case, vague references weren't enough. He had to be told several times, and he still didn't believe it. His state of denial was so deep that Stempel was forced to outline the news in a note delivered to O'Connell's hotel room the day before the board meeting.

Dallas—April 1992

THE SETTING for the dismantling of the old order was the Dallas headquarters of the company's Electronic Data Systems (EDS) subsidiary—ironically, Ross Perot's old stamping ground. The modern building was located in a pleasant parklike complex. Perot, a severe critic of the company, might have enjoyed being a fly on the wall. As it was, his presence was keenly felt. A large bronze eagle dominated the lobby, an ode to Perot's fabled act of heroism, as recorded in the Ken Follett book *On Wings of Eagles*. Perot was not above reminding others—especially the wimpy corporate executives he most disdained—that he was a "real man."

It was customary the evening before a board meeting for the members to join company executives for dinner. Normally, these occasions were friendly bonding sessions, but this one was different. "It was the most excruciating few hours of my life," Jack Smith later recalled. Given what was about to take place, there was no way to make small talk. Instead, furtive whispers and last-minute politicking (especially on O'Connell's part) made the meal hard to swallow.

The next day, as the directors gathered, their mood was somber and there was nervous tension. No one knew quite how to act. There was no predetermined protocol for this. A revolutionary action was about to be taken by the most visible board in America. It was an awesome moment.

One board member appeared lonely and out of place. Roger Smith, who only two years earlier had been the number one man in the auto industry, now seemed irrelevant. No one said it openly, but the board's decision was a complete repudiation of Smith's tenure as chairman. But Smith refused to admit it. Later he would tell reporters and some of his associates that he thought the board's action was unnecessary, that time would have healed General Motors. When Smith retired from the chairmanship in 1990, he had said, "I want to be judged in five years," as though the company would magically turn around in that period. He still believed it and felt the board was acting hastily, since only two years had passed. He seemed to be living in an almost pathological state of denial about the state of the company and his own role in its decline. But if Smith believed the one million dollars a year he was collecting in pension was reward for a job well done, he stood alone in that belief. Indeed, many considered it scandalous that the former chairman was pulling down such a hearty pension when the seeds of GM's near destruction were sown on his watch. Smith's handsome pension package was the product of his own design. Only four months before he was scheduled to retire, he initiated a change in the retirement package, claiming that a study of comparable companies, conducted by the finance staff, showed that GM's benefits weren't competitive with business in general.

After the regular board meeting, Jack Smith and the other insiders, except for Stempel, were asked by the board to leave the room and wait in offices down the hall while the deed was done.

The board's action amounted to more than a simple reshuffling of the cast of characters. The very dynamics of leadership were also being challenged. For many years, the chairman had been the most powerful executive in the company, the one who set the agenda and stood in the public eye. The president was the inside man, obedient to the dictates of the chairman. During the 1980s Roger Smith's president, Jim McDonald, was practically invisible, a worker bee whose name was rarely in the news. Smith was a very public chairman who became even more well known after Michael Moore's film became a big hit across the country. Under Stempel, Reuss's role was a bit more public, in part because the two men had risen up through the ranks as equals and Reuss had built an independent power base. But Stempel, not Reuss, was most often called to account in the press.

Now the board was suggesting that Jack Smith should be given a freer hand to run the company. The removal of Stempel as head of the executive committee implied that his role would become more ceremonial—interfacing with government regulators, dealers, and others outside the company. In truth, it was a role better suited to a man who had never been comfortable wearing the mantle of chairman. At least one executive close to Stempel speculated that he might be secretly relieved to be pulled off the hot seat.

After the board meeting, F. Alan Smith was asked by the board to write the press release that would tell the world about the change. The bland release, which, incidentally, made no mention of F. Alan Smith's removal from the board, stated the facts plainly and without drama.

Oddly, Jack Smith, waiting in an office down the hall, was never called before the board for a formal passing of the baton, congratulations, or a pep talk. Instead, he, Hoglund, O'Connell, and F. Alan Smith were collected and taken in cars to the airport without being told the details of what had occurred. Only as the company plane headed home did F. Alan Smith give Smith a copy of the press release that had already been sent to the media. The press and public knew about Smith's elevation before he officially had the news. His wife, Lydia, heard about it when she was deluged with phone calls from members of the press and family friends—while her husband was still en route from Dallas. Stempel and Reuss, smarting from the events of the day, returned to Detroit on a different plane.

News of the "bloodless coup" at General Motors made the front pages of every newspaper in America the following day. As word spread down the ranks of the company, there was an air of celebration. "This is how it must have felt when the Berlin Wall fell," gloated a longtime employee.

Keeping a stiff upper lip, Reuss appeared on schedule the evening after the coup to receive an award from the Engineering Society. And the next day, O'Connell was present on the dais during a speech this author delivered to the Detroit Economic Club. Both appearances were greeted with embarrassment. No one knew quite what to say. It seemed easier to pretend that nothing had changed.

Jack Smith returned to Detroit still not knowing the full scope of the board's intentions. Many of the details had been left unspoken, and this made him uneasy. But he forged ahead, strong and decisive in his approach because that was his style. His first actions rang like loud symbolic bells of a new era. He began by announcing a review of executive perks. Then he moved most of his business from the bunkered location on the Fourteenth Floor to the GM Technical Center ten miles away in Warren, Michigan. No longer would the chief executives of the company be removed from the main operations. The Fourteenth Floor had lost its cachet.

Almost immediately after the change, GM announced that it would sell shares of stock in the largest public equity offering ever. The company desperately needed the cash, so Smith's first action was a globe-trotting road show to convince investors that GM had a bright future. It was an eye-opening experience for Smith. On the road, he learned just how deep the skepticism about GM had become. At one early morning meeting during which he was interrogated by angry portfolio managers, he wasn't even offered a cup of coffee while the managers ate breakfast. The symbolism of his empty cup demonstrated how far GM had to climb.

The transition to power was anything but smooth. For one thing, Stempel wasn't being a good soldier in his newly revised role. Although it had been made very clear to him and everyone else that the buck stopped with Smith, Stempel was still telling the press, "I'm in charge," and Smith had to acquiesce at public meetings to the titular head. The only one who didn't seem to know he wasn't in charge was Stempel himself, and since he was out of the loop, his public pronouncements didn't necessarily reflect the strategy being devised at the Technical Center. Furthermore, Reuss was still around, and with the passage of time, the effects of the April board action seemed less radical.

In the months to come, it became increasingly clear to Jack Smith that the board had only done half the job. Stempel wasn't settling into a new role, and what was worse, the minuscule first-half profits had nose-dived into a megabucks loss for the second half. Smith could not fudge the books, in the GM tradition. The results would be honestly reported, and they were grim. Bill Hoglund later described the situation, saying, "When I took over the financial job, I was stunned by how every time something went wrong, it shot right down to the bottom line. There was no rubber in the system." Smith and his hardworking crew felt no euphoria as they faced the bitter truths. And meanwhile, the vultures were still circling.

THREE

The Road Warriors

Let us protect our own castle with our own hands.

—Taizo Ishida

BY BULLET TRAIN, traveling at speeds of more than one hundred miles an hour, the city of Nagoya is an easy two-hour commute from Tokyo and one hour from Osaka, Japan's major urban centers. The sleek white train, with a blue bull's-eye on the pointed nose of its locomotive, is the favored form of travel between distant cities, and so reliable you can set your watch by it. Nagoya Central Station stands at the center of town, a fifteen-minute ride from the Nagoya Castle, constructed in 1609. It is a colorful, bustling place, with subterranean shopping arcades and food kiosks. The latter are a staple feature of Japanese life, as travelers are always eating *bentos* (rice, pickled vegetables, scrambled egg, and slices of fish or meat packed in small boxes) or buying gifts of carefully wrapped fruit, rice crackers, or red bean paste confection to present to business associates, customers, friends, and relatives. The prices would stun American visitors—such as the hundred-dollar melons nestled in brocade boxes.

At certain times of day, throngs of uniformed schoolchildren—

the boys in black pseudo-military jackets and the girls in blue middy dresses—besiege Nagoya station, which also receives trains from several private, regional railroads. Outside, Toyota taxis line up to collect passengers exiting from the continuously arriving and departing trains. Toyota's influence is so pervasive that there are few Japanese cars in evidence that are not Toyotas.

Nagoya today is an important commercial city. It was once one of the great castle towns of the Edo period, and the rebuilt castle and surrounding walled moat of Tokugawa Ieyasu, the first shogun, remains the public centerpiece. The city and most of its cultural heritage was destroyed during World War II, and later the main streets were rebuilt to wider dimensions. At the central intersection of Hotta-dori and Sakura-dori, the streets are one hundred feet wide to prevent fires from crossing—a precaution from the days when wooden buildings, cramped housing, and open cooking fires resulted in frequent blazes. The street leading to the Tomei Expressway is decorated in a stylish fashion that belies the deeply conservative nature of the locale and people. Modern art sculptures adorn the sidewalks, and blue and white ceramic lampposts shaped like torchères line the avenues—oddly out of place in this no-nonsense city. The medians are bright with azaleas and grass. To the surprise of visitors, whose image of Japan is manicured gardens, there is quite a lot of litter tangled in the shrubs.

Nagoya is the regional and cultural home of Toyota Motor Corporation, although the company's real center is Toyota City, formerly the town of Koromo, about thirty-five miles away. Honored visitors to Toyota, arriving at Nagoya Central Station, are met by white-gloved, blue-suited chauffeurs driving black company cars. One can determine the importance of the visitor by the model of the car.

If Nagoya is physically an easy commute from Japan's major cities, temperamentally it is like a different country. The American notion that all Japanese businesses operate as one—like a large invading "Japan Inc." spider—is nonsense to anyone who understands the all-consuming nature of location, family, and local culture. In Japan Toyota is defined by its Nagoya roots; even its great wealth is attributed to the tradition of frugality. It is not uncommon for young men from other parts of the country to aspire to marry Nagoya girls because they know they will be thrifty. Although Toyota is a model for modern companies, and has been Japan's most profitable industrial company for years, Nagoya and its people remain the humble citizens of their feudal castle town. In many ways they embody the Japanese stereotype of hardworking, humorless people who keep their noses to the grindstone. They are less likely to be inspired by a national spirit, especially since they view Tokyo as the home of free-spenders and less disciplined workers. People in Nagoya are suspicious of national goals that appear to be at the expense of local prosperity. (That is why Toyota so often went head-to-head with MITI about complying—or not complying—with national trade goals and expansion plans.)

To understand Toyota and the region from which it sprang, one must remember that until the last thirty years, Nagoya was completely rural. After World War II its struggling farmers saw the company as the fulfillment of a dream for their children, who might work in the factories and prosper beyond the poverty of the agricultural life. It was this dream that inspired the extraordinary dedication and drive of Toyota's workers.

On the whole, Japanese car companies are more different from each other culturally than the Big Three in America, which all share a common epicenter in Detroit. The Japanese companies are not located in a single place, but are scattered across Honshu, the main island of Japan. Mazda, headquartered in Hiroshima, bears the mark of the city's tortured history. Flattened by the A-bomb, the city was rebuilt, but its wide streets and modern buildings mask the victim mentality that permeates everything about the otherwise bustling town.

Honda was created as an upstart motorcycle company by a talented engineer who prized independence and refused to be intimidated into giving up his dream of building cars just because he wasn't a founding member of the industry. To this day, Honda is an outsider in the industry, resented for being so successful when nobody believed it could be. Its late start in producing cars forced it to become international faster than its rivals, who found fortune in the home market first. Honda is headquartered in a steel and glass building in the Aoyama district of Tokyo. This is one of Tokyo's most fashionable and affluent areas, and it includes the city's most prestigious funeral house and cemetery.

Nissan is Tokyo-based, its urban prestige covering up for poor performance. In its dazzling Ginza headquarters, executives (mostly graduates of the prestigious Tokyo University) are stylishly dressed, well coiffed, and appear more sophisticated than many Japanese executives. Most high-ranking managers speak English and are not uncomfortable using it.

Toyota is provincial by Tokyo standards—a badge the company wears proudly. In Tokyo people often tell jokes about the "country bumpkins" of Nagoya, criticize their lack of sophistication, and denigrate their frugal, workaholic natures.

The Japanese are always creating new words to express ideas—kind of a fractured form of English. To illustrate Toyota's provincialism, the word *koromopolitan* was coined: Koromo is the original name of Toyota City; *politan* is the second half of the English word "cosmopolitan." To be referred to as *koromopolitan* is to be mildly ridiculed.

Toyota's headquarters is small by Western standards. The office buildings are surrounded by carefully trimmed azaleas and sculpted pine trees. Inside, there are few private offices and many open, cluttered bull pens with desks and filing cabinets. Uniformed office ladies (OLs), young college graduates hired to make tea, answer telephones, and perform limited clerical tasks, are stationed throughout the building. The most attractive OLs are located at reception desks on the ground floor and executive floor, ready to escort visitors to meeting rooms. They perform this task with lowered heads, shy smiles, and a demur wave of the hand to direct their charges to the correct room. Their style of practiced charm seems very Old World.

On the executive floor it has become customary for the chairman of the board and the president to share a single office, the better to collaborate. Theirs is a very different style of leadership from the Lone Ranger quality in American and European corporations. Indeed, the entire company is different. Lower-level executives don't even have offices, much less private secretaries.

The lobby and hallways are decorated in an eclectic mix of

cloisonné vases, ornate clocks, paper paintings, and Japanese and Impressionist Western art. There are special visitors rooms on the second floor, set aside for VIP meetings, which are rarely held in executive offices. These rooms are spacious and spartan, decorated in quiet tans, grays, and golds, with low chairs that leave long-legged Westerners with their knees higher than their hips. Large, low coffee tables hold tiny model Toyota cars filled with cigarettes, ashtrays and lighters, and clocks facing guests, which remind them they have a specific amount of time in which to conduct their business. Meetings always begin precisely on time and never exceed their stated length. If a foreign visitor fails to note his time is up, an OL will appear to gently remind her boss of an urgent meeting.

Toyota is unique among powerful Japanese companies because its wealth has given it a measure of independence from the influence of government, banks, and associated corporations that few companies enjoy. In 1991 it had around $18 billion. It is not dependent on a *zaibatsu*—the powerful group of banks, trading and insurance companies that surrounds most companies in Japan. To the contrary, Toyota's *zaibatsu* is dependent on it. Its family of parts suppliers has prospered along with it, and many businesses owe their prosperity to Toyota.

Toyota's stature leaves it unencumbered by the need to seek approval and advice from the outside. This was not always the case. Toyota was once loaded with debt, but it escaped from the clutches of its banks after learning that they exacted too high a price in exchange for their loans.

It is hard not to be impressed by the vitality and action of Toyota City, perhaps the largest company town in the world, which is extended further by the large number of suppliers whose operations spread into the surrounding towns and villages. Everything seems to be in motion at all times—an enormous industrial dance of parts delivery and production. Within a few miles of the headquarters, there are four assembly plants and dozens of factories run by Toyota affiliates. The streets are jammed with parts delivery trucks day and night, and caravans of cars being taken to their destinations for shipping. Uniformed workers scurry to and from factories. With the exception of a few rice paddies, persimmon trees, and small plots for growing onions and other vegetables, the entire landscape is devoted to cars.

Toyota City, Japan—January 1992

TOYOTA PRESIDENT Dr. Shoichiro Toyoda, sixty-seven, was a short, stocky man, intelligent and strong-willed. He was notably formal in his management style, even for the Japanese, who always observe the explicit rules of etiquette that accompany rank. The son of Toyota's founder, Kiichiro Toyoda, he ruled the company like a dynasty and was privately called the Crown Prince. Yet he spoke in customary humility about his own contribution, saying, "I am a son unworthy of his father. I am surrounded by these worthy souls and that is how I manage to get by even though I am mediocre." His words reflected the standard Japanese greeting, which always understated one's importance. For example, it is traditional for guests visiting a Japanese home to be greeted with a variation of, "Welcome to my unworthy home, please meet my inadequate wife and stupid children, and eat my unpalatable food."

Japanese businessmen are the most circumspect in the world, and Shoichiro* was a master of the art. He had limited fluency in English, but like so many Japanese, he understood more than he could speak, and often grasped the nuances of conversation that were beyond a translator's ability to provide.

As he presided over the unveiling of Toyota's new line of luxury cars at the 1991 Tokyo Motor Show, Shoichiro already knew about the serious challenges the company was facing at home and abroad. In no way was Toyota "on the ropes" in the manner of General Motors, but all big companies shared some common problems, and Toyota was not immune from them.

The success of the past twenty years was one part genius and one part good fortune. Every time a potential disaster struck, events would take over and turn things in Toyota's favor. The Japanese called it *kamikaze,* or "lucky wind." Also, Toyota seemed to do everything right. Like the prize student who always

---

* There are several Toyodas appearing in this book. To avoid confusion, they will generally be referred to by their first names.

scored straight As, it earned its share of both praise and resentment. A company that had never mass-produced cars before 1955, it had skyrocketed to the top in Japan, reaching around 41 percent in domestic market share (equivalent to GM's 1980s peak in America), and went on to achieve a powerful position in the international market. It was envied for its status as the world's low-cost producer, for its formidable wealth, and for its ability (prior to 1991) to launch one successful vehicle after another. Shoichiro and his second cousin and mentor, Eiji Toyoda, who now served as chairman of the board, had jointly presided over two decades of achievements.

But now both internal and external problems were beginning to impose themselves on Toyota's vision and strategy. Japan's struggling economy was only one part of the headache. Toyota had just completed a massive spending binge that had stretched its resources. New factories in Tahara, Kyushu, Great Britain, and Kentucky, along with heavy investments in new models, had dangerously raised its fixed costs.

To add to the company's troubles, there was also the prospect of trade barriers and quotas in the United States and Europe, and MITI was pressuring Toyota to pull back from its expansion plans. Shoichiro's stated goal had been "Global 10," achieving 10 percent of the world market by the end of the century. Now he was being urged to stifle the company's aggressiveness because of the wave of anti-Japan backlash and the drain Toyota's continued might was causing the other Japanese car companies, who felt compelled to play follow-the-leader, even though they lacked the means to keep up.

Other problems were surfacing. The acclaimed Toyota Production System needed an update, and declining birthrates and the reluctance of young people to work in factories were creating a labor shortage in Toyota City, where nearly everyone worked for Toyota or one of its affiliated companies. More and more, Toyota and its suppliers had to rely on older workers and foreigners. There was even talk of hiring some women, as if to demonstrate how great the crisis had become.

Although Toyota remained one of the most successful companies in the world, with its $18 billion in cash reserves, the challenges were a shock to the system of a company that had seemed invincible to many of its competitors.

To complicate matters further, Shoichiro was pondering a major management change. After ten years as president, it was time for him to move up to chairman and choose a new president. Eiji, now seventy-nine, was prepared to be less involved in the daily business of the company. In addition, Shoichiro, despite being firmly rooted in Nagoya culture, was taking a more active role in national Japanese business issues, and was spending more of his time in Tokyo, where Toyota had built a gleaming new office tower. He served as vice-chairman of the Keidanren, the Japanese Federation of Economic Organizations, and now he was angling to become its chairman. While Keidanren was no longer as influential as it had once been, it was still the most important organization representing Japanese industry. The chairman had a prestigious platform from which to express ideas, and the importance of the position reflected back to his company. Traditionally, the chairman of Keidanren was chosen from a Tokyo company like Nippon Steel or Tokyo Electric Power.

Shoichiro's chief competitor for the chairmanship was Yutaka Kume, chairman of Nissan. In Shoichiro's view, it was unthinkable that Kume, who had been a strident critic of Toyota's aggressive behavior, could win the position. Besides, Nissan was being soundly beaten by Toyota in the market and was bleeding financially. But Tokyo-based companies like Nissan, even if they were not the largest or wealthiest in their industries, were part of the ruling elite in Japan, and this gave Kume an advantage and made Shoichiro the underdog. Since the chairman of Keidanren was required to be chairman of his own company, Shoichiro had good reason to appoint a new president at Toyota and step into the more ceremonial role.

The rumors about Shoichiro's decision began circulating in early 1992, and attention quickly shifted to his successor. Speculation was high that Shoichiro would name his younger brother, Tatsuro, sixty-three, to the presidency.

In most Japanese companies the real influence rested in the president's office. The chairman of the board was the more ceremonial position. Unlike American companies, the board of directors was composed entirely of insiders—really a glorified executive committee.

At Toyota, with Eiji as chairman of the board, the dynamic was a little different, since Eiji's role in the company was so great and his influence so long-standing. As a result, it had taken Shoichiro about four years to truly take over as number one. Now that he was in firm control, the decision about a replacement was his alone to make.

As the busy rumor mill cranked out its scenarios for Shoichiro's replacement, there were some faint whispers that it might be a nonfamily member, not Tatsuro, but this speculation was never serious. It seemed unlikely that Shoichiro was ready to take the bold step of placing the company in the hands of a nonfamily member, especially since there were no strong candidates of the appropriate age at the executive vice-president level. It was the kind of dilemma that would be unheard-of in America's multibillion-dollar public companies, and it bespoke Toyota's entanglement in a tradition-bound society. In Japan the relationship between family and company was symbiotic, with firstborn sons of company founders being groomed for the top from the time they were children, but having to prove they deserved it. If there were no sons, the eldest daughter's husband could assume this role by being officially adopted by the daughter's family. This occurred early in Toyota's history and was currently the case with Osamo Suzuki, the dynamic leader of Suzuki Motors.

Although Toyota was a public company, its mentality was one of a private company, dominated by the founding family. Even the best and brightest executives at Toyota have always known there was a glass ceiling separating them from ultimate power. Blood was thicker than water, with the thickest blood belonging to the line of Kiichiro Toyoda, the founder.

The sole exception to this was Eiji Toyoda. Kiichiro and Eiji were cousins but they had become like brothers. In the 1930s and 1940s Kiichiro depended on Eiji to help build and operate his first factory, set up a research laboratory, and create prototypes of cars. Kiichiro shared his dream with Eiji when others in the family resisted his attempts to build a motor vehicle. Eiji was

Kiichiro's right hand, and his ascendancy through the company as it grew was well deserved.

Eiji was a remarkable man. Short, stocky, and gruff, he was the brains behind many of Toyota's product and marketing successes, and he remained the wise elder—the only one who had been with the company since its founding. He was also an engineering genius who had very definite ideas about how things should be done, and he knew how to challenge the organization to get the best out of it. Personally, Eiji was quiet, aristocratic, and decisive. Once he made up his mind, that was it. He was a natural leader who delegated authority well and created a powerful team around him. He encouraged the members of his inner circle to be independent and view themselves as his partners in making the company great. To him, that meant concentrating on quality as the ultimate means to success.

For many years it had been Eiji's dream to beat America and become the number one car company in the world. He had been surprised to observe how critical Americans were of their car companies, since in Japan the concept of consumer advocacy didn't exist. As Eiji watched the outcries from people like Ralph Nader during the 1960s, he was amazed to see what he considered to be the vulnerabilities of Americans. Everything was laid out on the table for public examination, and what he saw convinced him that Toyota could take advantage of the weakness of American companies. Along with his executive team, he devised a strategy that would ultimately make Toyota the most successful foreign import in America, gobbling market share from the American Big Three in their own country—initially from Ford and Chrysler, then, in the 1980s, from General Motors.

Shoichiro was similar to Eiji in bearing and temperament, but he had different ideas about running the company. He was less interested in input from others, preferring to manage things more autocratically. Even after he had turned the presidency over to Shoichiro in 1982, however, Eiji participated directly in the course of events from the chairman's seat. Shoichiro paid him quiet respect, but over the years, all of the strong executives loyal to Eiji retired and were replaced by Shoichiro's people. This changed the character of the company just as it was reaching maturity. It was no longer the small creative firm. It was now huge, resilient, and proud, manned by people who had no memory of the deprivation of the early years.

Eiji and Shoichiro sometimes disagreed about policy—especially about how far upmarket Toyota should move with new models. For example, Eiji promoted the development of a luxury car for the U.S. market, believing it would be the car that proved Toyota the engineering equal of BMW and Mercedes. Shoichiro questioned the project and voiced concerns that the consumers, even in America, wouldn't buy Japanese luxury cars. He wanted to build more cars for traditional Toyota customers, not for the wealthy few. This was where Toyota had proven success—by giving customers a bit more value for the money than their mass-market rivals. But Eiji always believed in challenging the organization through its products, and in the case of the luxury car, he was right. When the Lexus LS 400 was introduced in late 1991, it became an immediate success, outselling by three to one the luxury Nissan Infiniti Q-45, introduced just a few months later.

Fundamental to the difference between the two men were the separate challenges each faced as president. When Eiji was president, between 1967 and 1982, the issues were always related to product, productivity, and expansion. The company was filled with the zeal to beat America and make Toyota number one in Japan, and it possessed the passion of budding dreams. These were Japan's hidden years before it became viewed as a "threat" on the world stage. Shoichiro, on the other hand, had to respond in the 1980s to political and economic issues that were more complex. The passion of the early years, and the image of the underdog who made small, humble cars, were impossible to sustain once the company became established and wealthy. Shoichiro became president just as everyone was talking about the secrets of Japanese management and business practices, and the unfair regulations and impediments to exporting to Japan. By nature as well as necessity, Shoichiro was more worldly than Eiji. He understood that the Nagoya mentality would be insufficient for the new era of national and international challenges. During his presidency, Shoichiro talked about moving the company away from its provincialism, although in doing so, he was bucking a deeply entrenched local culture.

Now Shoichiro was faced with a decision: whether to keep the power in the family or to return the presidency to an outsider. His own son, Akio, thirty-six, a manager in the Toyota Corolla Domestic Administration Division, was too young and inexperienced to be president. Eiji's three sons all worked in the Toyota group of companies, but were also considered too young and inexperienced for the job; his eldest, Kanshiro, fifty, was executive vice-president of Aishin Seiki, a major Toyota supplier of mechanical components. (Fifty years old would hardly be regarded as too young in any Western company, but this was Japan.) The only logical family candidate was Shoichiro's younger brother, Tatsuro, currently an executive vice-president in charge of international sales.

In his own way, Tatsuro was also caught in a cultural bind. Corporate family dynasties in Japan were based on the succession of the firstborn son, who was cultivated for the position his entire life—not unlike a royal heir. The secondborn was not groomed for leadership, either by training or by design. In the Toyoda family, Shoichiro had been the golden child, destined to take over his father's company. His mother, Hatako, who had been quite a catch for the country boy Kiichiro, being from a prominent Kyoto family (the founders of the Takashimaya department stores), often said in the press that she expected her firstborn to assume full control of his father's company. Before her death in 1984, Hatako was a powerful matriarch who controlled her family with an iron will in the custom of Japanese grandmothers, who were the most honored members of the family, since they usually outlived their husbands. For example, when Hatako's grandchildren attended school in Tokyo, they lived with her rather than at school, so she could closely supervise their development. She always knew everything that was going on in the company, and she was Shoichiro's greatest promoter. Hatako was never heard to discuss the future of her secondborn, Tatsuro.

When Tatsuro was first brought into Toyota Motor Sales, he was not "mentored" as Shoichiro was. Although Shoichiro was carefully groomed, Tatsuro was basically left to sink or swim alone. Many people in the company believed that Tatsuro was temperamentally a very weak candidate. Having never been groomed, either practically or psychologically, for the top job, he could hardly be faulted for having poorly honed leadership skills, even though he spent his entire professional life at Toyota or in its affiliate companies. They feared that he would be inadequate at a time when circumstances required an articulate vision for the company, and decisive leadership in a less hospitable world. He lacked both the communal style of Eiji and the independent forcefulness of Shoichiro. Down the line, the whispered word was that Tatsuro's appointment would be difficult at a time when Toyota needed forceful leadership.

This reaction was not entirely fair. In almost every respect, Shoichiro's status and birthright as the heir apparent had effectively clouded the way for Tatsuro, who was never given the same chances his brother had to gain the right kind of experience. Shoichiro was carefully guided by his father and later, after Kiichiro died, by Eiji. The difference was apparent. As one insider observed, "At Toyota, regardless of how high the rank might be, everyone bowed to Shoichiro. But at Toyota Motor Sales, Tatsuro bowed to others."

The alternative of choosing a president from outside the family would not be without precedent, since Toyota had once before, in 1950, chosen a nonfamily member to serve as president. However, the circumstances of that selection were highly unusual. Indeed, the story of how Shoichiro's father, Kiichiro, stepped down from the presidency was the type of drama that could only be played out in a Japanese company, and spoke volumes about the unique cultural themes of honor and personal responsibility that were central to Japanese life.

In 1950 Japan was on the brink of depression, and Toyota Motor Company, the company Kiichiro Toyoda had lovingly nurtured for nearly twenty years, was on the verge of collapse. Although it had miraculously survived World War II, Toyota was a struggling small company that had yet to successfully mass-produce a car and had assembled only trucks for the military. In near financial ruin, there was little hope that it could survive without concessions from the labor unions and help from the

banks. Both prospects distressed Kiichiro. He had always promised his workers that they would have job security, and he understood he was turning over control of his company to impersonal
bankers who could not imagine the pain of losing one's lifelong
commitment. One of the demands of the Nagoya branch of the
Bank of Japan, which agreed to back Toyota, was that Kiichiro
lay off sixteen hundred workers. It filled him with agony. He
struggled over the mandate, deeply ashamed that it would cause
him to break his word to the workers about their job security,
but he finally bowed to the bottom line: either lay off the workers
or lose the company. He asked Eiji to help convince the union
that the layoffs were the only way to survive.

Standing before an assembly of two thousand angry workers,
Eiji pleaded with them to save the company by making the ulti-
mate sacrifice: "Toyota is like a boat that is foundering," he said.
"Unless someone jumps off into the water, the boat will sink."

The workers were outraged. They surged forward crying out,
"Call off the cuts! Call off the cuts!"

The situation was not that different from crises that had occurred in Western corporations, but Kiichiro's personal response
to the crisis was unlike any that would be seen in America or
Europe. In Japan, when a company is in trouble, the first person
who is called to account is the president. He is the one who takes
responsibility, who suffers first financially, and who, if necessary,
gives up his job. In Kiichiro's heart, he believed he had broken
faith with his workers and failed his company. With tears filling
his eyes, he told the workers, "Much as I am against it, unless we
make these cuts, the company doesn't stand a chance. I'm personally taking responsibility for this by resigning."

Hearing of Kiichiro's decision, Taizo Ishida felt his heart sink.
Some weeks earlier, Kiichiro had come to him and said that if it
became necessary for him to resign, he wanted Ishida to take over
the company. Ishida had replied, "If that's what you want, I
will." But he had dreaded the prospect. Toyota was Kiichiro's
company—his child. A humble but very competent finance man,
Ishida did not feel he had any right to the position. As the president of Toyoda Automatic Loom Works, the company established
by Kiichiro's father, Sakichi, he knew little about carmaking. But

he nevertheless accepted Kiichiro's decision to resign and his own ascendancy, since there was no other natural replacement. Kiichiro's firstborn son, Shoichiro, was only twenty-five. Eiji was also too young, at thirty-six, to take over.

In this way, Ishida, an outsider, became president of Toyota, although he never saw it as anything more than a temporary measure. "When the company becomes stable, you will return," he told Kiichiro repeatedly. And it was always assumed this would happen. After two years, with the company again prosperous, thanks to the purchase of trucks by Americans for use in the Korean War, Ishida urged Kiichiro to return. The Toyota founder was eager to do so, but he died suddenly just weeks before his scheduled comeback. The company remained under the direction of nonfamily members until 1967, when Eiji became president. It is notable that during Ishida's era, the company began to emerge as a strong contender. It would be Ishida who would lay the foundation for Toyota's other successes, such as its ability to control costs and make money without sacrificing growth, something no other Japanese car company had done.

When Eiji was president, it was always assumed that he would someday turn over the reins to Shoichiro. Ishida had privately voiced doubts about Shoichiro, but they were not shared by Eiji, who had formed a close relationship with the younger man. He was uncle, "godfather," protector, teacher, and guardian. When Shoichiro became president, he inherited an incredibly powerful company that was the product of Eiji's creation and was well run by his formidable team. It took years for Shoichiro to feel that he was really in charge—which didn't happen until the last of Eiji's team retired in the mid-1980s.

Now the question was whether or not the entire philosophy of the family-run business was suitable for the times. Toyota was the only large automaker in the world with the son of the founder or any family member still sitting at its head. Although Shoichiro had 20 million shares of Toyota stock (valued at about $200 million), it was not the shares that gave him power but rather the fact of his direct descendancy from the founder. Tatsuro may have been a weak candidate, but he shared that heritage.

In some respects, it could have been argued, Tatsuro was the right man for the times. Educated in the United States and conversant in English (which, unlike Shoichiro, he would use in casual greetings, though not in formal meetings), he had worked in America and was sent to oversee the start-up of NUMMI, the successful GM/Toyota joint venture in California. NUMMI wasn't the result of Tatsuro's efforts, since other executives effectively laid the groundwork. His presence there was not a true test of his abilities. Having spent much of his career in marketing, however, he appeared to possess many traits lacking in the typical Toyota executives who rarely ventured beyond the comfortable isolation of Nagoya. His visibility on the business scene was also a point in his favor. Some people suggested that Tatsuro had to be chosen because he had just, in April, become vice-chairman and president of Keizai Doyukai, the Japanese Association of Corporate Executives. This was an important industrial group, not unlike Keidanren, although somewhat less influential. There was a particularly cynical cast to this suggestion. Keizai Doyukai's chairman was T. Ishihara, the former president of Nissan; it was he who encouraged Tatsuro's appointment to vice-chairman. Some said it was a deliberate strategy. One Japanese magazine suggested that Ishihara knew if Tatsuro was made vice-chairman, Toyota would have to promote him to the presidency, since the position would not be fitting for a lowly executive vice-president. The magazine said this might be Ishihara's way of giving Nissan some room to maneuver around Toyota by weakening the latter's leadership.

In spite of Tatsuro's ease with international customs, and his notably warm personality, he was seen as having weak managerial skills, and this troubled many. In a time when hard decisions and innovative thinking were clearly the mandate, Tatsuro lacked the personal characteristics consistent with strong leadership. Diminutive almost to the point of appearing frail, he had a reputation for getting involved in the smallest details—such as planning a luncheon for foreign journalists and car dealers—while ignoring the substantive issues surrounding the meetings. (There was a story repeated so often it had become company legend. A group of American dealers were scheduled to meet with Tatsuro. Instead of preparing for the meeting, he spent half a day debating whether to serve fish or meat at lunch.) When the American operation was ready to introduce Toyota's new pickup, Tatsuro waffled on making the announcement, creating great frustration at all levels and infuriating dealers who had already been promised its delivery. Since Toyota's entry into large pickup trucks was viewed as a potential threat to U.S. companies who earned the bulk of their profits in these and other light trucks, Tatsuro delayed, hoping that an economic turn in the U.S. economy would seem to minimize the threat of Toyota's latest challenge. But the incident left the executives around Tatsuro worried that his lack of decisiveness would complicate the other adjustments Toyota had to make.

A retired company executive who had worked for Tatsuro confirmed that he had difficulty taking charge. "On most important issues, he couldn't make a decision," the executive said, still remembering his own frustration. "There was no response from him at all, even when there were several alternatives with one clearly being better. No response; nothing happened. Eventually, I would simply decide myself and inform him of what 'we' had decided. I would present it to him and he would agree, gaining confidence from the fact that someone else had taken responsibility."

It was no secret that Eiji was very demanding of Tatsuro, possibly trying to coax out of him the leadership that he felt was lacking. At meetings, Eiji was tough with him, pressing for details and explanations that Tatsuro was not always prepared to give. It would be unthinkable for Eiji to raise any public objections. In Japan the solemn privilege and responsibility of each president was to choose his successor, which meant that the future of the company was entrusted to a single individual. Eiji and others might have wondered about Tatsuro's appointment, but nothing was done, out of honor for Shoichiro's privilege. Nevertheless, those who knew the revered chairman well could see he was concerned about the prospect of Tatsuro at the helm.

By spring of 1992, however, Shoichiro had made his decision: Tatsuro would succeed him as president.

Tokyo—July 1992

THE FORMAL ANNOUNCEMENT that Tatsuro would be appointed president was made at a press conference on July 29 at the Keidanren Hall in Tokyo, a site Shoichiro preferred, for public relations reasons, to use for major announcements. Seated at the table were Tatsuro on the left, Shoichiro in the middle, and Masami Iwasaki, the new vice-chairman, on the right. Eiji was not present.

Shoichiro did most of the talking, couching news of Tatsuro's appointment in a carefully crafted set of unspoken caveats, which the Japanese press quickly latched onto as evidence that Tatsuro wouldn't be the independent executive his brother had been. Most revealing was the elaborate support system that was created around the new president. He was cushioned from the top by Eiji and Shoichiro, who would respectively assume the positions of honorary chairman and chairman; and from the bottom by an impressive buffer group of executive vice-presidents who would help him make decisions. Shoichiro diplomatically avoided directly stealing Tatsuro's thunder, but he did say, "In the future, managers should not depend on a single leader. All eight [referring to the five executive vice-presidents and three top executives, including Tatsuro] will be consulted in decisions of the company. So final responsibility may not be so clearly defined."

On September 28 there was a second press conference at the Hotel Okura to make the management shift formal. Eiji, Shoichiro, Tatsuro, Iwasaki, and the executive vice-presidents were all there, and this time Tatsuro did most of the talking. He seemed eager to soften the blow of his appointment, responding vaguely to questions about his plans, saying, "I will consult with the new honorary chairman and the new chairman to formulate a new policy." At the same time, he argued that his selection was based on experience and merit. "I don't think my being a Toyoda is the reason for my becoming president," he said with an entirely straight face. "I have no doubt that I was chosen because I have the right kind of experience. Allusion to nepotism is simply ludicrous." Nearly twenty-five years earlier, Eiji had made the same claim, as had Shoichiro in 1982. These men possessed such unquestionable stature that no one doubted the truth of their statements. Tatsuro's claim that his appointment had nothing to do with his family ties was received with a certain degree of incredulity by the press, however, and people in the company didn't buy it at all.

On October 29 Toyota hosted a huge party in honor of Tatsuro at the Hotel Okura, and hundreds of business leaders came to pay their respects and offer congratulations to the new president. The party was a customary rite of passage for those who had been promoted, but it wasn't altogether celebratory for many in attendance.

After the formal announcement, there was no dissent inside the company; that wasn't the Japanese way. But one executive admitted that there had been numerous meetings among senior executives to discuss how to deal with Tatsuro's management style while still remaining faithful to traditional management culture.

As evidence of Eiji's displeasure with the selection of Tatsuro, *Sentaku,* a respected Japanese magazine, reported that Eiji would continue attending meetings of Senmukai, the regular conference of Toyota's top management. As honorary chairman, he should not have attended those meetings. His presence was seen by *Sentaku* as a vote of no confidence in Tatsuro. Nevertheless, his role was uncertain. Although he was an elderly man, Eiji was still energetic and clear thinking, but he was from another generation. The company operations were being run by people thirty years his junior. He did not know them; they were not "his" people so he could not influence them. It seemed his role would be to stand as the personification of Toyota at ceremonial occasions.

Some observers assumed that Tatsuro's reign would be short and that he would retire within four years. This raised the long-term question of how Toyota would structure its management.

With the forces of global change challenging the company as never before, it was an odd time to be creating short-term stopgaps. Like its competitors, Toyota needed strong leadership more than ever. Even as he chose Tatsuro, Shoichiro was beginning to acknowledge that perhaps the company was headed for a great cultural upheaval; the end of the old family dynasty was near. "Look around," he said sadly. "We are the last generation."

For Toyota, the emerging problems and challenges ran wide and deep. On the international front, the company was clearly struggling with what it meant to be global—not just as a sales strategy but as a fundamental grounding. "Being global means that the personnel who run the company must be of many nationalities," warned one critic who believed that Toyota, along with many Japanese companies, "just doesn't get it." As an example, he mentioned the closed doors that greeted Americans and Europeans who worked in Japanese companies. "In America and Europe, there are opportunities for foreigners to be promoted, but not in Japanese companies," he said pointedly. Furthermore, the Japanese who lived and worked in Western countries remain isolated from the host culture, settling in Japanese ghettos that exist in the upscale districts or suburbs of every major city in the world.

Even some of Toyota's marketing strategies reflected a startling racial disharmony with the rest of the world. An example: A few years ago, Toyota opened a design center in Tokyo as a way of absorbing cultural influences outside its Nagoya center. One of the company's chief designers gave a lecture on why it was important to place design centers in the markets they serve. He gave a detailed analysis of the relationship of color choices to cultural preferences—why some colors were preferred by Europeans, others by Americans, and others by Japanese. He concluded his remarks by observing that color preferences were different in Europe and America "because they see out of blue eyes."

Historically, Toyota had shown itself to be brilliant when it came to the practical matters of production and product development, and in designing the cars people wanted to buy. These new challenges were different. They involved brand-new considerations such as cultural conflicts with the West, the pressure to stem growth for the sake of Japan's entire industry, and the emerging dissatisfaction of a new generation of workers who no longer wanted to be pushed so hard. In the old days, when building cars and getting them to market was the only focus of the company, the simplicity of the mission energized the workers at all levels. Now there was uncertainty about the future direction.

Recession at home rocked the economy, making the formerly invincible juggernaut vulnerable. The shock of simultaneous downturns in Japan, Europe, and North America, and harsh questioning of some of the basic principles that made Toyota great, were forcing a reassessment of strategy—especially whether it was feasible to continue pursuing market share above profits. Looking to the future, one Toyota executive voiced the sentiments of many when he said, "We have to change our financial constitution. We have to get away from the continuous growing circle: economic growth leading to more productivity leading to more investment leading to more productivity. Quality of business must come first rather than only pursuing continuous growth or enlarging sales volume."

His opinion represented some of the new imperatives facing the company. Growth had always been Shoichiro's main priority; he often spoke of how big the world was, and how much room there was for expansion. Global 10, his proud goal of achieving 10 percent of the world market, was now being challenged by MITI and the other Japanese car companies who blamed Toyota's aggressive growth for many of their own problems. But what would be Toyota's new emphasis, if not growth?

The pressure to pull back was coming from both government and business leaders in Japan. In essence, they accused Toyota of being too successful at the expense of other Japanese carmakers. Such a criticism would never be leveled against a Western company, where the rubric was survival of the fittest. But in Japan the concept of kyosei—literally, "symbiotic competition," a mandate to cooperate with one's competitors—was deeply rooted, although many modern thinkers believed it was an excuse for supporting losers and was not in the best interests of Japan.

Like a team whose star player was accused of stealing the show, Toyota, as the largest and wealthiest of the auto companies, was being charged with poor sportsmanship. Nissan complained that Toyota was so powerful that other companies had to follow its lead or perish, and they lacked the resources to do so. Others said that Toyota's relentless pursuit of global market share made exporting to the West more difficult for them. As one official said, "Unless Toyota changes its expansionist policy, Japan itself will die."

Rumblings in the ranks added further tension. Long-held worker policies were being directly challenged by a new generation who decried the rigidity of working in manufacturing. There was a distinctly hierarchical quality to Toyota's corporate style, even inside the factories. The younger generation of factory workers was bucking at a system that stifled personal growth and creativity, demanded absolute loyalty to the company, and forced a deadening work pace. In 1990 Toyota fared poorly in a ranking of Japanese companies that rated them according to originality, vision, adaptability, perception of goodness, and whether parents would recommend them to their children. In the latter category, Honda scored number one, while Toyota scored number nineteen.

There were even suggestions that employees of all Japanese companies, blue- and white-collar alike, were systematically cheated out of their fair share of profits. When Sony chairman Akio Morita boldly suggested that Japanese workers created wealth but did not share in it, the accusation stung. The charge seemed the height of disloyalty, given that Japanese companies had fought for decades perceptions from abroad that their success was built on the backs of exploited worker bees. But the statistical evidence supported Morita's point: The low standard of living of Japanese workers was a stark contrast to the supposed wealth of its companies, although that wealth had recently been undermined by deflation in real estate and stocks. Like others, Toyota was being pushed to adopt more benevolent work practices, especially since the shortage of young male factory workers promised competition within the industry. Toyota, like other companies, had a surplus of white-collar workers. The young people of Japan simply did not want to work in factories anymore. Japanese parents wanted their sons to work in offices and their daughters to marry men who worked in offices.

In 1992 the Japanese government announced its goal of *jitan*—shorter work hours—stating that all companies should strive toward 1,800 hours by 1996. Since the current Japanese auto industry level was more than 2,200 hours, it was quite a stretch. The goal of shorter work hours was a hardship for an industry that had traditionally relied on ten-hour days and Saturday work to meet normal demand. The combination of a shortage in factory workers and the mandate to institute shorter hours was placing unexpected stresses on the industry.

With all of these problems swirling at the company's center, the future suddenly didn't seem as certain as it had in the heady days of the late 1980s when Toyota could do no wrong. These were challenges that would humble the most self-assured and brilliant leader. Yet here they were, falling directly in the lap of Tatsuro Toyoda. These issues contributed to speculation that Tatsuro would hold the position for only a short time, and that he would be followed by an outsider. Leading the pack was Iwao Isomura, executive vice-president of personnel. In Japanese companies the personnel department was considered a status position —unlike American companies. Another contender was Hiroshi Okuda, executive vice-president of finance, known for his keen mind and broad experience.

But it also remained a distinct possibility that another Toyoda would again assume leadership down the road. Shoichiro's son, Akio, was quietly being groomed by some senior executives and might emerge as a force within the company. Akio could turn out to be the ideal representative of a new era at Toyota. A graduate of Babson College, he worked in an American brokerage firm before returning to Japan to work at the Motomachi factory for three years, then in Toyota Motors Credit Corporation before assuming his current marketing position. One person who knew Akio well observed that "he wears two hats—one to work with dealers and one as a member of the founding family." In the latter, Akio was said to be quietly working to understand how the company should change.

In any case, that was the future. For the short term, it could be Tatsuro's ill fortune to preside over two or more years of falling profits at Toyota, due to circumstances that were totally beyond his control. Unfortunately, in the Japanese tradition, he would have to assume personal responsibility for all of Toyota's problems, whether they were his fault or not. Unlike General Motors, where the buck had often seemed to bypass the man in charge, the Japanese tradition held the president accountable for the rise and fall of a company's fortunes.

While the company continued to expand beyond its provincial Nagoya base, there were warning signs that it may need to return, at least in spirit, to the Nagoya tradition of frugality, "guarding the castle" by its own hands. In other words, it was time for Toyota to get its house in order.

FOUR

Tumbling Walls, Changing Vistas

Looking out of my office, you see a marvelous sight. You don't see an Iron Curtain anymore. Instead, you see a beautiful landscape, which is open now all the way to Moscow.

—CARL HAHN

Frankfurt—October 1990

DR. CARL HORST HAHN settled into his seat on the Volkswagen corporate jet and picked up the notes for a speech he was preparing to give the next day. Behind him, his bodyguard, and journalist Christiane Oppermann of *Stern* magazine, belted themselves in. It was only a short hop—less than an hour—from Frankfurt to Prague. The Volkswagen chairman seemed a little more tense than usual. Normally, he would have been chatting warmly with his companions, but on this day he was lost in his own thoughts—shuffling papers, making notes, and occasionally stopping to gaze distractedly out the window.

The official reason Hahn was traveling to the still elegant if frayed Czech city was to deliver a speech at an international management conference. But his private and more compelling agenda was to use this platform to persuade Czech politicians that Volkswagen, not the French company Renault, was best suited to revive Skoda, the state-owned carmaker that was the subject of a heated bidding war. Nearly every important automaker in the world had given Skoda a once-over, including General Motors. Now the bidding had narrowed to two. Hahn believed Skoda's engineers and workers preferred Volkswagen, although President Václav Havel and his ministers felt a sentimental draw toward the French company. Hahn's task was to convince them to set aside their emotions and understand why Volkswagen was the best choice.

Hahn, then sixty-four but looking much younger, was a man well suited for international gamesmanship. He possessed a charming, cosmopolitan personality and spoke several languages, including Czech. After eastern Europe opened up, he was intrigued with the opportunities that might exist in its underdeveloped markets. After the Berlin Wall fell, he liked to point to a map and boast of Volkswagen's home, "Wolfsburg used to be at the edge of Germany, and now it is in the center of Europe. It is only 360 kilometers from Prague, 670 from Warsaw, 1,300 from Barcelona and 470 from Brussels." His intention was to gain favor with eastern Europe by showing that VW was closer to it than to western Europe.

Hahn was equally at ease across the ocean in America, which was the home of his greatest personal and professional success, the establishment of the Beetle as the most popular import in the United States. In 1959, when Hahn was sent to America to sell Volkswagen's odd little bug-shaped car, he didn't expect much, especially since early forays by others to the States had been abominable failures. But the Beetle became a cult car and Hahn received the credit. By the time he returned to Wolfsburg in 1964, Hahn was known as Mr. Volkswagen throughout America and sales had reached 500,000 cars a year.

During his stay in America, Hahn met his wife, Marisa, the sister of popular novelist Danielle Steel. He enjoyed his sister-in-law, and even though his reading tastes were notably highbrow, he always made a point of saying he read Steel's novels. The Hahns' four children were born in the United States before he was called back to Germany. There, he entered a rocky period, which culminated with him challenging management and being

fired from the company. He was named chairman of the floun-
dering Continental Tire Company and regained his reputation by
turning the company around. In 1982, when he was asked to
return to VW as chairman, it was a victorious homecoming.

Because of his international experience and his preference for
the world outside Wolfsburg, Hahn seemed to be a Renaissance
man. But he was also very much a product of his cultural heritage, displaying what might be described as good old-fashioned
Prussian values. He was disciplined, well mannered, and a master
of ritual who possessed an elegant, near regal bearing. Unlike
most auto executives, who were not known for their fashion
sense, Hahn was a very stylish dresser. In the company of executives and people of influence, he had a commanding presence. He
drew people to him who wanted to know what he thought on all
subjects political, social, economic, and environmental. During
these discussions, he carefully couched his true opinions in statistical analyses, and he was adept at beating critics to the punch
with a full defense before they could get their mouths open. He
frequently quoted noted writers and philosophers, which could
be intimidating to those who were less well schooled. Hahn was a
natural leader, and as the head of Europe's largest car company,
he was the de facto spokesman for the European auto industry. It
was a role he relished.

Hahn's arrival at the Prague airport was treated with a flurry
of activity of the kind usually reserved for celebrities. As he and
his companions waited for passport clearance, Hahn was his
usual charming self, graciously ordering coffee—in perfect Czech,
of course—and serving it himself. Outside of the terminal, two
Audi sedans were waiting, with drivers and security guards from
President Havel's staff. Hans Holzer, Volkswagen's liaison officer
in Prague, joined Hahn in one of the cars and filled him in on the
behind-the-scenes intrigue surrounding the widening rift in
Czechoslovakia.

Less than a year after the nonviolent revolution of November
1989, there were already rumors that the Slovaks were pressing
for independence from the Czechs. They felt like second-class citizens in the country where Czechs held control of every major
industry and all important government jobs. The conflicts be-

tween the two groups were much older than the communist government; they stemmed from the times of the Austrian monarchy when the Czechs had many rights to which the Slovaks had no access. The Czechs enjoyed political power and had developed a broad-based intellectual elite. The Slovaks were peasant farmers and later factory workers who resented their inferior position.

Hahn listened to Holzer's reports without much comment, but deep down he was on the side of the Czechs and believed the Slovaks would be sorry for pressing for a separation. Naturally, he was concerned about a new fracture in the eastern nation that was exposing the tenuous structure of the region, not only wrecking business opportunities but destabilizing Germany by flooding western Europe with refugees. But still he believed the market there was wide open, since there were currently so few cars on the road. He also felt a personal need to play a role in both Germany's and eastern Europe's revival. Hahn had an altruistic side to him that was part hero complex. He believed he could make a difference and it gave him a great deal of satisfaction. Hahn frequently talked about the void left by communism and the threat of the newly opened borders. He worried about the consequences of inward migration, as people fled eastern Europe for a better life.

Hahn felt the Czechs would win this skirmish, but he was hedging his bets. At the same time he was chasing Skoda, he also made a bid for the Bratislava Motor Company in the capital of Slovakia. The deal was still under wraps; Hahn had asked the Slovakians to keep it that way until his negotiations with Skoda were complete.

It was Hahn's philosophy that in Europe it was better to take over a local car producer and develop it into a flourishing business than it was to set up a new operation or open a subsidiary under the VW name. Until Hahn, all of VW's expansion had been based upon producing Beetles and later Golfs in satellite factories. Hahn argued that the company benefited from customer loyalty to homegrown brands, and used Opel as an example. Most German consumers didn't consider Opel American-owned; its cars never suffered when the people were in a nationalistic "buy German" mood.

As they drove toward the hotel, the scene outside the car was vibrant evidence of Hahn's greatest hopes. Prague was noisy and bustling—a cosmopolitan, now free city, whose people still seemed to be trying on their new status. The avenues were crowded with young men and women dressed in fashionable Western clothing; some of their hairstyles were right out of MTV. Cafés and restaurants spilled open with overflow crowds, laughing and drinking. Beer and wine were very cheap, and the food was solid, home-style fare, served in abundance. A full meal, including beer and coffee, cost the equivalent of a dollar. The sounds of jazz drifted into the air, and it was hard to imagine that only a few years ago many musicians had been in jail. Prague might have been any other European capital except for the shabby, crumbling buildings (some scarred with bullet holes as old as World War II) and the absence of cars on the road. Nearly everyone was walking, biking, or riding in trams and buses. The price of gasoline was so high that even if the people could afford to buy cars, they could not afford to drive them; a full tank of gas averaged one-fifth of the average citizen's monthly income. Nevertheless, the air was heavily polluted—not from cars, but from the coal that was used as a primary source of fuel.

When the cars carrying Hahn and his group arrived at their destination, the lavish Hotel Praha, former guesthouse of the communist government, Hahn turned chatty. He loved to share his knowledge of small cultural details and now he pointed out the architecture, explaining that all state-owned buildings were decorated with acres of marble that had been procured from Cuba in exchange for oil and machinery. Marble and sugar were the two major exports Cuba used to buy energy and industrialization from its communist brothers.

Later that evening, Hahn left the hotel for a private meeting in town. On the way, he stopped at the Hradčany, Prague's famous castle, which served as Václav Havel's official residence. As he entered the courtyard, he was brought up short by the sight of about fifty soldiers in full military dress, performing ritual marches in the darkened area. The scene held an eerie sense of déjà vu, and Hahn watched uneasily as the soldiers clicked their heels in unison and stamped their rifle butts on the pavement.

Momentarily alarmed that this scene signaled some kind of coup against Havel, Hahn turned to Holzer. "What's going on here?" Holzer assured him that it was just a training session of the presidential guard. Hahn relaxed a bit but he could not suppress a sudden shudder. "They are really good at it," he marveled. "Even better than the Russians, and they were known for their excellence."

Hahn's speech the next day in front of about two hundred business people, mostly local, took place in an auditorium at the former Communist Party headquarters. He talked about the necessary process of economic transformation and warned his attentive audience of the pitfalls inherent in such dramatic change —especially the danger of excessive wage escalation and the need for an investment in modern technology. Czech industry, like those of all former communist countries, was notoriously overmanned and underdeveloped. To be competitive with western Europe, it needed a massive infusion of technology and a plan for patient, steady growth.

After lunch, Hahn participated in a panel discussion in a smaller room. Although it was built to accommodate thirty, more than one hundred people crowded into the room and it was stiflingly hot. They seemed most interested in hearing from Hahn, and the other panelists were virtually ignored. Hahn was charming and effusive. He used the forum as a sales pitch for VW. He boasted about VW's technological and engineering successes. Again and again, he referred to the company's turnaround of SEAT, the Spanish carmaker it had taken over in 1986, as if to say, "Let us show you what we can do for Skoda."

The acquisition and revival of SEAT was one of Hahn's great success stories. When VW purchased the company, it was a losing state-owned carmaker, administrated by a dusty crew of has-been military leaders from the Franco regime. It was not regarded as a viable producer. Other companies, including Fiat, which held a minority interest, found the idea of investing more money in this sorry company laughable. But Hahn said, "Let's do it." Within two years, SEAT was making a profit—an overnight reversal that amazed even Hahn. Although part of the growth came from the sudden explosion in car demand in Spain, Hahn was happy to take the credit.

What VW got from the deal was the opportunity to establish a low-cost manufacturing foothold in Europe. For one thing, Spanish wages were only about one-half that of Germans. SEAT produced the small VW Polo, but retained its national character and its own unique models, which it carried over from the previous owner. Volkswagen was a benign and generous parent, willing to provide whatever its Spanish offspring needed to prosper. Now Hahn promised he could achieve the same thing with Skoda, especially in light of the similarities between the two companies.

Skoda was the most modern auto manufacturing operation in the East Bloc, which didn't make it exactly "modern," since postcommunist nations were stuck in a time warp. Its factories were vintage 1960s, and one of its cars, the Favorit, was comparable to Western cars of the early 1970s—sturdy but crude transportation, produced in only two colors. The Czechs were proud of the Favorit. For many years it had been, as its name implied, the favored vehicle for East Bloc countries. The brand name Skoda was also known in western Europe, so Hahn believed there was a good chance of opening new markets there. Although the conditions of Skoda were archaic by contemporary standards, Hahn believed it provided an opportunity for VW to play a seminal role in shaping the industrial destiny of the most promising of the newly opened nations. In the process, he hoped to help VW mitigate some of its own problems at home—in particular, the high cost of labor.

Hahn wanted Skoda desperately. He hoped that it would give Volkswagen a crucial foothold in eastern Europe, even though it was impossible to say how many years it would take for the investment to pay off. He was convinced that whoever got there first would be the ultimate victor, and he hated the thought that it might be the French or, worse still, the Americans or Japanese. "In the next five years, as the Japanese begin to move into Europe, I think European manufacturers will be well advised to compete with the Japanese by concentrating on engineering and manufacturing," he said. "We also have to face the fact that the eastern European countries will not be blind to selecting their partners. They will not look only at the Germans, Italians or French. They will look at the Americans and they will certainly also look at the Japanese. The Japanese have already made cooperative ventures with East Germany."

Hahn's position—that first is better—was not shared by all. As Red Poling, chairman of Ford, liked to point out, the most successful carmakers in the United States were the Japanese, and they were the last to build factories there.

Skoda was an opportunistic venture; Hahn was buying it because it was available and he didn't want to miss the chance. He also felt the Czech company was well suited to the Volkswagen temperament. Although there were still remnants of hostility in Czechoslovakia toward the Germans, dating back to Hitler, there were many cultural similarities between the two countries. Hahn appreciated the fact that workers there were well trained, industrious, and orderly. This compatibility of engineering skills and values would make them potentially good partners and kindred spirits with the Germans. His favorite example of the mutual thinking was that Skoda had copied an axle from the Golf.

He also felt he needed Skoda in the same way he had needed SEAT. As long as Germany's overall economy was thriving, Hahn could not address the pork-barrel labor practices without alienating those who represented his power base on the supervisory board. Yet he knew VW costs were so high that he had to do something. So he sought to solve his catch-22 by making investments outside of Germany that would reduce the overall average cost per vehicle in the company.

After returning from his Czechoslovakia trip, Hahn sat down with his executives and began to develop a bid that would be more attractive to the Czechs than the one being proferred by Renault and its partner, Volvo. VW's plan was generous and appealing. It promised the modernization of existing facilities, the construction of a new car plant, doubling of capacity to 400,000 cars by the end of the decade, development of new models, and the creation of a separate Skoda dealer network across Europe. It also promised to retain the twenty thousand workers currently employed by Skoda. Although Renault was turning around after forty years as a government-owned disaster, and the French government was prepared to be generous, VW prevailed because Hahn promised a larger investment and no labor reductions.

On December 9 the Czech government officially approved Volkswagen's bid. The agreement called for VW to start with a 35 percent stake in the company and build it to 70 percent by 1995.

Hahn was elated, and to the outside world, including others in the auto industry, the deal was viewed as a major coup for the German company. The only voices of doubt came from the financial community, which wondered where the money would come from to pay for VW's largess. There was concern that VW would take all of the risks of pioneering, then other companies would move in after the political and economic climate in the country had stabilized. "Volkswagen will spend billions of dollars to come in first as a local producer," observed Stephen Reitman of UBS Phillips & Drew Securities. "But their rivals may reap a big share of the rewards without having invested nearly as much money." There was also concern that Skoda would compete with SEAT and stress the company with the challenge of selling two cheap car brands.

But overall, Hahn's stature was boosted by the deal, and many thought him to be a visionary. It appeared that under Hahn's cool direction, VW was adding to its position as an international company. In every way, Volkswagen was well cast for the role of third participant in the Global Big Three. It was the largest and most aggressive European carmaker, now poised to become even stronger if the promises of German and European unification were fulfilled. Like GM and Toyota, VW was responding to the need to confront the saturation and high labor costs in western Germany by expanding abroad. Yet also like GM and Toyota, it refused to confront the most difficult home-based challenges that could ultimately stifle its ambitions.

Wolfsburg, Germany—April 1992

THE VIEW from Carl Hahn's thirteenth-floor office at Volkswagen headquarters in Wolfsburg, Germany, was not one to lift the spirit. When the chairman turned away from his desk for a moment of reflection, he couldn't gaze contemplatively at the wide, open sky or the bucolic country landscape that surrounded the VW complex. His view on all sides was of the long gray brick buildings of his company with their smokestacks—"built for eternity" by Adolf Hitler—and the lots filled with cars. The sight could seem oppressive, even on a sunny spring day. Darkened by time, the buildings gave the complex a somber look, and the constant disquieting vibration from the nearby stamping presses put visitors to the corporate office on edge. Nevertheless, Hahn was comfortable here. It was his domain.

Adolf Hitler had once dreamed that Wolfsburg would become the shining industrial center of his European empire. That never happened, but by the 1990s it had achieved its goal of being a modern industrial city, albeit one dependent on a single company, Volkswagen, for its existence.

Wolfsburg's monoculture could be depressing. All life revolved around Volkswagen and it tended to be dreary and regimented—a large, gray company town. Since Wolfsburg was an artificially created city, built around the company, it lacked the quaint charm of old Europe. There was no sense of history or culture. For example, it was characteristic of old European cities to have a well-defined town center, usually marked by a church and a town hall. All the streets led to this center, like arteries spreading to the heart. Wolfsburg possessed no center or focus of history and culture. And, since the partitioning of Germany after World War II, it was not a place to pass through on the way to somewhere else. German companies avoided Lower Saxony despite favorable tax treatment on investments, and this added to its isolation.

The lives of the 130,000 Wolfsburg residents revolved around work in the factories, where they operated on a two-shift system. The typical worker was on a 5:30 A.M. to 2:00 P.M. shift one week, and a 2:00 P.M. to 10:30 P.M. shift the next week—hardly an arrangement that encouraged socializing. Those who had to get up at 4:30 in the morning retired early, and those who worked late into the night were satisfied to collapse in front of the television with a beer.

But even a change in the shift schedule would have done little to enhance community life in Wolfsburg. According to sociologist

Martin Schwonke, who conducted a study of cultural life in the industrial town, human social relations depend on more than work schedules. Professor Schwonke found that only four out of ten citizens had a positive opinion of their neighbors. Interviews revealed "unqualified collective prejudices." Examples of remarks included "Wolfsburg citizens per se are awful because they are so arrogant." And "Everyone wants to show off and prove he is better than the other." And "Solidarity does not exist. The population is mixed up and bigheaded."

From the beginning, the population of this artificial city had been a melting pot of people from different regions, all attracted by Volkswagen's need for workers. There were refugees from East Prussia and Silesia (territories that came under Soviet occupation after World War II), people flooding in from the Rhineland, and guest workers from Italy, Portugal, and Turkey. The mix of mannerisms, languages, and expectations worked against all efforts to create an assimilated community. Like the Japanese, Germans struggled with a history of racial exclusivity that prevented outsiders from becoming readily accepted. For the most part, the various groups in Wolfsburg kept to themselves.

Not that anyone was particularly interested in socializing. As it was, they encountered people from work wherever they went—at the hospital, the pub, or the sauna. And the hierarchy within the company was carried into the leisure environment. "It is a fact," grumbled one worker, "that a hall supervisor [plant manager] will not talk to a press worker outside the factory, even if they are both dressed in the same suits." Such elitism was characteristic of German society in general. Everyone was very conscious of status. In meetings between two companies, or even between two groups within the company, they would make sure that the contingents included exactly the same number of people with equivalent titles and degrees.

Resentments festered between workers and management, but in the closed society of Wolfsburg, it was hard to escape. As Professor Schwonke noted, "The subtle hostility of the parents is carried out among the children in violent attacks and open disputes. The parents very often react to the outbursts of temper and violence with strict control of the social groups their kids are in and with prohibitions against playing with certain other children."

In some quarters of the city, people built walls to fence out their unwelcome neighbors. Houses were constructed with walled-in mini-gardens, and many homes had no windows facing the street, the better to avoid contact with others.

The shining industrial city was better appreciated in vision than in reality. Even the cleanliness of the streets and the absence of dark alleys made Wolfsburg seem cold and unreal—unlike a pulsing, live city. The sterility of the city, its distance from Germany's urban centers, and the fact that for most of its history it stood in the shadow of the Wall with its barbed wire and grim guards pointing automatic machine guns, made it hard for Volkswagen to attract the best and the brightest. Managers from other companies flatly refused to accept positions in Wolfsburg, even for premium pay. In spite of its sterility, Wolfsburg was a relatively affluent community, with the highest per capita income in Lower Saxony. It had twenty tennis complexes, seventy gymnasiums, and numerous swimming pools and sports facilities, all open to the public.

Still, the monoculture could make life dull. Carl Hahn's penchant for travel might have been partially attributed to his boredom with the headquarters town, which was a two-and-a-half-hour drive from Berlin, three hours from Hamburg, and one hour from Hanover.

Nevertheless, the man loved his job and basked in the glow of his position as leader of the European auto industry. That was why, on this particular April day, he slumped in his office chair, staring out the window and wondering if he should have retired on schedule a year earlier instead of extending his contract only to face a shocking and unexpected humiliation.

The man who had been frequently cast as a heroic figure, a widely proclaimed visionary whose attention and image spanned the world, had just been unseated by one of his own. Now he sat in his office reviewing the message he would be delivering that afternoon—the announcement of his retirement a year earlier than expected. Despite the fact that he had just been named Man of the Year by *Automotive Industries,* which lauded his dar-

ing global expansion strategy, Volkswagen was suddenly overwhelmed by problems at home, and these led to Hahn's prema-
ture departure. Ferdinand Piech, fifty-four, chairman and chief
executive officer at Audi, the luxury car operation owned by VW,
and the nephew of Ferdinand Porsche, who designed the first
Volkswagen prototype, had forced Hahn out of his job.

It was a bitter blow for a man who had known no other life
than the auto industry. He had been born into it. His father, Carl
Hahn, Sr., founded a carmaker, Auto Union, before World War II
and was active in the industry until after the war, when his plant
was dismantled by the Soviet forces. He eventually rebuilt the
company as Audi NSU in Ingolstadt, West Germany, and it was
taken over by Volkswagen in 1965. In a piece of historical irony,
Hahn's father and Ferdinand Porsche, a relative of Piech's, were
on different sides of the debate over Hitler's plan to mass-produce an inexpensive "people's car." Ultimately, Porsche won
both Hitler's favor and the debate.

The signs that the end was near for Hahn were clearly visible
by the first months of the year. In early March, when the international automotive industry gathered at the Geneva Auto Show to
look over the newest models, renew old acquaintances, and talk
casually about business, the major topic of discussion was who
would be Hahn's successor. Rumors were growing stronger every
day that Hahn would be asked to retire early. At the show, journalists and his fellow industry leaders seemed to avoid him with
embarrassment—a sign of how fast and gracelessly the mighty
could fall. Hahn didn't seem like himself. The normally confident
leader was quiet and moody, especially striking since only
months earlier he had been the subject of praise because of the
success of the latest version of VW's popular car, the Golf, which
had been named Europe's Car of the Year; his widely acclaimed
strategy in negotiating the takeover of Skoda; and his growing
stature as a "statesman" who was eloquent in understanding and
addressing the industrial and social problems of eastern Europe.

Walking alone around the competitors' stands at the Geneva
fair, Hahn could already sense the waning of attention and deference to which he had grown so accustomed. It was a great blow
for him. Only seventeen months earlier he had been honored by

the *Aufsichtsrat,* VW's supervisory board, with an extension of his contract beyond normal retirement—a very unusual event in the German business community and a great honor for him. In some circles, and perhaps in his own mind, he had risen above the mundane problems within his own company. Perhaps he was so preoccupied that he was unaware of how quickly the situation was deteriorating beneath the veneer of triumph. But the crisis within Volkswagen was steadily mounting, though perhaps obscured to the outside world by booming German auto sales and Volkswagen's rising European market share. In reality, VW's underlying financial stability was severely threatened by an organization that didn't work and a cost structure that was out of control. For example, although orders were pouring in for the Golf, parts shortages resulted in thousands of unfinished cars being stockpiled in every available space in the cavernous Halle 54, Volkswagen's main plant, as well as on the lawns and lots throughout the VW complex. It looked more like a vast parking lot than a corporate headquarters.

The biggest issue was how to address the high cost of production—a problem systemic to the company and to Germany in general. Although car demand was still high, it was obvious that Germany would soon begin paying for the costs of reunification with a recession. The dire situation would be complicated by a huge labor surplus, especially in the former East Germany, and a tenacious resistance to wage cuts for workers—a condition that had made Germans the highest paid laborers in the world.

For years, the German car industry had lived off its ability to continuously pass along higher costs to consumers because of the superior engineering technology of its cars. This was especially true of BMW and Mercedes. In many ways VW suffered from the same problems as the entire German auto industry. But it was unique, too. For one thing, it sold relatively inexpensive cars compared to Mercedes and BMW. For another, it was partially owned by Lower Saxony, now governed by a coalition of Greens and Social Democrats, making it nearly impossible to force the supervisory board to deal with the labor cost problem.

It was easy to see how the system was out of control. There was little a single company chief like Hahn could do about it, unless he was willing to go head-to-head with the union, which was his strongest ally and the support behind his power base. But the high labor costs and plant inefficiency were sucking the life out of the company. Despite VW's ability to charge higher prices than its competitors because of its image, its after-tax profit margin of 2.8 percent was low, even considering the peculiarities of German accounting, which allowed the company to shield its profits.

Hahn's overseas maneuvers, though praised for expanding VW's empire, added more financial and business risks to the relatively provincial company. No one could predict what would ultimately come of the changing European configuration, and making investments in politically chaotic and economically depressed nations was risky, as VW discovered when transmissions it was purchasing from Yugoslavia ceased to be available as that country tore itself apart. Furthermore, Volkswagen failed miserably in the world's most competitive market, the United States. After establishing the small-car standard with the Beetle and holding a singular edge for a decade, Volkswagen gave it all away to the Japanese.

Throughout the 1980s Hahn and his lieutenants offered no clear vision for reasserting themselves in the United States and Canada. They simply cut their losses by closing their only plant in Westmoreland, Pennsylvania, and located the few remaining cars they sold out of Mexico. The new design studio erected outside of Los Angeles to monitor emerging trends did nothing to boost sales, since the company lacked the vehicles and marketing. Nor did a clever ad campaign launched shortly after George Bush's disappointing trip to Japan. VW briefly aired television ads promising loans and insurance payments to customers who lost their jobs. The American public didn't buy it. The company sold fewer than 100,000 cars in the United States during 1991, and there was no sign of a turnaround. Meanwhile, the aging men who ran the company remembered fondly the glory days of the Beetle, and they found it hard to comprehend that a new generation of Americans had never heard of or seen the once-popular car. They were out of touch with reality and they didn't grasp the permanence of the failure or the fact that Volkswagen had become irrelevant in

America. There was always a sense that they'd be able to regain strength in America whenever they wanted to. But it was wishful thinking. VW cars were no competition, either in price or in design, with Japanese and even many U.S.-made cars.

More fundamental still to the future of Volkswagen was the absence of any product development strategy that could free it from total dependence on the Golf. At Volkswagen, the car—or more aptly, Hitler's vision of the car—created the company, rather than the company creating the car. Volkswagen never went through the necessary infancy and growth period that builds substance and maturity. In a sense, the broad-based skills needed to be a car company were stunted even as sales of one model soared. VW was all engineering and production, with none of the refinements of knowing how to market the cars. The first postwar president, Heinrich Nordhoff, who had recovered VW from the wreckage of Hitler's lost dreams, had understood how to build cars, but he assumed they would sell themselves. He didn't see the need to develop a broader range of models. Nordhoff became obsessed with building more and more Beetles, not with understanding its consumers or creating the expertise found in well-rounded companies. Since the 1960s, VW had never managed to repeat the international success of the Beetle, even with the Golf, which was the best-selling model in Europe. More than any other factor, this challenged Volkswagen's future: It was still a one-car company and very much a German company, despite Hahn's international investments.

For too long a time, Hahn refused to be distracted by the problems at home. The transformation of eastern Europe invigorated him and gave him a rationale for coping with VW's costs and selling more cars. The *Aufsichtsrat,* the governing board of Volkswagen, was happy to go along with Hahn's plan and praise his strategy. Hahn was pleased to receive word that his contract had been extended through 1993. He wasn't ready to retire. "When you do something you love, that all your heart belongs to, this is not something you give up easily," he said with a vigor that belied his age.

But he did not know that his professional sibling, Ferdinand Piech, was already busy organizing a power play.

In early 1992 reports were leaked to the press, detailing Volkswagen's problems. Pretax profits were down, from almost 3 billion marks in 1989 and 2.4 billion in 1990, to only 1.785 billion for 1991. The greatest decline was in the Volkswagen brand; by comparison, Audi appeared very profitable, but the report avoided several key facts. It did not consolidate the losses from its sales in the United States, which had to be carried by Volkswagen. It was also not mentioned that in 1991 Audi had liquidated reserves of about 200 million marks to pump up its profits. Nevertheless, Audi, which operated independently from the parent company, was the financial star in the VW empire and Piech was the man who made it so by slashing costs and developing salable cars.

It was rumored that the leaks about Volkswagen's poor performance came from Piech's operation, Audi, which was owned by VW but operated like an independent company. However they reached the press, the reports began chipping away at Hahn's veneer of greatness. Journalist Günther Ogger wrote sarcastically, "In the tenth year of his job at the helm of the Volkswagen Corporation, the former Beetle salesman accomplished the miracle of losing 770 million marks during the biggest car boom of all time."

The gloomy reports made the supervisors of the *Aufsichtsrat* sit up and take notice. For the first time, there was serious concern about the company's financial health—so serious that the board decided to ask Hahn to retire early. In many ways, the wake-up call received by the *Aufsichtsrat* mirrored that of the GM board. Like the GM directors, they had given Hahn a free rein. They ignored the implications of his actions and didn't question his policies and priorities. The board went along with Hahn's program as long as it didn't disturb their constituencies in the unions or Lower Saxony. The news from Hahn always seemed good: great sales, high European market share, growing prestige as an international company. The members of the *Aufsichtsrat* assumed —and they were led to believe—that tremendous profits would follow.

But now, with rumors of Hahn's demise in the air, executives began furiously jockeying for his position. There was no shortage of candidates. One was Martin Posth, who had started and managed VW's Shanghai operation and had become manager of personnel upon his return from China. Posth was known for his blunt way of describing the company's cost problems, and for his frequent demands that the company find ways to increase productivity.

Other candidates included Dieter Ullsperger, head of the finance division, and Eberhard Koerber, the former sales head of BMW. It was even reported that Lou Hughes, the highly regarded head of GM's Opel, had been approached about the job by Hahn and members of the executive committee, the *Vorstand*. Another serious contender was the Frenchman Daniel Goeudevert.

Goeudevert, the former CEO of Ford-Germany and currently the head of the Volkswagen car division, had tried to establish himself as Hahn's ideal successor—a man of the nineties with a modern, sometimes unconventional approach, especially regarding environmental issues, which had become quite important in Germany.

But topping the list was Ferdinand Piech, who was said to be the source of negative rumors about Hahn. Piech's primary strength was his solid record managing Audi. When he took over in 1988, Audi was a poor stepsister to the great luxury cars of Europe. Now it challenged BMW for the lead among higher priced German cars. Piech also had some very powerful connections, perhaps because of his position among Germany's elite. (Piech's personal fortune, estimated at 5 billion marks, made him the richest man in the auto industry.) One of these connections was Roland Berger, the founder of the German consulting firm that bore his name, and one of the most influential businessmen in Germany. He had grown friendly with Piech and advised him on family business dealings. Berger lobbied members of the *Aufsichtsrat* on behalf of Piech, singing his praises as a no-nonsense fiscally responsible leader whose record at Audi was evidence of what he could do for the entire company. He was convincing enough that the advisory board agreed to appoint Piech.

In April the board asked Hahn to resign and appointed Piech chairman, effective January 1993. As a sign of its new get-tough mood, the board also announced that 12,500 of the company's 130,000 workers would be laid off or retire by 1996.

In spite of what some people regarded as personality flaws, Piech might have been the right man for the job; VW's home base could certainly use a little of the micromanagement that was Piech's forte, and he was the only one of the candidates with a proven track record. Before Volkswagen could hope to build a broad international base, it first needed to address the critical production problems at home, and it was fairly certain that Piech's preference would be to stick close to Wolfsburg and not shy from making hard choices, including plant closings and a tougher position with suppliers. Unlike Hahn, who never pushed the overpriced German suppliers or threatened to take his business elsewhere, Piech was a master at putting the screws to suppliers, often conducting the negotiations himself. Hahn had never challenged them, but Piech did.

Financial analysts were pleased with the choice. "They have put into the job the guy who won't shirk from making difficult decisions on what has to be done with VW," said Carl Ludvigsen of Ludvigsen Associates in London. Stephen Reitman, referring to Piech's well-known testiness, commented, "It is not the time to be courting popularity. He will be the man who rattles the cage."

In most ways, Piech was cut from a different cloth than Hahn. While Hahn was smooth as silk, a consummate charmer who enjoyed the public stage, Piech was balding, slope-shouldered, and haggard—always uneasy in the spotlight. He tended to speak slowly (his English usage was fractured), his eyes trained awkwardly on the floor. Although he was a gifted technician, many people wondered how he would stand up as a leader.

The assessment of his former colleagues could be harsh. Said one distastefully, "Piech is a master of intrigues and walking over the dead bodies of those he stepped on to get to the top." Said another, "Virtues such as fairness, humanity and tolerance are not for him."

Insiders at Audi still remembered, some bitterly, Piech's brutal firing of Fritz Indra, the head of engine production, and Jürgen Stockmar, head of development. Stockmar had brilliantly constructed a new six-cylinder engine for the new Audi 100 in only two years, but shortly after had been forced to leave the company. Many believed that Piech had fired Stockmar because he couldn't bear to see him so lavishly praised in the media.

One man who was most definitely concerned with Piech's appointment was his old rival Goeudevert. Goeudevert was an unusual auto executive in that he was both a scholar (and former teacher of literature) and a savvy salesman. In some ways he was many of the things Piech was not. His tall-blond good looks and confident demeanor were in direct contrast to Piech's discomfort in the public eye, although some of Goeudevert's critics said he had more style than substance. Now he would be Piech's deputy, and this could be considered both good and bad news. The good news was that Goeudevert might take the edge off of Piech's sour demeanor. The bad news was that the two men never got along.

Goeudevert was outspoken, sometimes to a fault, and he'd made no secret of his feelings about Piech. He once publicly called his views on cars a "fossil from a bygone chapter of automotive history." On another occasion, he said of Piech's leadership, "Talking to him is not a problem. The problem is, he does not like to listen."

As for Piech, he quickly set the tone for his future relationship with Goeudevert, letting everyone know who was boss. "I do not expect from a salesman as much honesty as from a technician," he said cavalierly. "I do not like people who try to sell a grandmother as a young girl."

Goeudevert was not the only person wondering what a Piech regime would be like. From the moment the announcement was made, the company was cloaked in intense political intrigue as managers maneuvered for Piech's favor. Many of them knew their days were numbered.

Piech went to work on updating his style. He was said to be frequently closeted with public relations director Lutz Schilling, who coached him on public speaking—trying to transform the uneasy public man into one more suitable for the position. He also went to work on improving his English and learning other languages. The transformation of Piech from provincial workman to acceptable spokesman became the job of several staff persons.

Not that Piech would be a global gladiator in the way Hahn was. His major problems were at home.

Even if his image were to undergo complete renovation, it would not change the growing crisis that faced the company. If Volkswagen was to climb out of its hole, Piech would have to find a way to cut costs fast while juggling the complex global network of operations set in place by his predecessor. Almost immediately it became clear to Piech that a complete reorganization of top management was needed. It was rumored that he would slash the old team and bring in a cadre of his allies from Audi.

Those almost certainly set to go included Dieter Ullsperger, the finance director, who should have known how bad things were, but instead painted rosy pictures (a la Bob O'Connell) that taxed the credulity of the board members. His "Group Plan 41," presented to the board in the fall of 1992, when they were already educated about the problems of the company, was a perfect example of his failings.

Group Plan 41 was to be Hahn's swan song, his last report to the board before he stepped down. Although it carried Hahn's signature, it was prepared by Ullsperger. It included the current status of the company and a five-year projection. The 1992 figures told the harsh truth about Volkswagen's losses, showing the company to be one billion marks in the red, in spite of the fact that it was selling more cars than ever. But what really shocked the board members were the future projections, which seemed unbelievably optimistic. Alongside the grim 1992 figures were projections for 1993–97 that showed Volkswagen making a phenomenal financial comeback, breaking all sales records to achieve a one-billion-mark profit. Nothing in the presentation suggested a way to make this happen. It was just one more sunny picture, unsupported by reality.

The report was strongly criticized by the board and robbed Hahn of his chance to make a proud exit. Perhaps he felt bitter because his many achievements seemed forgotten in the emerging gloom of the incipient German recession and the staggering losses that now required a tough workman rather than a statesman. He might have felt that Piech would have no better luck than he in dealing with the company's problems.

But Piech could no doubt look forward to more cooperation in making his changes. The extent of the crisis was so great that he had people's attention in a way Hahn never had, and a crisis always makes it easier to solve problems. Meanwhile, Piech made sure everyone knew that he was inheriting a mess. He didn't want to be blamed for it.

As 1992 drew to a close, Hahn was still in the chairman's seat, still hoping that a miracle could rescue his reputation and vindicate him. He had always been an optimist, but this time it seemed his hope was in vain. He had been transformed from a hero to a villain in less than ten months.

Piech hovered in the wings, sharpening his warrior skills. To those who wondered what was ahead, he liked to reply, "Sharpshooters have to move to the front line of the battlefield."

FIVE

Whose Century Is It?

Success is as dangerous as failure.

—*Tao*

THE AUTOMOBILE created Detroit, and the automobile has destroyed it.

Once Detroit was throbbing with the vitality of the growing auto industry, as waves of people flocked there to be a part of its work force. They were whites, blacks, immigrants, people from the poor areas of Appalachia—all seekers of a better life. And they realized that dream.

A bustling economy rose up around the assembly of cars. In the 1920s, when GM broke ground for a magnificent building in the heart of the city, it was a symbol of all that the new invention would become. And for many decades, that promise was fulfilled.

It is a sad irony that the very vehicles that made Detroit a thriving metropolis eventually became the means of escape for those who were lured away from the urban chaos to the peaceful suburbs to the north, with their hilly woods and quiet neighborhoods. Businesses and highways followed, then industrial parks and office complexes, then massive malls to support the burgeoning suburban population. Those who remained in Detroit could not afford cars or the life-style they supported. Those who could afford cars used them to get out.

In 1992 Chrysler announced that it would move its headquarters to its new billion-dollar Technology Center in Auburn Hills, a distant suburb of Detroit. It would leave behind its office and engineering complex in Highland Park, a now derelict neighborhood that once housed some of the industry's elite.

Ford's assembly plant on Woodward Avenue was long ago abandoned as Ford concentrated all of its operations ten miles to the west of Detroit in the community of Dearborn. Although the building is regarded as a landmark, only its shell remains, the wind whistling through broken windows, boards nailed across doorways to keep out vagrants.

The General Motors building still stands in the middle of a manicured island, just two or three blocks beyond the evidence of urban blight—in spite of the company's many attempts to revive the neighborhood. Although it long symbolized the potency of the industry, increasingly, the building has a hollow feel. Jack Smith has moved most of the staff to Warren, ten miles north of Detroit, as he disperses the central bureaucracy among the operating divisions. Now, entire sections of the vast floors are empty. The abandonment of the auto industry from its urban center, and the shambles it has left behind in Detroit, tell much about the rise and fall of the American century.

For the entire century, automaking has been America's most important industry. Directly or indirectly, it has supported the livelihoods of millions of people. A car company is much more than a collection of factories and a corporate office. It is an enterprise system that includes thousands of parts and components suppliers, thousands of dealers, and a massive assortment of supporting industries from truckers to railroads.

America's industrial might was unchallenged for most of this century. How, at the peak of such power, could it suddenly fall so far? Countless theories have been proferred about how America lost its "competitive edge." The auto industry is often used to symbolize what was happening throughout American industry.

The decline wasn't accidental. There wasn't a sudden earthquake that struck down American industrial might. It was a slow, steady process, the ironic lesson of history that makes the most powerful also the most vulnerable. As an old saying warns, "Power is precarious."

The story of the global auto industry is also the story of the rise and fall of individual men, who staked their fortunes and their dreams on their belief in the power of the automobile to create wealth and transform societies. Often, these men learned the bitter lesson that success can be even more dangerous than failure. The story of the growth of General Motors and how its might was challenged by Toyota and Volkswagen is a cautionary tale for all companies that would aspire to be great.

New York City—August 1920

ALFRED SLOAN felt as though he might explode with the frustration of working for Billy Durant. As he sat in his office at GM's New York headquarters and listened to his boss enthusiastically describe yet another wild scheme to bail out the company, he could barely contain his growing anxiety. It didn't matter that the country was in recession, that there was a near panic in the stock market, or that General Motors was almost out of cash. Durant was confident, almost cheerful. He seemed to like it best when times were challenging, as they certainly were now. He was sure his newest plan would work. It was very simple. He would personally support the price of GM stock by buying additional shares on his own margin accounts from the people whose companies he had acquired through stock swaps.

Sloan couldn't believe his boss was serious. It sounded like a mad plan. As he would say later, "I felt he had about as much chance for success as if he had tried to stand at the top of Niagara Falls and stop it with his hat."

The plan was vintage Billy Durant. The founder of General Motors had never been a romantic about cars themselves, but he unabashedly loved the thrill of high-risk business gambles. The early years of this century, when Durant founded GM, were a heady time of mechanical miracles and inventions that would change the world. It was an unprecedented period of economic expansion, as luck and determination transformed ordinary men into tycoons. Capital was available and labor was mobile. The industrial surge spawned giant companies that dominated whole industries, led by men like Andrew Carnegie, John D. Rockefeller, and Pierre du Pont. Durant was seduced by the mood of the age—the belief that anything was possible.

Nothing represented this time of sweeping change more than the car, with its promise of mobility and freedom. Along with such legendary men as Henry Ford and Ransom Olds, Billy Durant viewed the automobile as symbolic of a grand wave that would rise and crest as the car became a reliable means for getting from place to place. It was a speculator's dream: In time, every household in America would own an automobile. Durant saw the chance to make a fortune. And unlike others, who actually invented cars, Durant's invention was the car company itself. His philosophy was, the bigger the better, but almost from the start, the road was rocky.

Billy Durant could easily be cast as a romantic firebrand among early twentieth-century business leaders. He was a brilliant but flawed genius who managed through sheer force of determination and personality to keep GM afloat during its first twelve years. His wiry, 135-pound body was a force field of energy and he was a nonstop talker always angling for a deal. His enthusiasm for the automobile business was so infectious that normally conservative businessmen like Pierre du Pont became investors in Durant's company.

Unfortunately, Durant had little interest in day-to-day management. He naively believed that if the money was there to build the cars, people would buy them and the company would prosper on the strength of sheer momentum.

At forty-four, Alfred Sloan was Durant's vice-president and polar opposite. Tall, tense, and stern, he became the grim holder of accountability whose thick Brooklyn accent forbade levity. From the moment he joined the company in 1916, Sloan had been persuaded that Durant was setting an insane course. He would later say, "I was of two minds about Mr. Durant. I admired his automotive genius, his imagination, his generous human qualities, and his integrity. But I thought he was too casual in his ways for an administrator, and he overloaded himself. Important decisions had to wait until he was free, and were often made impulsively."

It was the latter characteristic that almost drove Sloan to resign. By 1920 General Motors was no mom-and-pop shop. It was a massive company with seventy-five factories in forty-five cities, all under the personal supervision of Durant. Furthermore, it was struggling with phenomenal debt in the aftermath of Durant's twelve-year spending spree, during which he acquired most of the innovative automobile builders of the day, and many parts producers, placing them under GM's tent. But now demand for new cars was declining in the face of the recession, and the company's cash reserves had disappeared. Sloan could not fathom the mind of a man who believed he could single-handedly supervise such a giant enterprise. Nor could he grasp Durant's logic that increasing company debt would lead to prosperity. For a long time, he had been urging his boss to reorganize the company, hoping to make it more rational, manageable, and efficient, but Durant refused to listen.

When he learned the details of Durant's latest scheme, Sloan felt nothing but despair. Instead of resigning outright, he decided to take a thirty-day vacation to think things over. When he returned, he found the company in turmoil. The value of GM stock was plummeting, and Durant's brokers were demanding that he cover his margin calls. Of course, he couldn't come up with the cash.

In the end, Pierre du Pont and J. P. Morgan arranged a joint bailout—with the provision that Durant resign from the company. Durant accepted the inevitable with a quiet dignity, but when he arrived home on the day of his resignation, he greeted his family with tears running down his face. He was sixty years old and his last gamble had failed.

To reassure the nervous financial community, Pierre du Pont reluctantly took over as chairman. At fifty, du Pont knew little about the auto industry, and his passion was more in the greenhouse at Longwood Gardens, his estate on the Brandywine River, than in the factory. He agreed to assume leadership only because he was convinced by the bankers that it would save the company. He asked Sloan to stay on as vice-president of operations and spearhead a reorganization of the company. By 1923, when Sloan replaced du Pont as chairman, the changes were well under way.

Billy Durant would hardly have recognized General Motors over the next few years with its new emphasis on a logical internal organization, financial discipline, and coordinated product and marketing strategies. He felt pushed aside, bitter, and misunderstood. In a melancholy letter to Sloan, Durant wrote, "I do wish, Mr. Sloan, that you had known me when we were laying the foundation—when speed and action seemed necessary."

Sloan maintained a quiet respect for Durant and made sure that he was financially supported throughout his life. But times had changed. His mandate was different.

Alfred Sloan, the quiet, clearheaded Brooklynite, did not create General Motors, but in a sense he fathered it. In the process he set the course for all big business in America. Sloan viewed GM's dilemma this way: As a big company, it needed centralized control, and yet that control could not be divorced from the real know-how that existed at the operating level. Nor could it be a one-man rule, subject to the whim and style of a single leader. This was no longer feasible for a company of GM's size and complexity.

Peter Drucker, the noted business professor, would later describe the uphill battle Sloan faced. Since Durant had left the heads of the companies he bought in place, GM had never become a cohesive organization. Drucker wrote that when Sloan took over GM,

> it was a loose federation of independent chieftains. A few years earlier, each of the men had been running their own companies, all of which were now part of something called General Motors. The route that Durant had taken was to hope that the strong-willed men would temper their independence with a desire to maximize their profits, and act in the best interests of the entire company. Sloan recognized that the refusal of these men to work together had all but destroyed the company. This was not a short or long term problem, but rather a generic problem of a big business. A big business as Sloan saw it needed unity of direction and central control. But it equally needed the energy, enthusiasm and strength of its operations. The operating

managers had to have enough freedom to do things their own way. They had to have the responsibility and authority that goes with it, the scope to show what they could do, and the recognition that goes with performance.

Sloan's plan called for a balance of central control and operational autonomy, a kind of corporate democracy with a coordinating center supporting individual divisions that held hands-on responsibility for developing, producing, and marketing cars.

There was plenty of resistance to Sloan's plans, especially from the heads of car divisions who were reluctant to relinquish any control to a central authority. Sloan set a new standard for leadership—accountability to the corporate good. He achieved this in part by setting up a bonus system in order to encourage pride of ownership among employees at all levels.

With the new organization taking shape, Sloan turned his attention to the cars themselves. What did consumers want? How could GM keep them coming back for more? At the time, GM's car lines were an irrational jumble, burdened by duplication and arbitrary pricing policies that had divisions competing with each other rather than with other companies like Ford. Sloan chastised the division heads, reminding them there was no point in building cars for the sake of building cars. Car lines must be distinct from one another and designed to meet perceived customer need. He wanted to broaden sales and encourage repeat buyers, so that people who owned cars that were still good would want new ones. He described the automotive industry as having gone through three phases: The first was the early car era prior to 1908, which was a "class" market, since the expense of the new invention limited its access to a privileged few. Then followed a "mass" market period, which was dominated by Ford with its cheap cars and concept of basic transportation for all. Now, he proposed, the potential was there for a "class-mass" market, served by better and better cars with increasing diversity. This, he proclaimed, was to be the General Motors era. The motto: "A car for every purse and purpose."

Each GM car was given a position on a pyramid of price and consumer demographics. Cadillac was the high-end car, at the pinnacle of the price pyramid, followed closely by Buick. The midprice cars were Oldsmobiles and Pontiacs. Chevrolet was at the base of the pyramid with the inexpensive mass-market models. "During that time, you could go into a neighborhood and tell everything you wanted to know about the residents from the cars parked on the streets," a GM executive once said. "Sloan defined the market for the first time, and directed that cars be built to fill each niche."

But even with Sloan's reorganizational principles and strategy for car models, GM could not have succeeded had he not also understood the importance of financial discipline to provide standards and guidelines for investment. It prevented excess spending and kept costs under control. Donaldson Browne, Sloan's one-man financial brain trust, devised a method called standard volume accounting, which set controls in place to achieve the needed return on investment while operating at a standard volume of 80 percent capacity. All costs were scrutinized for reduction, and the manufacturing processes were reviewed each year to keep the company financially sound at 80 percent capacity. This discipline imposed on costs helped General Motors survive the Depression without suffering crippling losses.

In the early 1930s automotive supremacy belonged to American carmakers, which dominated the industry at home and abroad. GM and Ford had accumulated massive holdings overseas, building and selling cars throughout the world, and even purchasing foreign companies—like GM's ownership of the German carmaker Opel. There was little competition from Europe. Although Germany had an auto industry, and the Germans were known for their engineering excellence, no German carmaker had yet discovered how to mass-produce cars at a profit. Even if they could, the standard of living in Germany severely restricted car ownership. Japan was decades away from producing a viable car. The only cars on the road in Japan were exported by GM or Ford, although the American ambition to assemble cars in Japan had been short-circuited by a law that restricted foreign auto production.

America owned the car world—and the grandfather of them all was General Motors.

Berlin—May 1933

FERDINAND PORSCHE, a young Austrian engineer and designer, was excited. In only a few hours he would be seeing Adolf Hitler. It would not be the first meeting between the two men. They had been briefly introduced nine years earlier in a racing pit. But Porsche doubted that Hitler would remember him.

Hitler's love of car racing was legendary, and on this day Porsche had been invited to accompany Klaus von Oertzen, a German auto company executive, and Hans Stuck, the famous racing car driver, to pay a social call on the Führer. Hitler was delighted to see Stuck and greeted him effusively. Porsche stood in the background waiting to be introduced. But suddenly Hitler's eyes lit on the young man and he smiled in recognition. "Ah, Herr Porsche," he said, "we have met before." Porsche was surprised when Hitler remembered to the last detail their momentary greeting in the racing pit. He was truly amazed when Hitler pulled him aside and asked if they could meet privately.

For years, Porsche had been working on various designs for a car that could be produced inexpensively, and now it seemed this was exactly what Hitler wanted to discuss. The two men ignored the others and spoke together at length. Porsche told Hitler that mass motorization was a reachable goal for Germany. After all, he said, it had already been achieved in the United States. There, one of every five people owned a car, compared to one of every fifty in Germany.

As Hitler continued to ask questions, Porsche tantalized him with an outline of the car design he was currently working on. He assured Hitler it was possible to assemble a car profitably that would reach a speed of one hundred kilometers per hour, travel more than fourteen kilometers per liter of petrol, seat four passengers, and be priced at around 1,000 reichsmarks (or about $142, compared to the cheapest American car, which cost about $425). Hitler was impressed. By the time the two men parted, Porsche hoped Hitler would engage him to create the automobile that he had envisioned as the birthright of the German people.

Soon after the meeting, Hitler made a public announcement to

German carmakers: Give the highest priority to building an inexpensive "people's car," suitable for the German masses.

The response of the German car companies was lukewarm. The idea of a mass-produced car had been attempted before by companies such as BMW, Adler, and Auto Union, but each time they concluded that it could not be done profitably. At the time, the German auto industry was conservative and cash poor, having barely survived the Depression. The general attitude was that Hitler's vision was pie in the sky for an industry that was struggling just to stay alive.

The lone exception was Opel, which was then launching the P4, a small, fuel-efficient vehicle priced low at 1,450 marks. But Opel was a special case. A General Motors subsidiary since 1929, it was backed by the resources of the American company that was on the cutting edge in production technology and product development. Opel was able to build the P4 at a relatively low cost because it had access to GM's know-how.

The association of car manufacturers, the Reichsverband der Automobilindustrie (RDA), considered the situation. It was doubtful that any German car company could match the P4's low price. Even if it were possible, the very idea of producing a car for the masses was ludicrous considering the high cost of gasoline and the low income of the German people. Who would be able to afford to drive this dream car? The RDA quietly buried the idea and hoped that time would turn the Führer's attention to other matters.

Among the strongest opponents of Hitler's plan were Carl Hahn, director of Auto Union, and Heinrich Nordhoff, a young engineer who was the RDA representative at Opel. Nordhoff was daringly outspoken against Hitler at a time when this was becoming dangerous. Refusing to cooperate with Hitler's program, he boasted, "In the near future, Opel will bring out a people's car by themselves." Hahn, father of the man who would later become chairman of Volkswagen, sided with Nordhoff and warned against the folly of thinking a company could succeed and profit with "a single uniform model," no matter how advanced the model might be.

In May 1934, a full year after they had first met, Hitler summoned Porsche from his office in Stuttgart to discuss plans to build a people's car. He was tired of waiting for the industry to fall into line.

Suddenly, Porsche became Hitler's auto-darling—the man who agreed with him, amid all the naysayers, that mass motorization could be achieved. At the 1934 Automotive Exhibition in Berlin, Porsche was the talk of the show, as leaders of the RDA stood miserably by and tried to downplay his newfound influence.

By 1936 Porsche was ready to test-drive his prototypes of the people's car. Each of three different prototypes had been driven fifty thousand kilometers, supervised by the RDA and the Technical Universities of Stuttgart and Berlin. At the end of the tests, a car was presented to Hitler at his summer house at the Obersalzberg. Hitler examined the car happily, and lavishly praised the engineers. The RDA offered grudging approval: "The construction of the car has proven to be capable," the report read. "In general, the test cars did the job on the 50,000 km run. The vehicle has showed a remarkable performance, which makes further development recommendable."

Porsche continued to test variations of the prototype as other German car companies watched the process with chagrin. How could any of the other companies hope to compete with a vehicle that was subsidized and literally mandated by the government— especially this government? Shortages of raw materials, construction supplies, and labor haunted the other companies, but Hitler made certain that Porsche got everything he needed. He wanted a state-of-the-art factory and an elite work force to build the cars, and he promised that the resources of the Reich would be put behind this effort.

The new company was to be modeled after the Ford Motor Company. Twenty technicians were hired from Ford to oversee the process. Most were German nationals working in the United States; a few were American citizens of German descent, and these returned home when the war started in 1939. With American expertise at his disposal, Porsche began to realize the dream he shared with Hitler of creating the greatest car company in the world.

Lower Saxony—May 1938

PORSCHE AND HIS COLLEAGUES reviewed a variety of sites for construction of the factory where the new car would be assembled. It was Hitler's desire that a town be built around the factory site to house the thousands of workers who would be needed to assemble more vehicles in one place than was ever conceived of before or since. Porsche finally settled on an area in Lower Saxony that seemed ideal for the project. Ten thousand acres of lush farmland would allow enough space to build the most impressive manufacturing complex and a shining industrial city. The land was owned by Count Werner von der Schulenberg, whose castle, Schloss Wolfsburg, sat at the edge of the estate. The count was informed that the Nazi State would be taking over his land for its own use. He tried to fight the takeover, but by that time there was really no defense against the will of Hitler. And so, a city was incorporated where the count's private estate used to be. It was called Volkswagen City. The ceremony of incorporation on May 26, 1938, was a grandiose affair, and seventy thousand people attended. Hitler himself laid the cornerstone, saying, "I undertake the laying of this cornerstone in the name of the German people. This factory shall arise out of the strength of the entire German people and it shall serve the happiness of the German people." Thus was created the rhetorical name for the new vehicle: the Strength Through Joy Car. The goal was to produce 1.5 million vehicles each year.

Hannoverscher Anzeiger, a major daily newspaper in the region, wrote glowingly of the opening ceremony:

THE FIST OF A CYCLOPS

A small world is going to be created. The peaceful region of Lower Saxony came under the grip of a cyclops. But it is a modern cyclops who understands the beauty of work. From the main area where the ceremony takes place one can see the channel and the soft rolling hills and forests. This will become the home of the most modern and beautiful worker's city of the German Reich. Happy people, who will find their homes here!

It was a majestic beginning, but almost immediately, everything changed. With the declaration of war, the mass production of Hitler's people's car was abruptly put on hold. Overnight, Volkswagen City became the site of the massive production of war machinery. The equipment procured for building cars was put in storage. Given how quickly the change from car building to war manufacturing took place, some cynical observers speculated that Hitler never had any intention of building a car in the first place; the plant was merely camouflage for his military buildup. More likely, Hitler really wanted the car, but not until the war was over and the Nazis would be in control of Europe.

With the shift to war-building efforts, the idea of training an elite work force was also discontinued. Now the focus became procuring masses of workers who would be employed as slave labor in the factories. The logical candidates were the POWs and concentration camp inmates. Thousands were brought to the plant, housed in barely livable conditions, and forced to work in the most brutal environment. They labored in sweltering plants until they literally dropped dead and were dragged away.

Volkswagen had the dubious distinction of being one of the first operations in Nazi Germany to use concentration camp inmates to work in its factory. Porsche, who was visibly distressed by the turn his vision had taken, used what influence he had to get more food and supplies for the workers. But he also received the choicest selection of able bodies from the camps.

The war took its toll on the struggling production town, and the Volkswagen plant, an easy target on the open farmland, was devastated by Allied bombing. Two-thirds of the site was destroyed by air raids and many people were killed. But the production lines kept moving, cranking out the equipment for Hitler's war.

In May 1945, when the Allies marched into town, what they found was far from a "city of joy." Seventeen thousand people existed in the most primitive conditions, trying to survive in the midst of rubble. The great shining city had never materialized. There were no paved roads and no houses—only rugged barracks, ugly huts, and thousands of half-starved, war-stunned people.

Nagoya, Japan—May 1936

WHEN KIICHIRO TOYODA heard about the fantastic people's car that had been designed in Germany, he recognized the outline of his own dream. He knew little about the details of Hitler's regime, or that the Reich's car was at the time more rhetoric than reality. All he knew was that building a car for the masses had been his dream for most of his adult life.

Japan was an industrial infant compared to the great Western nations like Germany and the United States. In the 1920s, when America's Big Three car companies were already dominating the globe, there was no substantial industry in Japan except textile manufacturing. Kiichiro's father, Sakichi, invented an automatic loom, which revolutionized textile production in Asia. His company, Toyoda Automatic Loom Works, was an international success, and Sakichi was considered a man ahead of his time in the provincial environs of Nagoya. He sent his son Kiichiro to Tokyo Imperial University, where he received a degree in mechanical engineering. All along, Kiichiro assumed that he would one day take over his father's company and spend his life producing textile machinery. But Sakichi had a saying, "One generation, one enterprise." He told his son, "I have built the loom; you must build something else."

Kiichiro chose the automobile, a fairly remarkable decision in light of the fact that 1920s Japan was still a primitive country with limited use of motor vehicles and no technological infrastructure to produce even rudimentary parts for engines, transmissions, and other components. But Sakichi encouraged his son and sent him to the United States to observe how automobiles were made. When he returned to Nagoya, Kiichiro began a long process of trial and error, frustration, and ultimately success. He began to tinker with an experimental engine based on a Chevrolet design, using workers from the loom factory to help him. Eventually, an official car-building division was added.

Sakichi's dying wish was for his son to prosper in making cars. But he passed on responsibility for his company to his son-in-law, Risaburo (who was also his adopted son), who was less enthusiastic about the venture. Risaburo was a realistic businessman. He understood how risky the auto venture would be, given the fact that all the great *zaibatsu* companies like Mitsubishi had so far failed to establish a viable auto industry. Risaburo felt responsible for the management of Sakichi's holdings, and he was reluctant to commit the family fortune to this risky venture. Had it not been Sakichi's expressed wish that his son be given support in his endeavors, the car-building enterprise might have died with Sakichi. With the rest of his family and most executives at the loom works unsupportive of his plan, Kiichiro enlisted the help of his bright young cousin, Eiji, and together they created the genesis of a real company. They chose to name it Toyota Motor Company.

There is some debate about why the company was named Toyota and not Toyoda. One theory is that it was an effort to distinguish the new enterprise from the loom works. A second (less likely) theory is that it was the result of a misspelling on the registration. But a more convincing reason is Japanese superstition. The word *Toyota* takes ten strokes to write in Japanese, and *Toyoda* eight. In Japan ten is luckier than eight. In fact, many goods are sold in groups of five, and it is considered unlucky to sell in multiples of four. The word for four is *shi,* the same as for death. Thus, Toyota was luckier than Toyoda.

Koromo, Japan—November 1938

ON A COOL MORNING in early November, Kiichiro, dressed in a factory uniform, stood with his brother-in-law Risaburo, his cousin Eiji, and a handful of others, and offered a dedication for the small plant he had built in Koromo, thirty-five miles from Nagoya. (It would later be renamed Toyota City.) In a quiet voice, he offered a dedication: "My late father left behind as his parting wish that Toyoda build automobiles, and we have made that wish come true. We are gathered here to witness the birth of a domestic Japanese auto industry."

Kiichiro was emotional as he recalled his father's dream which had brought the company to these beginnings. Privately, he felt melancholic with the realization that it might well be a dream deferred even longer. The forces that would bring Japan to war with the United States seemed unstoppable.

Kiichiro was opposed to the war, not because he was a pacifist, but because he was a realist. He openly expressed his belief that the industrial power of America (which he had seen firsthand) could never be conquered by a country whose industry was largely on the drawing board.

At that time, Japan's meager motor vehicle industry produced only a few thousand trucks, used mostly for military purposes. America, on the other hand, was manufacturing more than 3.5 million cars a year. "That's the real truth of our chances of victory," Kiichiro said. "We are outranked by a factor of one thousand."

As Kiichiro predicted, the war was a major setback for Toyota and Japanese industry in general. Materials were scarce, the labor force vanished as all able-bodied men were conscripted into the military, and all plans to build passenger cars were shelved while makeshift, barely operational trucks were hastily produced to support the military effort.

During the war, many Japanese businesses were bombed out of existence. It was serendipitous that Toyota survived without being totally destroyed. Later it was learned that the "Toyota Motor Factory" was marked on U.S. aerial maps, but it was spared attack because it wasn't on a list of vital plants. Perhaps its slow development, a constant frustration to Kiichiro, was lucky after all.

Not that anyone felt so lucky after the war. The whole nation was in chaos, shell-shocked by the defeat. The barest essentials—food, water, and shelter—were scarce. Businesses were shaky and jobs were uncertain. Kiichiro promised his workers job security, but things were not good for the auto industry. Neither the government nor financial institutions considered it a developmental priority. There was a preference for investing in industries where there was a comparable advantage with the West. The auto industry, with barely a passenger car in production, was certainly not one of them. In 1950, when Kiichiro resigned in shame from the company to which he had given birth, it seemed as though all the hard work and dreams for his great car company had come to naught.

The three great founders of General Motors, Volkswagen, and Toyota—Billy Durant, Ferdinand Porsche, and Kiichiro Toyoda—were similar in many ways. In each case, they began with a dream to create wealth and national pride through mass motorization. None of them reached the point of carrying out his dream. Durant was forced to resign, Porsche was jailed after the war (and his sponsor, Hitler, committed suicide), and Kiichiro resigned, humiliated by his broken promises. In each case, these men were replaced by technocrats who were less enamored of the car but had a firmer handle on the business of creating them. They were Alfred Sloan, Taizo Ishida, and Heinrich Nordhoff. Each of these men fulfilled the goal of bringing his company to a state of maturity. In a sense, these men could have been at the helm of any company. It was not a love of cars that inspired them, but a grasp of business principles.

Sloan understood that workers had to be motivated, and this understanding was at the core of everything. He established financial incentives based on the idea that to stay in business, a corporation had to earn enough money to be self-perpetuating. This resulted in a system of financial controls and the transformation of the car from merely transportation to a desirable luxury good that symbolized status and personal image.

Ishida established the strict financial controls that became the foundation of how Toyota ran itself. Toyota became great because of Ishida's cost-control system. He maintained low fixed costs (thanks in large part to an efficient production system that included the Just-in-Time method of delivery) so the company could earn consistently high profits.

Nordhoff was more engineer than financial wizard, and he was less successful in establishing a long-term financial discipline over Volkswagen. But in the short term, he succeeded in putting a devastated company back on its feet.

The United States came out of the war the unquestioned conquerer on the two fronts of Germany and Japan. General Motors was only strengthened by the war, even as the fledgling Volkswagen and Toyota struggled for the barest survival. It was a bitter irony for the American giant that in the coming forty years, a complete turnaround of this situation would prevail.

The decline of General Motors might be compared to the process of collapse in a marriage. It doesn't happen overnight but slowly, almost imperceptibly, over time. The chasms begin as small fissures, ever-expanding. Once-careful gestures grow sloppy. People stop listening. Dullness sets in. For a while, maybe even for years, the problems are camouflaged by brave cheer and superficial fixes. There can be a false security in sameness, as though an unchanged course is the equivalent of stability.

The fallacy of such blind hope is apparent, but it was nevertheless the way General Motors conducted itself in the decades following World War II. The company drew comfort from its history, its size, and its power. When GM president Charles Wilson declared in 1952 that "what is good for the country is good for General Motors, and what is good for General Motors is good for the country," it was accepted as obvious and true. GM was a great intractable force in business and culture, a carmaker second to none and an organizational model for other companies.

In a sense, success spoiled GM, but there is much more to it than that. The roots of General Motors' decline are complex. It would be tempting to pin it on one or a dozen failed leaders. But although the leadership after Alfred Sloan did indeed fail, perhaps the true blame rests with the underlying culture of the company that spawned them.

Every corporation has a culture that is distinct from the larger business or social culture. It is born partially of environment and nursed by tradition. Corporate identity is usually reflective of its place of origin. For example, someone once sarcastically described General Motors as a "midwestern car company," a description that speaks volumes about the company's inherent parochialism. For while GM is unquestionably a global company, its decisions have been colored by an isolated Detroit mentality—a bedrock Americanism that prevented true global understanding. In part because of this parochialism, inbred among generations of midwesterners, the nurturing ethic of the company has tended to focus inward.

Alfred Sloan was the organizational guru of GM and, indeed, of American business in general. Under his guidance, GM grew and prospered and by the 1950s it was a massive, profitable enterprise whose success was confirmed year after year by a supportive buying public. Its domestic market share held steady in the 50 percent range.

But as time went on, and especially after Sloan was no longer in charge of day-to-day operations, a new mentality began to emerge. In itself, corporate evolution is not bad; change is a necessary component of growth. In the 1950s GM had the opportunity to re-create itself in light of new socioeconomic imperatives. But instead of growth and change, it chose to turn inward and rest on its laurels. The emerging General Motors culture of the 1950s and beyond showed that GM's method of change was to shrink into itself rather than grow outward; to become conservative and risk-averse.

Human beings on the whole are resistant to change—an irony when you consider that change has always been one of the most consistent features of life. As a corporation, GM developed a finely tuned behavior of self-protection. In spite of all evidence to the contrary, it maintained a conviction that the cars that made it great were the cars that would continue to keep it great. There was, from the 1950s on, an almost pathological resistance to the glaring shifts in American life and values—and how these changes might translate into automobile purchases. Serious market research and long-range planning were practically nonexistent, although it was not for lack of committees. As a GM executive once noted grimly, "The worst news you could hear was that a task force had been assigned to study the problem. Task forces were the black hole at GM."

Although General Motors was a global car company, it never occurred to the leadership that other companies, from Europe or Japan, might grow into global car companies, too. It has been said that the eye cannot see what the mind does not believe. On the Fourteenth Floor of the General Motors building, where executives were cushioned from the influences of the outside world, they remained blind to the change that was occurring in society. Foreign competition was viewed as a nagging tic, not a major assault. The fiction was reinforced every day inside the bunker as General Motors kept building its big, gas-guzzling cars.

No one saw it coming. The Volkswagen Beetle was a joke—a "personal insult," one Detroit executive sniffed. Writing about the strange bug-shaped car that was a new arrival on American shores, a writer observed: "While Detroit sells power, style, and a soft, quiet ride, the Beetle persists in being homely, noisy, cramped and powered by a tiny engine—air cooled not water cooled—located where the trunk ought to be."

The phenomenal success of this odd little car in the land of the giants was a mystery to American car executives, who scratched their heads while Americans flocked to buy the German car that had become a reverse status symbol for the postwar generation. Even the advertising poked fun, perhaps the first time blatant self-deprecation was employed to such great effect. Ads typically featured the bug itself, looking lost and somewhat dumpy, and a simple caption like "Ugly is only skin deep" or "It won't drive you to the poorhouse."

"Someone actually stole one," marveled the copy beneath a picture of a stocky VW microbus.

The advertising humanized the Beetle, giving it feelings and a personality. In one ad, a lonely bug sits in a two-car garage in the dark gloom of night. The headline: "It does all the work but on Saturday night which one goes to the party?"

Given the origins of the Beetle and the devastation of Hitler's car company after the war, it was a miracle that the car ever reached American shores—much less was built at all. It might never have happened were it not for Heinrich Nordhoff. Before the war, when Nordhoff worked for GM's Opel, he was an influential and outspoken member of the German car industry. During the war, Opel was confiscated by Hitler and made to produce trucks for the war effort. He did this so well that he was awarded honors by Hitler's regime. Even if he didn't sympathize with the Nazis, he put his production skills to work for them. When GM regained control after the war, it fired Nordhoff because of his collaboration with the Nazis. Stunned by the events of the past few years, and desperate for work, Nordhoff reluctantly accepted the offer of the British military to take over the plant at Volkswagen City, now renamed Wolfsburg.

When Nordhoff arrived, he was shocked by what greeted him. As he would later recall, "I found desolate ruins, a group of desperate people, the remains of a city which had never been built nor completed, an amorphous mass without an organizational principle, structure or program—without the possibility of rational work. I had to create something new. Something which had never existed before." He put on a brave front and attempted to deliver an inspiring speech to the ragtag band of workers.

"It is up to us," he told them, "to turn the largest German automobile facility into the most influential contributor to the German peacetime economy. It will be up to us whether Volkswagen's future course will rise or fall."

Nordhoff's greatest worry was the technical prowess—or lack thereof—of his new company's car. Some experts, Nordhoff himself among them, had criticized the Beetle as being outdated before the first prototypes were ever tested. After the war, criticism grew louder, with people complaining, "You have to change this car! It looks like the Third Reich." But there was no money available to develop a new model. Thus hampered from research and development, Nordhoff set out to build twenty thousand Beetles, working from the original blueprints. By the time the twenty thousandth car rolled off the line in January 1948, Nordhoff had become its most avid supporter.

As a leader, Nordhoff was inspirational and hardworking. He literally dedicated his life to the success of the company. Frequently, he spoke to his factory workers via a company radio channel, praising their efforts and asking them for even greater commitment to the future of the company. He believed in rewarding that effort. In September 1948, on the occasion of the rollout of the thirty thousandth Beetle, he announced a 15 percent increase in wages. "As long as I am in charge of the company," he promised, "the workers will always benefit."

There were gradual attempts to modernize the old model, eventually replacing most of the parts. But it was still not perfect.

Complaints flooded into headquarters from the German consumers, but Nordhoff simply ignored them, putting a bright spin on the Beetle's problems. When drivers complained about the difficulty of shifting into the rear gear, he replied ingeniously, "A Beetle always runs ahead."

Although Nordhoff was bright and benevolent, he possessed the same flaw that would hamper his colleagues in America: He was autocratic and rigid, and he didn't see the car as a complex effort. He was only a production engineer—a good one but not someone who could build a major company. One did not argue or even suggest. "I cannot be provoked," he often said ominously. His response to those who suggested that the company should expand to include other models was to take them to the company mausoleum which housed thirty-six Volkswagen test models, each rejected. His point: There is nothing better than a Beetle.

It was hard to argue with success. By the mid-1950s Nordhoff had worked miracles at the company. Profits were high, the plant was fully rebuilt, and a network of repair operations and dealers was established. Germans finally had their people's car, and the expanding economy allowed many of them to buy it. It was time to consider the American market.

The teams Nordhoff sent to sell the Beetle in America during the early 1950s were nearly laughed off the continent. U.S. dealers had no interest in selling such an ugly, underpowered car when their customers were buying large, stylish, well-equipped models. Eventually, Nordhoff realized that America required a different approach. He set out to build an entirely separate organization, and Volkswagen of America (VWoA) became a wholly owned subsidiary of its German parent. VWoA established a network of one thousand dealers (marked by the "lollipop" blue and white sign). Perhaps most important, the dealers took the issue of service seriously. At the time, foreign car owners in America were plagued by the frustrating lack of parts and service outlets for their Renaults, Fiats, and British roadsters. VWoA guaranteed that parts would be on hand for every car sold, and service was assured through the large dealer network. Coupled with the counterculture mood building in America, the strategies worked.

In 1958 more than 100,000 Beetles were sold in the United States.

In 1959 Carl Hahn was a rising young executive working in the export department in Wolfsburg when Nordhoff tapped him to run the American operation. Hahn had energy, style, a good team, and plenty of innovative ideas. But most of all, he had luck. Even with the best dealer/service network in the world, it's arguable that anything short of a cultural revolution could have created such a consumer craving for a car like the Beetle in the land of sleek, sophisticated, high-powered cars. By 1962 one million Beetles had been sold in America, and Hahn received much of the credit. But there were critics back in Germany and they were becoming more outspoken. "What happens," one asked sarcastically, "when the Americans stop being amused by the Beetle?"

It was a good question. Unfortunately, the Beetle's American success created false confidence in a company that was functioning with a prewar concept and model. The glory days of VWoA bought time for the company, but that's all. For all his engineering skill, Nordhoff failed to understand the importance of new product development. He never imagined there would be a day when the Beetle would become obsolete. He just kept building more and more Beetles, spreading the word of their superiority around the world like a proselytizing missionary. Even efforts to create new models never amounted to much. When people stopped buying Beetles in the early 1970s, it nearly killed the company.

Under Nordhoff, Volkswagen made so much money that the company stopped thinking about financial controls. It seemed like the flow of money would never stop. There was never any effort to control costs as long as the cash kept pouring in. It was simply assumed that as more cars were produced, efficiency would increase and the cost per unit would fall. But it never made any effort to control the variable costs of labor and materials.

Volkswagen's failure to expand beyond its monoculture would be the source of severe problems in the years ahead—and nowhere was this more apparent than in America. By the 1970s young Americans were less interested in reverse status symbols than they were in good, durable, affordable cars. Volkswagen was losing its punch in the market just as the Japanese were poised to begin their long seduction of America.

Toyota City, Japan—August 1957

SEISI KATO felt equal parts of awe and humility. "Exporting Japanese passenger cars to America, the 'home' of the passenger car," he marveled. "It seemed like some wild dream come true."

But that was Kato's charge. Since World War II, Kiichiro's company had continued to grow slowly, cautiously, and quietly from its home in Nagoya. At times, it seemed the company wouldn't make it—such as the jarring recession in 1950 that forced Kiichiro to resign and appoint Ishida president. Part of the outcome of that crisis was a dramatic split of the company into two independent parts: Toyota Motor Company, which built the cars, and Toyota Motor Sales, which sold them. This separation of manufacturing from sales was designed to place more rigid sales discipline on the company. It would remain divided until 1982.

With Eiji at his side, Ishida pulled the company back to life and set it on a course of steady growth that would continue for decades. Even so, it would not be until 1955 that the company produced its first passenger car. The Crown was unveiled on New Year's Day. A celebration was held at the plant, and a beaming Eiji, dressed in a tuxedo, drove the first car off the line.

It became an immediate hit in Japan—so much so that Shotaro Kamiya, president of Toyota Motor Sales, began urging Ishida and Eiji to test-market it in the United States. Kamiya was impressed with the success of the Beetle; he believed there was an open market in America. "We've got to get in there now or never," he urged.

Thus was the conservative company pushed headlong into its first American venture. It was not a particularly auspicious beginning. "The reception [of the Crown] was horrible," Eiji would say later. "To begin with, the car didn't have enough power to travel on high-speed roads. In retrospect, the first initiative of ours was very poorly thought out indeed, but our timing was definitely not off. In fact, having this bitter experience behind us helped us work that much harder afterwards to build cars for the U.S. market."

Seisi Kato recalled the failure of the venture more vividly. "As our dreams sank out of sight like a ship with a giant hole in its bottom, we wrote to Tokyo that it was advisable to simply throw in the towel. But we were instructed to proceed, even if only with the registration of our company in the United States. The strategy was to try to sell the Crown, even if only 50 or 100 of them, just to establish a beachhead."

It would take another seven years before Toyota launched its first successful American import. The Corona, priced at $1,700, was the cheapest car on the road and was an instant success. It was followed by the Corolla, which was more popular still. Unbeknownst to the blind executives overseeing their sprawling domain in the American auto industry, people were developing quite a taste for these inexpensive, well-built little cars. All it took was an oil crisis to push them over the edge.

Many American executives believed that the early success of Toyota's imports was a direct result of the 1973–74 oil embargo, which created a demand for fuel-efficient cars. That may have been partially correct, at least in the short term. But these same executives were ignoring a deeper reality. They simply could not believe that, given the choice, Americans would prefer small foreign cars. They didn't believe it when Volkswagen was burning a path across the country. And they didn't believe it when Toyota handed enthusiastic car buyers the Corona on a silver platter. Instead of listening to the consumers, they denied reality and formulated excuses. And that's how, by the middle of the 1970s, the American century had come to an end. Detroit's glory days were over.

In 1980 a CBS-TV documentary, titled "The Toyota Invasion," seemed to revel in the contrast between Detroit's stagnation in the midst of a severe recession, and Japan's vigor. The documentary featured miserable, dark scenes from America's factories, set against what appeared to be an autoland fantasy: the gleaming factories of Toyota City, manned by proud, energetic workers.

Documentaries like this one and another aired by NBC that

same year exaggerated the contrasts between the two nations, but the underlying message could not be ignored: The Japanese had to be taken seriously. That summer, as 250,000 U.S. autoworkers faced layoffs, and Detroit continued to fumble in its attempts to build successful import fighters, the UAW stepped in with a suit against Japanese car companies. Citing Japan's unfair trade advantage as the source of Detroit's problems, the UAW called upon the International Trade Commission to impose stiff restrictions on Japanese car companies.

Certainly, it was true that Japanese imports were gobbling up market share in the United States. But the source of Detroit's decline was open to argument. In a formal statement to the ITC, MITI suggested that "the sluggishness of the American auto industry did not originate in imported cars but from the fact that the American automakers' response to the abrupt change of the American market in favor of compact cars had been too slow." This was true, although the malaise ran much deeper. Why was their response too slow? It was a failure both of imagination and of systems. They could not fathom the idea that cheaper cars could be profitable. Nor could they see how their systems could be changed to make that happen.

The ITC agreed with MITI and dismissed the suit, but that did not end the debate. Even after MITI agreed to a three-year slow-down of Japanese exports to the United States, the idea was firmly planted in America's industrial heartland that Japan was to blame for its problems. At General Motors, Japan became the scapegoat for a host of problems of its own making. The most notable of these was the deterioration of its cars.

During the 1960s and 1970s GM was lulled into a false sense of security by its dominance of the market. There was certainly a bottom-line mentality, but this mentality dictated that additional costs be passed on to customers. There was little effort to control costs from within.

GM didn't seem to understand that to achieve a high return on investment, the company must coordinate the design and production of its vehicles to that end. The corporate office set goals that it forced on the divisions, without also asking how to develop more efficient production systems. Cost-cutting measures were often penny-wise but pound-foolish.

The corporate offices of GM might have benefited from the warning of an old Japanese saying: "Let not the work of creating a great mound fail for lack of one basket full of soil." Penny-pinching was the rule, but too often it was in ignorance of the big picture. For example, the attitude about defects in cars was to ignore them with the rationale that "business is business," and companies had to accept a certain number of defects. One example, which would lead to hundreds of lawsuits against GM, was the Chevy Vega's tendency to flip over on sharp turns. The engineers sent a proposal to the Fourteenth Floor recommending the installation of a stabilizing bar in the rear to reduce the problem. The financial scorekeepers at the top calculated the expense: fifteen dollars per car to install the bars. Word came down that the cost was too high. It was only when the head of Chevrolet threatened to quit and go to the press that the company caved in and agreed to the installation.

It is remarkable that the corporate rule-makers were blind to their own tunnel vision. GM's entire strategy could be summed up this way: Pinch pennies and wait for the Japanese to go away. Blame the competition for your own failures. Live on the hope for a miraculous turnaround. It is revealing and somewhat sad that as late as 1991, when Japan held 30 percent of the American market share in vehicles, Bob Stempel was still telling the press that once the Japanese threat was gone, General Motors would be great again.

SIX

Boardroom Battlegrounds

Iron rusts from disuse; stagnant water loses its purity and in cold weather becomes frozen; even so does inaction sap the vigors of the mind.

—LEONARDO DA VINCI

Warren, Michigan—October 1992

DURING THE SIX MONTHS since his appointment as president of GM, Jack Smith had been encouraging a sense of urgency and camaraderie among his lieutenants. Camped out at the GM Technical Center, he worked long hours trying to find solutions to problems that had taken decades to overwhelm the company. The problems were worse than he had ever imagined, yet Smith realized that GM had to own up to them quickly and spread the sense of urgency beyond the upper ranks to every level of the organization.

Warren, Michigan, was an ordinary suburban community, like thousands of others in America. Its side streets were filled with clusters of modest ranch houses and two-story garden-apartment complexes, and its thoroughfares were lined with strip malls. Alfred Sloan built the GM Technical Center during the 1950s to serve as an engineering hub, and it was physically designed as a "working" complex. Its buildings were long and modern, surrounding a man-made lake. During the 1980s it became the location of BOC and CPC, and Bob Stempel and Lloyd Reuss ran their car groups from office buildings in the complex. Jack Smith moved to the former BOC building, which had been renamed the North American Automotive Operations (NAAO) headquarters by Reuss.

Smith's move was a practical decision, but also symbolic, since one of his goals was to dismantle the central office bureaucracy that for so long had isolated the corporate staffs and executives from the operating divisions. He saw no need for the battalions of data massagers to run interference while providing little value to the process of building good cars. He wanted to be close to the action.

His plate was full. After a successful stock offering in May that raised more than $2 billion, the company seemed ready to confront the lack of cash flow that had delayed several important vehicle programs. The stage was also set to address the company's swelling health care burden, as white-collar employees were asked to pay more of their own medical costs.

Then, in August and September, GM experienced a series of minor strikes in factories which highlighted the tension between GM and the UAW. Although the company reached an accommodation with the UAW in each case, the strikes dramatized the fact that management lacked a plan to anticipate and cope with the situation. Stempel, who seemed completely caught off guard by the strikes, seemed to cave in to UAW demands.

Meanwhile, the initial shock of Jack Smith's appointment had worn off, and deep inside the company there was a return to some of the old complacency. Smith wasn't completely free to press his agenda, and he had to acquiesce to Bob Stempel in public situations. Stempel was still talking about going slow, effectively undermining the sense of urgency Smith wanted to create.

As Smith worked feverishly to make a dent in the company's heaping plate of problems, he tried to ignore Stempel, still firmly entrenched in his office on the fourteenth floor of GM headquarters in Detroit. It was becoming increasingly harder to do so. Throughout the summer and into the fall, the loose ends of the board's action lingered and grew irritating, both in practical ways and because of the message it sent. Many employees who were being told to retire early or who had to pay more medical costs resented the fact that the people who caused their distress still had jobs. Some of them privately complained that Stempel, Reuss, and others should have been fired, not just demoted. Keeping them on the payroll was a good example of the double standard that infected American business. It seemed clear: If you're high enough on the corporate totem pole, you'll keep your job no matter what folly you created. Meanwhile, the workers, the ordinary folks, would lose their jobs by the thousands. "In the real world, people get fired for ruining a company," grumbled one recently laid-off worker. "At least, that's what I always thought. Maybe it's the other way around."

Stempel's continuation as chairman was awkward for everyone. As long as Stempel continued to give interviews to the press and blame GM's problems on the recession, Smith would have a harder time making dramatic organizational change. Stempel reinforced some people's hope that the problems were self-correcting and simple. But as Smith quickly learned the magnitude of GM's cash problems and loss of market share, he knew that the situation wouldn't be resolved without drastic action.

It wasn't easy for Stempel, either. It was never the board's intention to be cruel, but the end result, as a Stempel supporter described it, was that "they left him twisting in the wind." In effect, the board had allowed Stempel to retain his title, but stripped him of much of the authority of the post. There had been those on the board who had lobbied for Stempel's dismissal in April, but most members wanted to move more cautiously. For one thing, there was no heir apparent. For another, Stempel's supporters on the board felt he should be given a chance to do something to turn the company around—although it was unclear what that might be. In effect, they were asking him to act in ways that were contrary to his very being.

Stempel could hardly be blamed for being confused by the board's mixed signals. "It's as though the board started surgery, but never sewed up the patient," an executive noted.

By October rumors were flying through the air like antiaircraft fire. There were stories circulating that the company was in such bad financial condition that bankruptcy was being considered. Though these stories were given little credence, they worsened the public image of the company and caused morale inside to plummet.

It was time to act—again. A large faction in the board, now growing more comfortable in its activist role, was beginning to consider more seriously the idea of replacing Stempel, not with another insider, but with one of their own. Their deliberations leaked into the press, and the name most often heard was John Smale, the board's main instigator for change.

The stress was getting to Stempel. It was slow torture. On October 13, while he was in Washington, D.C., he suddenly became ill and was rushed to the hospital. There, doctors found that his blood pressure was high and he was experiencing heart problems. Stempel lay in his hospital bed and contemplated his future. He knew he had supporters on the board. With the exception of a handful of detractors, he believed he could count on the board's backing. He thought he could still survive. But the loop was closing tighter, and it seemed Stempel was no longer inside.

A week later, back at work, Stempel told the press that things were okay with the company; the turnaround was progressing. He hung tough, refusing the convenient "resignation for health reasons." He was convinced that his optimism was warranted. Meanwhile, rumors continued that he was on his way out. GM's public relations staff pressured Smale and the board to issue a statement of confidence to squelch the rumors. Instead, Smale issued a press release that said the board "has taken no action regarding any management changes at GM."

Stempel was pained when he read the release. Smale didn't say Stempel was out, but the release was, by omission, the nail in the coffin. Suddenly, Stempel knew the board was going to ask for his resignation. For a moment, he considered fighting. But it was a fleeting thought. It was over, and he knew it—although a part of him would never accept it.

New York City—November 1992

FINALLY, COUP, PART TWO. On November 2 GM's board gathered in the teak-paneled offices of the New York headquarters—what the ever-colorful Perot had once described as the "Let 'em eat cake floor"—and finally finished the job they had started six months earlier. John Smale would become chairman, and Jack Smith would become chief executive officer in addition to president. In the coming days, the board's housecleaning would extend at last to Lloyd Reuss and F. Alan Smith. By the time the dust settled, most of Roger Smith's old team had been forced out. It was rumored that Roger Smith himself would be forced off the board. He was indignant when he heard this, and insisted it was a lie. But there was little doubt that he had been asked to resign. Smith's continued presence on the board seemed an insult to the board's new direction. Everything they did was a repudiation of his tenure, and his protestations that their actions had been unnecessary were becoming as annoying as his million-dollar pension. It wasn't so easy to force a board member out, however, since the position was secured through an election by shareholders. So Smith remained, all the while publicly defending himself to anyone who would listen. You'd think shame would get him, but Roger Smith had no shame. He still didn't seem to understand what had happened. "He has given no indication that he will leave voluntarily, even though he is excluded from most meetings and the board's actions are a clear repudiation of his leadership," said a source close to the board. "Roger Smith has impossibly thick skin. He thinks if he denies it long enough, people might actually believe him."

The one-two coup was a messy business and it left deep scars. In the days following Stempel's resignation, many people in the company and the Detroit press rushed to his defense, saying he was unfairly cast as the scapegoat for all the company's problems. Industry expert James Womack, coauthor of the MIT study *The Machine That Changed the World,* voiced the feelings of many when he said of Stempel, "He's a nice man who got hit by the bus because he was standing where someone else should be—

Roger Smith." Others grumbled about the precedent being set with Smale's appointment as chairman. The sixty-five-year-old former Procter & Gamble chairman was angrily dismissed by these detractors as a "toothpaste salesman." What did he know about cars? Their man, Stempel, was a "car guy"—the first engineer who had served as chairman for several decades. They didn't make the connection that he was more responsible than Roger Smith for the lack of competitive cars, low productivity in the factories, and soaring labor costs, which were now among the major problems confronting the company. Roger Smith was aptly portrayed as the biggest culprit, but Stempel and Reuss had to share the blame.

Smale's ascendancy to the chairmanship was hardly a power grab. He didn't really want the job—he would prefer to be out fly fishing than beating his head against GM's hardened corporate culture. His selection was revolutionary because it signaled a new direction that other corporations would follow: the chairman as outsider, a break in the incestuous relationship between directors and company executives. As one analyst said, "The CEO will look less like an emperor than like a congressman, trying to represent his constituents and to the extent he succeeds being re-elected."

In the aftermath of his resignation, Stempel could not contain his bitterness. "I think I had good support in some quarters," he said—the suggestion being that it was instigators within the board who had driven him out. He also blamed his ouster on press leaks—in particular, speculation about the board's continued displeasure. But there was much more to it than that. The board members regretted the stories in the press. It was not their intention to embarrass Stempel, only to act. Besides, as one board member said later, "It wasn't exactly a secret that we were unhappy with Stempel. He knew it. We gave him a chance in April and he just sat on it. Some of us were hoping he would resign voluntarily."

Even without the board's drastic action, GM might have pulled itself out of the mud during the next few years. But no one could be sure what the competition would do; if it continued to move forward, GM would have to accelerate change in order to hurdle the chasm that Jack Smith and the newly enlightened board members faced.

Furthermore, there was a corrupting influence at the heart of the company's culture. It was that which demanded the board's revolutionary attention. Had the company been allowed to go on operating the way it had always done, it would never catch up with the best in the business. Incrementalism never begat a revolution, and GM needed a revolution.

It is not unusual for American boards to be shaped by external forces—although the process is far from rapid. For example, social issues in the 1970s brought women and blacks onto corporate boards for the first time and their presence began to shake up the all-white, old-boys network. In essence, what occurred on the General Motors board was about more than the narrow consideration of a company's financial problems. It was about the shape of corporate governance in America. Over time, many company boards became clubby and inbred, without much visible distinction between insiders and outsiders. The chief mandate of the board—to represent the shareholders—was lost in the process, leaving companies with no functioning set of checks and balances to executive power. The interests of the shareholders were served when the company prospered and was able to invest in its future, thereby rewarding its owners as its profits grew. But with lax accountability, problems could go unnoticed for years. Management did what it wanted to do with little complaint from the board. On a deeper level, corporate boards lacked a sense of moral responsibility to the shareholders.

For many years the GM board failed the shareholders. It didn't oversee their assets effectively. The board permitted the company to borrow money to pay dividends in an effort to placate them and make them believe all was well. It failed to hold management accountable for its inability to produce cars people wanted to buy or its failure to control costs. The board accepted accounting compromises that were obviously disguising the financial deterioration.

In the past it was easier to ignore shareholders. They often did not consider themselves "owners," since they could freely sell their shares. But with the growth of institutional investors, ownership became concentrated in large blocks where a quick exit from a stock became impossible. These large shareholders began to demand stricter accountability for the use of their capital. Boards of directors often felt caught in the middle: appointed by management but responsible to shareholders.

At issue were the larger questions of why companies exist, what is their reason for being, who are their constituencies, and to whom are they responsible. These were questions that Ira Millstein loved to sink his teeth into. A quiet, brilliant New York lawyer, Millstein came into GM's orbit in 1986 after the board had bought back Ross Perot's shares for more than $700 million. They feared, rightfully, that some shareholders might find this lavish deal a little hard to swallow, and Millstein was brought in by Roger Smith's general counsel, Elmer Johnson, to protect the board members from the possible wrath of angry investors. Little did Smith or anyone else know that Millstein would be a significant behind-the-scenes force in encouraging members of the board to become activists.

It wasn't as though Millstein's feelings on the subject of board responsibility were a secret. During the 1980s he wrote and lectured often on the subject. His views were sharp and clear and they challenged America's corporate boards to undertake a serious reappraisal. In one thoughtful piece, he wrote:

> A relatively small group of men and women has been charged with great responsibility. They are more acutely aware of the seriousness of these obligations than ever before, especially of the risks to them if they are not careful. They spend more hours on the job. They appear, in theory, to have immense power and flexibility. They can help shape their corporations' missions in a great variety of ways, provided only that they offer plausible evidence that they have taken their primary obligations to shareholders adequately into account. . . .
>
> And yet, their gut feeling is that their role is exceedingly limited. They feel that they do not have time enough to get to know the company's products well, especially how competitive these products truly are. They do not have time enough to tour company plants, talk to middle managers, hear alternative points of view. While they can criticize CEOs, punish them, and even remove them, there is an im-

mense unwillingness to do so. This is an individual they themselves have selected, an individual who has far more information at hand than they do, who is (surprising as it may seem to many corporate critics) usually devoting every waking hour to the firm's affairs, and who is in need of every bit of support the board can give.

A former Harvard professor, Millstein thought hard about reinventing America's corporate boards. He viewed the change at General Motors with a great deal of satisfaction. After the November coup, he personally felt a kind of withdrawal. His job was done. Now others—some groomed with his encouragement—would continue the process of change. "The GM board has done an extraordinary thing," he said. "Before, being a board member was an honorary, part-time role. The GM example ended the corporate mythology about the role of boards. It took a long time, but they have set an extraordinary example for the rest of industry. They have empowered the boards of troubled companies to act." Indeed, in the months following GM's board action, IBM, Sears, Westinghouse, American Express (which, ironically, threw out its own chairman, a former GM director, James Robinson), and others convulsed from one rebellion after another.

Millstein reflected on the actions at GM and what they had meant to the people involved. He said of GM's board: "They were all scared when they were going through the process, but now they're very proud of what they have done. They see themselves as heroes. They have performed a revolution in corporate governance."

The question of how companies govern themselves is the core issue of the corporate world—and one that is coming under increasing scrutiny. Even though the form of governance differs among GM, Toyota, and VW, all three have a common need to articulate clearly, in words and actions, why they exist and to whom they are accountable. The identity and behavior of a company are shaped by its system of accountability, since corporations are products of financial and social systems. In the United States, public corporations are answerable to the owners, who are shareholders. Companies raise money and investors provide money based on their assessment of risk and returns. The goal of companies is to make profits, thus satisfying investors. This is not a system that gives priority to social objectives (like full employment). The assumption is that a healthy company that earns enough money to grow and prosper in the future will also provide full employment and contribute to society at large. In Europe and Japan the systems are different.

If the American system of corporate checks and balances has been visibly cracking after decades of hands-off clubbiness on the part of company boards of directors, the Japanese system has allowed little room for open acknowledgment that there might be a problem to begin with. In Japanese public companies, when heads roll the messy business is dispatched in private. At Toyota the board of directors is composed entirely of insiders. While shareholders include individual investors, they are mainly other corporations who are related to Toyota through business, and reciprocally, Toyota owns stock in those companies as well. Since only a small minority of shares is available for public ownership, it would be impossible for Toyota—or any other Japanese company—to be acquired. Corporate shareholders usually measure their "returns" not in dividends, but in business relationships between the two parties. In fact, it is almost a prerequisite of any deal that the players purchase one another's stock. For the most part, investments are not made with the expectation of capital gains or dividends. The ownership is symbolic of a relationship, with the "gains" coming from the implied common bond of working together.

The lack of shareholder participation in the process of accountability is especially true in a company like Toyota, whose wealth is so substantial that it is sometimes called Toyota Bank. Shareholders wouldn't dream of disputing Toyota's policies—and why should they? Even the banks are held in thrall by this powerful company. As one insider described it, "The banks bow their heads low and thank Toyota for accepting their loans." While most Japanese companies have long-standing relationships with the same banks, Toyota remains independent and can pick and choose to find the one with the best interest rate. "When Toyota has surplus funds," a Japanese banker said, "its finance department staff call all the banks every morning to search for the one that has the highest interest." For this reason, the term "Toyota rate" has been coined in Japanese business circles to describe the highest interest rate.

Toyota's informal *zaibatsu*—the group of companies that make up its business family—adds to its power. After World War II, the Occupation forces tried to dissolve *zaibatsus* and purge their leaders. Nissan was thus disbanded and suffered mightily as a result. Toyota tried to avoid having its *zaibatsu* disbanded by masking its existence, renaming its companies. For example, Toyoda Steel Works became Aichi Steel Works, and Toyoda Machine Tools became Kariya Machine Tools. In this way, Toyota was able to "disband" its *zaibatsu* on its own terms—in name, but not in reality. According to Shoichiro Toyoda, this gave it an edge over companies like Nissan.

Toyota's shareholders have tremendous respect for its management and are loath to complain. Monthly board meetings are pro forma; all decisions are resolved in advance. The process is called *nemawashi*—consensus building before the fact. Since, like all Japanese companies, the board members are insiders (usually handpicked by Eiji, Shoichiro, and a couple of other people), decisions can always be strictly controlled. A "coup," in the manner of GM's board, could never happen.

Toyota is perhaps more sensitive to the threat of shareholder interference than other companies. Its historical memory reaches back to Kiichiro's father, Sakichi, and his disdain for outsiders. He kept the shares of his company limited to those in his inner circle. Although Toyota eventually resorted to public stock, Kiichiro also maintained an attitude of independence. But he found himself in the painful position, in 1950, of having to depend on a bank to bail the company out. Were it not for the Bank of Japan, the company would have folded, but the bank exacted a high price in control and set harsh conditions for its support—including worker layoffs. It was this condition that led to Kiichiro's resignation, and the split into two companies. The bitter experience was branded on the consciousness of subsequent Toyota leaders who vowed they would never again be dependent upon the power of banks. When Ishida replaced Kiichiro, he vowed to create a no-debt company, once saying, "Toyota will survive even if it has 365 days of picnics"—in other words, even if it went on a year-long holiday. Eiji promised that a time would come when there would be no outside directors on Toyota's board, and that came to pass in the 1970s.

Toyota's annual shareholder meetings are carefully scripted and rehearsed to guard against the remote chance that there might be a bleat of protest. They occur in September, unlike virtually every other company in Japan (except Isuzu), which all hold their meetings on the same day in June. Simultaneous board meetings prevent shareholders who have interests in more than one company from attending all of the meetings—another way Japanese companies subtly undermine the influence of shareholders.

The day before Toyota's annual meeting, board members engage in a dress rehearsal, with the silent men lined up on the stage, according to rank, the CEO standing front and center. In hierarchical Japan, the protocol prescribes that only the CEO speaks during the meeting.

At the rehearsal, young company executives from the general-affairs staff are assigned to make strident comments and ask hard questions, in the nature of a U.S. presidential debate rehearsal. The alleged purpose is to prepare the CEO for any tough questions that might come from real-life shareholders. What makes the custom ludicrous is the fact that it is so unlikely any shareholder will open his mouth. Meetings are rigidly formated, precision-timed events, lasting no more than thirty minutes. It is considered a real victory if the time can be slashed to twenty minutes. Although shareholders are certainly entitled to ask questions, the practice is discouraged.

The annual meeting on September 25, 1992, at the company headquarters in Toyota City was a particularly important one, as its agenda included announcements regarding Tatsuro's appointment and the appointment of new directors. The meeting was attended by 498 people. Two of them asked questions about the domestic market. It was over in fifty-eight minutes—an exceptionally long meeting by normal standards.

In Japanese life the conformity and invisibility within a group is so intense that it keeps people in line. The shame of standing out is so great that one risks it at tremendous peril to his reputation and future. If a person's behavior doesn't conform, he is shunned—a fate too grim to contemplate. There is strong motivation to toe the "Japanese line." If one is different, he is accused of not "behaving Japanese." Life in corporate Japan is like participating in a group dance. If one deviates, it interrupts the flow. Conformity is not just valued in corporate life; it is carried into every aspect of social behavior, even the most mundane. A friend of this author's, an American living in Japan, told of how severely she was chastised and nearly ostracized by her neighbors when she put her trash out on the wrong day and in the wrong barrel. It was a monumental faux pas. The neighbors wrote letters to the authorities complaining about their rule-breaking neighbor. A more brutal example of what happens to those who are different is evident in the bullying that takes place in Japanese schools. The victims are always those who do not fit the norm, including children who have lived abroad.

The Japanese are taught from birth to be responsible to group norms. They dress alike, wear the same hairstyles, and drive the same-color cars (until recently, these were usually white). In school, children are taught that it is impolite to raise their hands unless others are already doing so. There's no jostling to be first with the correct answer.

The desire to be alike leads to intense fadism. For example, several years ago, there was the "*shochu* boom." *Shochu* is a powerful vodkalike brew that everyone drank, not necessarily because they liked it, but because it was the rage. The *shochu* boom was replaced by the *Beaujolais nouveau* craze, which was so fierce that some people rushed to the hotels near Narita Airport when a shipment of the wine was due, so they could be the first to "experience" it at mass tastings.

Such attitudes opened the way for a unique brand of corporate game-playing, compliments of the *sokaiya*.

The *sokaiya*—literally translated as "general shareholder meeting fixers"—are business-style extortionists who are perfectly suited to fill the immense gap between ritual and reality in Japanese corporate business practices. The *sokaiya* first emerged in the 1960s after one corporation paid gangs (*yakuza*) to beat up a group of renegade shareholders who were actually planning to challenge the company at its annual meeting. The *yakuza* wheels started spinning: If companies were so fearful that shareholders would speak out, why not stir the pot? Thus emerged the *sokaiya* —presentable "businessmen" who formed shell companies and became professional shareholders, for the sole purpose of extorting money from corporations.

Here's how it worked: The *sokaiya* would purchase a few shares of a company to make themselves legitimate shareholders. Then they would approach the CEO or his lieutenants (in many companies, there was actually a "department of *sokaiya* affairs") and demand money, threatening that if they weren't paid they would disrupt the shareholder meeting and embarrass the CEO. The prospect of *sokaiya* rising up in the midst of orderly annual meetings to shout questions or make shocking personal revelations about the CEO was unbearable. Nearly every company paid *sokaiya* to make sure shareholder meetings ran smoothly. It was illegal, but there seemed to be no choice.

A Westerner might ask, if everyone knew that shareholder meeting disruptions were being caused by *sokaiya* and were not "real," why didn't they just call the *sokaiya* bluff? Because this was Japan, where appearance and reality are often considered the same.

In at least one instance, a Toyota-affiliated company used *sokaiya* disruptions to its advantage. In 1986 T. Boone Pickens, the colorful Texas oilman, purchased 26 percent of Koito Manufacturing Company, a part of Toyota's extended family of parts manufacturers. Toyota owned 19 percent of Koito, and had three board seats and an active involvement in the appointment of key managers.

Pickens felt that in exchange for his substantial interest in Koito, which was even larger than Toyota's, he should at least get a seat on the board. Pickens charged that Koito was not providing its investors with a reasonable return because Toyota exercised too much control over its prices. But the swaggering Texan had no idea what he was up against.

No matter what he tried, Pickens could not get to first base in establishing his rights—or what he thought were his rights. He decided to use the shareholder meeting to state his claim that he should be allowed a seat on the board.

The *sokaiya* were out in full force that day as the Koito board gathered. Every time Pickens tried to speak, he was shouted down by a chorus of loud voices, while the stony-faced board members sat silently on the stage. The scene was so chaotic that Pickens couldn't get a word in edgewise—which was, of course, the point. In the course of their tirades, the *sokaiya* uttered every known four-letter word, which made for interesting reading in the Japanese business press the following week. By the end of the meeting, it finally dawned on the Texan that Koito and, indirectly, Toyota would go to any lengths necessary to keep an American—or any outsider—off one of its boards.

The *sokaiya* existed in a tense standoff with the companies they blackmailed until 1992 when the law stepped in. In a huge scandal that rocked corporate Japan, twenty-two companies were charged with making illegal payments to *sokaiya*. The CEOs of these companies were indicted and forced to resign in shame. But the scandal didn't necessarily mean the end of *sokaiya*—only that they would become more clever in the way they set up legitimate-looking businesses. The system of ritualized performance had not changed. The scandal isolated the problem as a series of illegal actions, while failing to examine the system that led to them. "Companies refuse to disclose most information to the public in Japan and try to keep it a secret," commented Takayuki Suzuki, an analyst with Merrill Lynch Japan. "The *sokaiya* love that. But the real point is that we have absolutely no shareholder democracy in Japan. Annual meetings are just ceremonies."

That might be changing. Because of Pickens's outrage and additional pressure from the United States, the slowly grinding wheels of change are in motion in Japan. In early 1993 the Justice Ministry announced that it was redrafting the country's Commercial Code and would press for the Diet to enact new policies of shareholder involvement in Japanese companies. The new code would make it easier for shareholders to protect their interests by forcing companies to hire outside auditors and provide full disclosure. It would also give shareholders a greater voice and potentially make it easier for non-Japanese shareholders to become directors. In the long run the code could reshape corporate Japan by making shareholders more active.

Of course, real power is not always so easily legislated, especially in a country like Japan where so much is controlled by nuance and where shareholders are accustomed to being "silent investors."

What lies beneath the appearances and proprieties of corporate governance in Japan? The Japanese structure of responsibility and corporate accountability is quite different from the one in America. The basis for this difference rests in Japan's "debt capital" as opposed to America's "equity capital."

In the early days of industrialization in Japan, banks provided the money that companies needed to keep going. Toyota was typical of companies in the 1950s that were forced to seek bailouts from banks. In exchange, the banks exacted a high price through control. The United States, throughout most of this century, has had an equity-based capital market which created the concept of shareholders as the owners of the company. Shareholders in Japanese companies like Toyota mostly consist of other companies that exist in Toyota's corporate circle. There is no value placed on individual profit—only on maximizing the strength of the entire system. There is a saying in Japan: "As a supplier to Toyota you will never get rich, but you will never go out of business either."

So, to whom is Toyota responsible, if not to its shareholders? Again, the system is less straightforward than America's, but it can be every bit as brutal, if not more so. If a large company like Toyota were to get into trouble, the pressures would be intense, with punishment exacted on executives through public ostracism, humiliation, and (something lacking in American corporations) personal financial sacrifice. It is a fate worse than death to be forced to resign one's position because one did not fulfill the corporation's promise. In Japan a man in Bob Stempel's or Carl Hahn's position would have resigned much earlier. It is the unrelenting strength of the cultural code, not precisely formulated checks and balances, that keeps executives in check.

Toyota is an independent company, but practically speaking,

there are three forms of external accountability: the press, the dealers, and government and social organizations that limit Toyota through public pressure.

By Japanese standards, Nissan and Honda have always been much bolder when it comes to taking business risks. Being a more conservative company, Toyota is very press-sensitive. It exerts tremendous energy in public relations, producing volumes of documents, brochures, and even books that chart the history of the company and its strong leaders.

Toyota's dealers gained special power during the 1950s when the manufacturing and sales operations of the company were separated from one another. Toyota Motor Sales, which operated as an independent company, built its power base among the dealers. TMS's first president, Shotaro Kamiya, a savvy executive who had previously worked for GM-Japan, understood that dealers gathered valuable information about customers, products, and competitors. He effectively used that information to help Toyota advance in the early days. Because Toyota listened to its dealers and welcomed their input, it gained an advantage in the market. When Toyota Motor Company and Toyota Motor Sales were remerged during the 1980s, the dealers retained much of their influence. But today, Toyota is very large, and the process of gathering information from dealers has become quite formal. Dealers try to influence company decisions, but they aren't always successful. For example, dealers told the company that the expensive Corolla wouldn't sell in Japan, and the company went ahead anyway.

MITI was fundamental to the postwar expansion of Japanese business. It represented national goals and held the tension between helping government achieve a broad industrial policy and promoting competition among businesses. For many years the goal was expansion—even if it did not lead to profits. But today, MITI is trying to put the brakes on expansion, and Toyota is one of the targeted companies.

In itself, MITI isn't strong enough to force Toyota to adopt policies with which it does not agree. But MITI's policies are often in line with public opinion, and although Toyota resents interference from national bureaucracies, it often goes along. Perhaps it seems like a phony game of compliance in form and resistance in operation. But until recently, it has hardly mattered. After all, Toyota is the most successful industrial company in Japan.

Beneath all of these pseudo checks and balances, the real form of accountability in Japanese companies, and Toyota is no exception, is the fear of *mura hachibu,* which means, literally, "ostracism from the village." The term is commonly used in businesses to denote one who has failed to abide by the established principles of behavior. "If you're a target of *mura hachibu,* it is a fate worse than dying," said one Japanese businessman soberly.

These rules are not ethical standards, in the manner of Western mores. For instance, there are plenty of stock scandals and other dubious business dealings that come to light all the time in Japan, but the participants are not ostracized—much less jailed. The code of behavior is social, not moral. A recent example is the company president who announced that he would lay off five thousand workers. When it was discovered that he had not first cut his own salary, he had to rescind the order. In Japan you might survive a stock scandal, but if you break social mores, there might not be rehabilitation. *Mura hachibu* is the ultimate form of corporate accountability.

Of the three global companies, Volkswagen has the most complex system of governance, thus making it the least flexible to change. Because its ownership is partly composed of the government of Lower Saxony and the labor unions, the issue of accountability to company stability is complicated by employment and compensation guarantees, and other issues linked to regional prosperity. It would be comparable to the state of Michigan having partial ownership of General Motors.

Volkswagen's board, the *Aufsichtsrat,* is composed of twenty members—eight shareholders, two representatives of Lower Saxony, and ten employees. Seven of the employee seats are elected by the general work force and three are chosen by the union. Shareholders have power to elect only eight members, making the *Aufsichtsrat* a hornet's nest of vying agendas.

The *Aufsichtsrat* selects the members of the *Vorstand,* which is comparable to the executive committee. *Vorstand* members must seek *Aufsichtsrat* approval for major decisions, but in the past the *Vorstand* has easily manipulated them. Consider how easily Carl Hahn won approval for his projects by painting rosy pictures of the great glory and windfalls that were just around the corner for the company. Like the GM board, *Aufsichtsrat* members lacked the information to question what Hahn and his finance chief, Dieter Ullsperger, were telling them. And as long as the company appeared to prosper, they had little interest in probing deeper.

What really distinguishes Volkswagen's governance from the other two is the concept of codetermination, which demands that the governing body, the *Aufsichtsrat,* have equal numbers of representatives from the labor and capital sides of the business. The chairman, elected from among this group, holds two votes to prevent a fifty-fifty tie in decision making.

A Volkswagen board meeting has a decidedly different character from the elite gatherings of General Motors or the insider collectives of Toyota. The VW board is composed of a diverse collection of blue-collar workers, office employees, professionals, and outside union members. Franz Steinkuehler, the powerful head of IG Metall, the metalworkers union, is a board member at both Volkswagen and Daimler Benz, and he serves as deputy chairman of the *Aufsichtsrat.* In no other system does labor exert such formal control over corporate decisions, which in the past included promises that no German working for VW would ever lose his job to a Spaniard or Czech. When the company invested in an East German plant, West German workers were assured that they would not lose their jobs to East German workers either.

But even though the official structure of governance is very tight, it has traditionally chosen to be an almost silent partner to the chairman's decisions. During Carl Hahn's chairmanship, he was given nearly a free rein to pursue his chosen policies. The board never challenged him until the end, when the company's problems had reached a crisis point.

According to industry expert Jim Womack, "German management is schlerotic—the worst in Europe. They don't think or recognize reality. The old boy network is cemented in place. Companies like Volkswagen are organized with very strong functional

managers who rise to the tops of their departments and then refuse to budge. One of the problems that the chairman faces is
that there are white collar unions as well as blue collar unions,
and they prevent a chairman from simply getting rid of staff."

Wolfsburg, Germany—January 1993

THE FAREWELL PARTY for Carl Hahn took place in Goslar, a
charming medieval town, with winding roads and Old World
stone houses, about fifty miles southeast of Wolfsburg. Goslar
was a prosperous town, surrounded by silver mines that were
long the source of its wealth. The ceremony took place in the
dramatic setting of the Palatinate of Goslar, a grand complex
constructed under Emperor Henry II in the years between 1005
and 1015. For many generations, the Palatinate stood as the center of the Holy Roman Empire. The gathering for Carl Hahn was
held in the Emperor's Hall, a majestic location for his send-off.

Present were the "old boys" of Hahn's career, who comprised
the cream of the crop of German business. Only two women were
in attendance—Hahn's wife, Marisa, and Ferdinand Piech's
mother. Mrs. Piech, the sister of Ferdinand (Ferry) Porsche, was a
powerful force in her own right, since she was a major Porsche
shareholder.

Only days earlier, Piech had presented his proposal for management and structural changes to the *Aufsichtsrat*. He felt confident as he prepared his laundry list of recommendations, which
included a formal request that members of Hahn's executive
committee be fired, and a plan to create a separate sales and
dealer network for Audi. It was important to Piech that Hahn's
allies be replaced before they could use their influence with members of the *Aufsichtsrat* to thwart his plans.

When he was named chairman, Piech was heralded as the man
who was tough enough to save Volkswagen. But now his honey-
moon ended before it even began.

Piech was stunned when the *Aufsichtsrat* refused to make any
changes in the *Vorstand*. He had been certain that he would be
able to start with a clean slate, and most company observers anticipated some big changes. But the management stayed in place,

even Dieter Ullsperger, who had been responsible for so many of the company's faulty financial reports. At the March meeting, Piech would have greater success, but for now the *Aufsichtsrat* made it clear that every concession would be a struggle.

Furthermore, Piech's request to set up a separate sales and dealer network for Audi was turned down on the grounds that it would be too expensive. So was his request to move company headquarters out of Wolfsburg.

Piech had expected full support. But the board was reluctant to move too fast, especially on replacing the management team. The members wanted more specifics about the replacements, and Piech didn't have the details.

Jim Womack wasn't surprised by Piech's failure to make management changes right away. "It's just about impossible to unload one of these guys," he said. "It was an interesting prospect that Piech might be able to get rid of a few, but in the *Aufsichtsrat,* the old boy network is stifling. They are all related to each other in one way or another. These guys make the GM board look like commandos!"

Detroit—January 1993

LLOYD REUSS no longer worked for General Motors, but he was finding it hard to make the break. Say what you will about his level of competence, the company had been his life. Forced into retirement by the board's action, he didn't know what to do with himself. For several weeks after he ceased being on the payroll, he would arrive at his office, day after day. There was no business for him to conduct, no decisions for him to make. He just wanted to be there.

In January visitors to GM's booth at the Detroit Auto Show in Cobo Hall were amazed to find Bob Stempel and Lloyd Reuss standing there, as though they were part of the official contingent. Reuss spoke freely to reporters about GM's new lineup of cars. "It was bizarre," one of them said. "He sounded like he still worked for the company."

Stempel looked gray and sickly. He had lost a lot of weight following open heart surgery. He told anyone who asked that the change of power wasn't caused by the failures of his management. He was tired but defiant as he spoke of the contingent of outsiders who forced the board to act.

Jack Smith was busy at the Technical Center and only briefly attended the show. But with Stempel and Reuss at the booth, many people avoided it, feeling embarrassed and not knowing what to say. Once the most powerful men in the auto industry, Stempel and Reuss were both out of jobs, and it seemed they still couldn't accept that fact. Falling from power is like withdrawing from a drug. It is a long, slow process, and it hurts a lot.

Within three months, Roger Smith would join them on the outside.

On January 26 an article appeared in the *Washington Post* quoting unidentified sources as saying Smith had agreed to leave the board. Smith went ballistic. None of it was true, he raved. Furthermore, he thought he knew which board member was responsible for the leaks. He accused Ann McLaughlin of being the source—perhaps because she lived in Washington and he thought she might be close to *Post* reporters. McLaughlin, who had served as secretary of labor during the final years of the Reagan administration, and had been an outspoken member of the GM board, was not known for being shy about stating her opinions. But in this case, she insisted the accusation was unwarranted. She was furious that she had been singled out, and she thought it was terribly irresponsible of Smith to make such an accusation without any evidence. "I vehemently deny that I am the source of anything," she said angrily. "It's a total lie. It's unfortunate, because we work hard to maintain our confidentiality." The *Post* would not comment on its sources, except to say that it had three of them and they were all credible.

But then a funny thing happened. The day after the *Post*'s story appeared, Smith announced that he was leaving the board, effective April 6. It was, he said, a decision he had made privately a month earlier. He denied that anyone was forcing his hand. The reason for his resignation was the fact that he was spending "too many nights in hotels, and not enough nights at home." He was sixty-seven. He wanted to shift "into a lower gear."

According to *The Wall Street Journal,* Smale and company had wanted Smith to resign along with Stempel on November 2, but Smith said he would only do it if the board reversed its decision to cut his $1.2-million-a-year pension by 15 percent. They refused, and he hung on to his seat. But he was effectively ostracized. Other board members made it clear that they didn't want him around. As the May elections grew nearer, perhaps Smith, in a rare moment of self-awareness, realized he might not be reelected to the board and decided he had better resign. But he still couldn't understand it. He had been such a good chairman. He had left the company so strong in 1990. What happened?

As late as February, Bob Stempel, looking more pale and haggard than ever, continued to come to his office on the Fourteenth Floor. During that time, he wrote a lengthy memo to the board, defending his record. Stempel refused Smith's offer of a retirement party, although others did not. On February 17 General Motors officially said goodbye to Lloyd Reuss, F. Alan Smith, and Bob Schultz with a big bash. Stempel could not bring himself to attend.

SEVEN

It's Just a Car

If you look up the word "engineer" in an English dictionary, you might find "technologist," while in Japanese, its meaning uses the character for "art."

—Taiishi Ohno

Warren, Michigan—January 1993

EVERY MORNING, J. Ignacio (Inaki) Lopez de Arriortua, fifty-two, rose early, took a brisk run, then ate a spartan breakfast of unpeeled fruit before leaving for his office at the GM Technical Center to start one of his typical fifteen-hour days as head of GM's worldwide purchasing operation. He usually started as early as five or six. The tall, lean Lopez favored early staff meetings—at which, incidentally, he allowed no poisonous substances like coffee or sugar to be served.

Nothing about Lopez was consistent with the old GM style, or, for that matter, with any style known to corporate America. Since May 1992, when Jack Smith brought the Basque purchasing whiz to Detroit from his prior tour of duty at GM's main complex in Rüsselsheim, Germany, he had become the most talked about person in the auto industry. In six months he gained notoriety as the most visible and controversial symbol of Jack

Smith's new regime. Some insiders called him "the alien," and in many respects, the description was accurate. Lopez was eccentric, a messianic figure to his team and a crazy Spaniard to his critics. But even those who were most suspicious of his style and tactics could not deny that the man was effective. He seemed capable of achieving (and motivating others to achieve) long-range goals almost overnight.

Bringing Inaki Lopez, his old ally at GM-Europe, to the United States was one of Jack Smith's first actions as president. He liked Lopez's way of doing things, and credited the tough purchasing guru for 40 percent of GM-Europe's $1.5 billion in profits, which were the primary source of income for the company in the lean years of 1991 and 1992. And Smith genuinely liked Lopez, considering him a friend as well as a colleague. If there was such a thing as blood loyalty in the corporate world, Smith and Lopez seemed to have that bond.

Lopez first came to Jack Smith's attention when the Spaniard was a production manager at the Zaragoza plant of GM-Spain. Hans Huskes, the head of GM-Spain, called Smith at his Zurich office one day and told him about this creative engineer who was full of amazing ideas that no one would listen to. Smith's curiosity was piqued, and he and Fritz Lohr, the chief engineer at Opel, arranged a visit to Zaragoza. They arrived to find Lopez standing amid the parts of a disassembled Corsa, Opel's Spanish-built subcompact model. Lopez greeted the two men enthusiastically and walked them around the pieces, pointing out where money could be saved by changing the design, parts, or materials. Lopez's suggestions were so good that Lohr said yes to many of them on the spot. Within a few hours, hundreds of dollars were cut from the cost of building the Corsa, without compromising its appearance, features, or quality. Jack Smith was sold on Inaki Lopez.

But Lopez preached more than just cost-effectiveness. He behaved as though he was on a religious crusade. One of the first things he did upon his arrival was distribute a copy of his "Warrior's Diet," which he urged his staffers and others to follow to maximize their energy. When people received their copies of the sparse, low-fat, almost monklike program, they thought Lopez must be kidding. The idea that a corporate executive in beef and dairy land would encourage his staff to partake of such a diet was initially cause for great hilarity. Xerox and fax machines were kept busy circulating the regimen across the country so that friends and colleagues could share in the joke. But Lopez was absolutely serious. He patiently explained his philosophy to the doubters: Overweight bodies led to overweight minds. He reminded them that the Japanese ate the leanest diet in the world— 2,850 calories a day to America's porky 3,670. There was, Lopez insisted, "a direct correlation between nutrition and professional efficiency, between health and the warrior spirit."

Lopez called his purchasing staff "warriors." He and they were engaged in no less than a crusade for the future of GM—a crusade whose goal was to beat the Japanese by outdoing them in lean manufacturing. As head of worldwide purchasing, Lopez would do in the United States what he had done in Germany: reduce supplier costs and help them learn better manufacturing practices so they could still make a lot of money. He knew that unless GM reduced its costs, it had no hope of turning around and competing on an equal footing with the Japanese. As a reminder of his goal, Lopez displayed a Japanese doll in his office, which he liked to show to visitors. "This," he said with a smile, "is all we want the Japanese to be able to build."

But initially, at least, it wasn't the Japanese who feared Lopez and his warriors the most. It was GM's own suppliers, who viewed Lopez's arrival as one more plague visited upon them by their most important and most difficult client. Being a GM supplier was an endless headache. The company was constantly demanding price concessions and free engineering and research assistance. Furthermore, GM chronically promised more than it could deliver, since it did such a poor job forecasting how many cars it would sell. Rarely did a contract with GM produce the revenues or profits promised at the time of negotiation. Disheartened suppliers now faced an adversary who pledged to deliver billions in savings to help the struggling auto company pull itself out of the trenches.

Lopez had a track record that lent credibility to his pledge. In Europe, and especially in Germany, where GM had most of its operations, the parts suppliers had grouped themselves into cartels that held companies hostage to their bidding practices. Lopez refused to go along with the system. He simply moved contracts to Spain, Italy, or wherever he could get better prices. His tactics worked. Soon the German suppliers were bidding more competitively in order to hold on to their existing business. Because prices had previously been so high, it was easy for Lopez to buy the same parts for 30 percent less.

Jack Smith had been lobbying to bring Lopez to America for two years, but Stempel and Reuss weren't interested. Lopez might have been effective, but they didn't like the idea of introducing such a controversial foreign presence into GM—even if he was brilliant. They were not prepared to stand behind him and give him unconditional support while he turned the supplier system upside down. Then, a week before the GM board action on April 6, Lopez received a long-distance call from Smith. "What would you do if you were asked to come to the United States and do the same job with our operations here that you've done in Europe?" Smith asked coyly. Lopez stared at the tree outside his office window and wondered what the call meant and how he should respond. Was Jack Smith going to be in charge?

It was ironic, really. Only three weeks earlier, Lopez had been talking by phone to his friend Father Coyle, a Roman Catholic priest in Three Rivers, Michigan, who was looking after his two daughters while they studied at the General Motors Institute (an engineering school no longer controlled by the company). At one point, Father Coyle asked Lopez what it would take to turn GM around. Lopez didn't hesitate. "It would take Jack Smith," he said.

"Well, then," replied Father Coyle, "this Sunday, which is the feast of St. Joseph, I will pray for his appointment."

Now Lopez considered the power of prayer and wondered if the priest's divine intervention had worked.

"I know it's difficult to move, and I will understand if you say no," Smith told Lopez.

Lopez replied immediately, "Jack, for you I have only two answers: yes, or yes, sir."

Just over a month later, he was in Detroit, which would be-

come his home base, although he retained responsibility for GM-
Europe.

On the job, Lopez's tactics were strictly slash-and-burn. He
would seek bids from many suppliers and choose several finalists,
based upon their price, quality, and service. Then he would name
a target price lower than any of the bids and ask them to match
it. The dubious winner would end up with a price far lower than
anyone originally thought possible. All contracts, large and small,
came under scrutiny. Within weeks, Lopez was the most feared
man in the industry, and "PICOS" became the new curse word.
PICOS was Lopez's plan, short for Purchased Input Concept Op-
timization of Systems. It was aimed at improving quality, service,
and pricing by focusing on all aspects of production. Lopez's
two-hundred-member PICOS team traveled the country, landing
like locusts at suppliers' facilities and, over a five-day period,
transforming their manufacturing processes. According to Lopez,
companies that went through PICOS training scored huge improvements in all areas of manpower, productivity, space utiliza-
tion, and inventory investment—enough to make profits even
with lower bids.

There were some true believers among the ranks of suppliers—
those who said PICOS exposed them to entirely new methods
that they had not considered or heard of before. But often the
reaction to Lopez was unfavorable. By August, when auto suppliers gathered at the Traverse City resort on the shore of Lake
Michigan for the annual University of Michigan automotive sem-
inar, there was an electric buzz of anger in the air over Lopez's
"one hundred days of terror." One man, who had yet to meet
with Lopez, remarked gloomily, "I haven't been to the dentist
yet, but I face the process of four root canals."

Lopez was criticized for trying to destroy long-term relationships that had been tough to establish to begin with, given the
traditional distrust between the company and its suppliers. Now
suppliers were in an uproar over what they felt were unfair bidding practices. It might have worked in Europe, but this wasn't
the way Americans did business, they complained. The UAW
wasn't in love with Lopez, either, fearing that if GM used his
methods internally, the improved efficiency would lead to mas-

sive layoffs across the board. Many of GM's factories were grossly overstaffed and unproductive. Lopez tried to allay fears by announcing that he would encourage suppliers to set up shop inside GM plants and use excess workers in their production.

At the August conference, there was some talk of suing over broken contracts, but as one supplier sighed hopelessly, "Suing General Motors is like making love to an elephant. You can get crushed in the process." It appeared there would be no end to Lopez's "reign of terror."

The man who had been called Hurricane Lopez, Vlad the Impaler, and Inaki the Terrible was, to many people's surprise, personally charming and easygoing—nothing like the military figure of his legend. He publicly expressed surprise at all the fuss being made. He insisted he wasn't trying to beat up on suppliers. He was trying to help them. His case was simple: Leaner production methods and better controls would benefit everyone, from GM to the suppliers themselves to the customers. Wasn't that what people wanted?

It was a rocky start, during which time Lopez populated the purchasing staff with the same Spaniards who were his core team in Europe. His people were swept up in a fervor—a personality cult formed around Lopez. As the results poured in, they grew even more energized by the simple fact that they were doing something important and had become the focal point of GM's plan to turn itself around.

As a symbol of his intentions, Lopez transferred his watch to his right arm. He told people he would only return it to his left arm when his task was accomplished and he could return to his farm in Bilbao. Every executive at GM and all of Lopez's staff took to wearing their watches on the right arm as a sign of changing times. Even Jack Smith's wife, Lydia, showed her allegiance to the movement in this way.

During his brief term on the GM board of directors, Ross Perot liked to say, "This isn't a moon shot; it's just a car." But that was a big "just." Building a car and doing it profitably was not a one-dimensional matter. It involved the efficient, cost-effective synchronization of people, machines, parts, and components, woven into a system that produced a high-quality vehicle for the lowest possible cost. Unlike a moon shot, it had to be done thousands of times every day, year in and year out.

GM's inability to get the elements of design, engineering, and manufacturing in sync had been its worst problem, and like it or not, Lopez was Jack Smith's angel of hope for a company that had existed for too many years on a fatty, steak-and-potatoes diet. Lopez often protested that he had nothing to do with GM's production system. His job was to deal with outside suppliers. But the relationship between supplier costs and quality and the final cost and quality in the factories was clear. Since he was producing such huge savings for GM on the outside, it seemed only a matter of time before his concepts would make their way to the inside. In addition, Lopez would gradually assert himself on more of GM's operations through the introduction of creativity teams—cross-functional groups that tackled a variety of issues. They brought together people from every department having anything to do with the design, production, and sale of a vehicle. By early 1993, Lopez was breaking down the internal barriers that had long precluded the resolution of fundamental design and manufacturing questions.

Although Lopez was loath to admit it, many pieces of his program were a Westernized takeoff of the Toyota Production System. What was so special about the way Toyota produced cars? In the 1970s, if one were to visit Toyota's Motomachi plant, the trip would hardly inspire oohs and ahhs. There was little automation in sight; it didn't look nearly as impressive as the huge factories one could tour in Europe and the United States. Instead, one saw hardworking uniformed men choreographed in an industrial dance, without a wasted motion or moment. The factories were clean but rather shabby, uncluttered and small, with an occasional bonsai plant to add some green to the gray cubbyholes used for the team meetings held at the end of each shift. When Americans toured Japanese factories, they thought the workers seemed like human robots, and they couldn't imagine American workers being made to perform so hard or diligently. Visitors from General Motors and other American companies, noting the low absenteeism, long workdays, discipline, and nonexistence of substance abuse and strikes, were sure there was no way to duplicate the environment in their factories.

Since Toyota always took foreign visitors to the older Motomachi factory, there was a suspicion that its newer factories held secrets that these clever people did not want to reveal. In fact, although Motomachi was old, it was quite typical of Toyota factories of the time. The line speed was unusually slow—about fifty-two cars per hour compared with sixty to seventy at GM. But this slow pace was deceptive, since high first-time quality allowed Toyota to produce cars at lower costs than the faster factories, and man-hours per car were less than half of GM standards. Visitors did not understand this. They assumed there was something else going on at other factories that was hidden from their view—perhaps more automation.

Western companies, especially those with financial resources like GM and Volkswagen, were in love with the idea of automation. With robots manning the factories, the lines would run faster, quality would be higher, and, best of all, the number of expensive human workers could be reduced. There was a naive faith in the power of machines: If the right technology was in place, everything would miraculously be transformed.

During the 1950s and 1960s, while Western companies were becoming more and more mechanized, Toyota had little money for machines, and plenty of human workers who were willing to labor long hours for low pay. The factory workers were trained to view their futures, goals, and values as inseparable from those of management. In exchange for this loyalty, the company promised lifetime employment to full-time workers.

Toyota couldn't afford and didn't need the high capital expenditures of automation, so it took a different route—one that would ultimately outshine all the sophisticated equipment Western money could buy.

Taiishi Ohno was a dedicated and talented engineer without a college education who was made general manager of the manufacturing department at Toyota in the early 1950s. There, he was inspired to look for ways to improve the efficiency of the assembly line. Ironically, part of his inspiration came, not from technology or what he learned by studying Western competition, but by his observation of an American supermarket. In essence, his thinking went this way: In a supermarket the shelves were restocked when they needed to be, as goods were sold to customers. The stock on the shelves was not controlled by the producer of goods, but by the shelf stocker and the end user. You didn't walk into a supermarket and see goods piled on the floor because there was no room on the shelves. The system of ordering was contingent on the demand for products at the store level, rather than decisions made by the supplier of the merchandise. A supermarket that ordered more goods than it could sell during the week not only had a storage and control problem, it also risked piling up inventory it would never disgorge. In effect, final demand pulled goods through the system rather than the manufacturer pushing them through.

Ohno's approach was also influenced by the state of the Japanese auto industry at the time. In 1950 total production in Japan was only about thirty thousand vehicles, so output of any one model hardly matched the definition of "mass" established in the United States. As a result, Ohno's system had to be designed for efficient low-volume production of many models. It also had to take into account small factories, the shortage of capital, the plentiful inexpensive labor, and the need to reduce investment in facilities and materials.

These considerations formed the basis of Ohno's creation of Just-in-Time (JIT) production, a process for reducing costs through the elimination of waste. Waste was defined as excess manpower, time, space, money—any resource that was involved in the assembly of the final vehicle. It also became the underpinning for the quality ethic. With no buffer in the system, quality problems were, by necessity, quickly corrected so the system would not grind to a halt. It conferred responsibility for much of the operation on line workers rather than on supervisors.

It soon became clear that the importance of the system transcended Toyota's unique circumstances and maintained its relevance as Toyota's production scale and product line complexity grew. Over time, JIT was implemented by all Japanese manufacturers, though rarely with the precision and perfection of Toyota.

But as simple as JIT sounds when it is described, it took the West more than twenty years to understand, and no one has yet entirely mastered this deceptively "simple" system. Western companies like General Motors failed to grasp that for JIT to work, dozens of other functions and operations had to be coordinated in the factory, among suppliers, and in overall production scheduling. You couldn't just change the delivery schedule and expect miracles. Everything was held in a fragile balance. The system had a choreography and a soul.

American and German companies tried and failed to infuse their assembly plants with elements of the Toyota Production System, but its premise was anathema to their organizations. When Henry Ford invented the assembly line, it revolutionized industry and reduced costs enough to make cars affordable to the masses. Before Ford, carmaking required numerous skilled craftsmen. Ford took unskilled workers and enabled them to build a car by doing the same repetitive, simple task while the gradually built vehicle was towed along on a conveyor. But he didn't take the idea beyond the concept of breaking down production into repetitive tasks on a moving line. Ford, and every other practitioner of traditional mass production, gave little thought to the whole system—the relationship of a car's design and the quality of its components, or the importance of worker involvement in the process. Ford's system has been sarcastically called Just-in-Case, since the continuous flow was ensured by huge stocks of parts and subassemblies piled around the line.

The Western mass-production system accommodated variable parts quality with buffer stocks to compensate for defective items. Frequent breakdowns of equipment on the line also necessitated extra supplies, so that the rest of the line could be kept operating while repairs were being made. Inspectors were needed to make sure quality standards were met. It was a rugged system, based on the assumption of failure, and this added costs to the process. By contrast, JIT forced companies to maintain equipment and anticipate overhauls before breakdowns happened.

It didn't seem to occur to American or German carmakers that they ought to modify the assumptions behind their systems instead of dismissing the initial success of the Japanese as the by-product of a workaholic nation. They were locked into a system that was virtually unchanged from the early decades of the twentieth century.

Furthermore, Toyota understood that to maintain quality and efficiency in the assembly plant, it would have to begin with the car's point of origin. Organizational discipline, which integrated designers, engineers, and manufacturing specialists into the creative and engineering process early on, minimized the use of resources needed for the creation and production of cars. The early collaboration by suppliers further contributed to efficiency and reduced vehicle-development lead times.

In the West there was traditionally little collaboration among the disciplines. Design staffs were often separate from the manufacturing process. Until recently at GM, the design staff reported to the chairman rather than to the car groups; that might have been the reason for the frequent styling mishaps that occurred during the 1980s. Vehicle engineering was in its own isolated world. General Motors, prior to the 1984 reorganization, managed most of its assembly plants through GMAD, which at least provided a consistent manufacturing discipline throughout the company. After the reorganization, GMAD was dismantled and the job of actually transforming the engineered prototypes into finished products was left to individual plant managers—each of whom had his own ideas about how to manage his plant and what kind of equipment to buy.

During its spending binge of the mid-1980s, six new assembly plants were opened, and they didn't have much in common. The most absurd example of the lack of coordination and flexibility in GM was found in the four plants that engineered and produced four versions of the midsize W-cars. Although the cars are identical in most ways, they are sufficiently different that two versions cannot be assembled in the same plant.

Toyota was unique because it incorporated all aspects of carbuilding into a single system, while General Motors abided by the long-held premise that product innovation had a strategic advantage over process innovation. Volkswagen's philosophy of manufacturing, developed by Nordhoff after the war, involved building more and more of the same car—the Beetle—in ever larger factories. It was as though the company was producing bread or beer, and never expected to change the recipe. Even when VW set up factories in Brazil or Mexico, they were always based on the notion of maximizing profits by producing the same car in huge quantities.

As long as demand for the Beetle grew faster than capacity, Nordhoff didn't have to pay much attention to the finer points of maximizing the use of resources. Cost per unit fell as the fixed costs of product development and production remained stable, and output soared. Germany was recovering from the war, the economy was booming, wages were low, and the reputation of VW's cars was strong enough to command premium prices. The biggest challenge was how to satisfy the world's insatiable appetite for the Beetle. VW made enormous amounts of money during this period, much of it reinvested in even bigger factories, but some of it simply added to the company's growing storehouse of hidden resources. By the 1960s, when Carl Hahn came to the United States, he was pleasantly surprised to find $300 million in a bank account earning interest. The pile of money that VW accumulated seemed to vindicate Nordhoff's philosophy, even though the company and the Beetle were living on borrowed time.

There was a concept in Germany called Technik, which was a combination of art and technology embodied in the craftsman worker. The skilled worker, who had labored at least three years as an apprentice, could be relied on to make good cars and put things right if machines didn't work or parts were less than perfect. He could be counted on to touch up paint, sculpt metal stampings, and use brute force, if necessary, to fit imperfect trim in place. The Germans thought the combination of machinery and well-trained men would provide a permanent cost and quality advantage.

In Germany, engineering (especially mechanical and chemical) was valued above the soft sciences, and machinery and metalworking companies dominated industry. Perhaps this tradition, reinforced in education and investment, explains why Germany has lagged so far behind Japan and the United States in biotechnology, electronics, and computer sciences. It might also explain why the Mercedes S class, the flagship of the line with a price tag to match, was a flop with the consumers. Mercedes engineers designed gadgets that provided solutions to things people didn't see as problems. Consider the model's double-glazed side windows to prevent fogging. Such windows made the car heavier, the door thicker, and the cost exorbitantly high—all for the sake of a fog-free window. Other companies solved the problem simply by directing heated air at the windows to keep them clear. (Helmut Werner, Mercedes' president, now admits that the company went too far and failed to understand the needs of the consumer. He promised to overhaul the entire Mercedes-Benz car line to make it more socially responsible and affordable.)

For decades German car companies boasted about their engineering brilliance and the resulting sleek, well-crafted cars. But because they never evolved a production *system*—beyond bigger and more costly machines—they found themselves unable to understand or match Toyota when it vaulted onto the world stage in the 1970s and threatened to destroy their companies. Toyota put manufacturing in the forefront and understood that in order to maximize productivity, quality, and resources, there had to be a predictable production schedule, good, reliable suppliers, and trained workers who could react to any disruption in the system. It was considered a "fragile" system, since everything was intertwined. Toyota's major rival in Japan, the once-wealthier Tokyo-based company Nissan, favored more automation, yet it would consistently lag behind Toyota in nearly every measure, especially in profits. Toyota was the only auto company that remained profitable during the 1973–74 oil crisis that sent Japan into a recession. Until the crisis, other Japanese auto companies functioned more or less like those in the United States, except for the advantage of having cheap, hardworking labor. But Toyota's profits were so much higher that the other companies started to learn from it, although they had a hard time replicating what Toyota had accomplished. One reason was that Toyota had a strong supplier network, all located around Toyota City. No other automaker had as many dedicated and technically competent suppliers situated so close to home.

What made Toyota's system function was the underlying emphasis on quality control, fast reaction to problems on the line, and an incredible attention to detail. Problems were seen as opportunities to do something better, rather than as interruptions and inconveniences. This was the exact reverse of the General Motors mentality. As a young GM engineer put it, "No one in a product development group solved all the problems that they knew of. You simply assumed that your replacements would tackle them when you were assigned to another task. It was the way things were done. And that's how cars got into production with so many problems."

Ironically, Toyota learned its valuable lesson in problem solving from an American. In the 1950s W. Edwards Deming, who would later be lauded as "the father of the quality management movement," tried to interest General Motors and Ford in his ideas about how to build a well-run company by instilling quality and pride in the workers. Feeling cocky and invincible, neither company was interested. But Japanese businesses, reaching for a postwar comeback, were. At the time, Toyota was a small, unimpressive company, with a dream to be great and a recognition that Japan did not have the resources to make that happen. It was eager to listen—especially Ohno, who tailored much of his philosophy after Deming's. One important lesson was to give workers a sense of "ownership" in the company by involving them in problem solving. As Ohno put it:

"When confronted with a problem, have you ever stopped and asked why five times? It is difficult to do even though it sounds easy. For example, suppose a machine stopped functioning:

"Why did the machine stop? There was an overload and the fuse blew.

"Why was there an overload? The bearing was not sufficiently lubricated.

"Why was it not lubricated sufficiently? The lubrication pump was not pumping sufficiently.

"Why was it not pumping sufficiently? The shaft of the pump was worn and rattling.

"Why was the shaft worn out? There was no strainer attached and metal scrap got in."

And so on. By asking questions until the source of the problem was uncovered, the correct adjustments and repairs could be made. Had the worker stopped at question number one, the response would have been merely to replace the fuse, thus leaving the door open for more breakdowns.

One of the main factors that distinguished the Toyota Production System from Fordism was the amount of responsibility and individual control given to workers. In the West the assembly-line worker was a cog in a large machine whose full responsibility was compartmentalized into the single task to which he or she was assigned—be it tightening a screw, attaching a door, applying sealant, or whatever the job. The task, which would take only a few seconds, would be performed exactly the same way several hundred times a day. The worker had to know very little if anything about building the car, or the purpose of the component they were putting together. He or she was detached from any understanding of how individual performance affected future work on the vehicle or its overall quality. The car itself was abstract to the task at hand, and the emphasis was on speed. The West ignored poor quality, assuming that repair stations at the end of the line would correct defects. There was little accountability for the quality of the final product. Even if workers tried to alert supervisors to problems with equipment or defective parts, they were usually told, "Just do your job; don't complain." The process alienated workers and bred contempt for managers.

At Toyota, factory workers also repeated tasks on assembly lines. But the difference was its philosophy of shared responsibility. Each worker was trained for a variety of jobs which they performed in teams, and the teams were the primary structure of accountability. Workers not only assembled cars, they also inspected them. They were expected to think about how tasks, parts, or equipment could be improved. Their suggestions were always carefully reviewed and incorporated if they were deemed valuable. To instill respect for the importance of the product and the difficulty of manufacturing it, every salaried worker started his career with three months working on the assembly line. Each person working on the line had the authority to stop the line to correct a problem. Although this is now common in U.S. factories, until the 1980s it was unheard-of. Managers assumed workers would stop the line on any pretext—to loaf rather than to fix a problem.

The Toyota Production System, in all its logic and simplicity, was the key to Toyota's market success and huge profits. Toyota is by its nature a slower, more risk-adverse company. Yet, like the fable of the tortoise and the hare, its habit of studying a decision thoroughly before making a move has resulted in fewer mistakes and thus more consistent growth. Other Japanese companies, in trying to beat Toyota, have taken risks without having the same cash reserves to protect them. But this fact was impossible for people like Roger Smith to wrap their minds around. Smith believed a Japanese secret weapon, not shown to outsiders, was really responsible for Toyota's efficiency and quality. Perhaps he suspected it was a dazzling piece of automation. NUMMI (New United Motor Manufacturing, Inc.), the joint venture Smith would enter with Toyota, was meant to give GM a small car and in the process teach the company Toyota's ways. At the time, GM calculated that it was costing them $2,578 per car more than the Japanese to produce a small car. Roger Smith was desperate to learn if the methods were transferable to the United States, and avoid investing in another money-losing small car. He also wanted the car because he needed a model for Chevrolet.

The plan for a General Motors–Toyota joint venture was two years in the making, and both Roger Smith and Eiji Toyoda were eager for it to happen, in spite of dissent from executives in the two companies. While Smith believed it was the way to discover Toyota's secret, Eiji regarded it as the perfect low-risk, politically appropriate opportunity for Toyota to learn if it could transfer its systems to America. Although Honda and Nissan were already establishing their own auto assembly plants in the United States, Toyota was always more cautious than some of its Japanese competitors. It was Eiji's way to move slowly—to learn first, then to act—all the while carefully trying to quell the flames of protectionism by appearing to be nonthreatening.

In March 1983 the two companies reached an agreement in principle to combine forces to assemble a small car. Toyota would contribute $100 million in cash and GM would contribute the equivalent in assets, primarily a closed GM plant in Fremont,

California, that had been shuttered because of GM's excess capacity, fractious labor relations, and poor quality. NUMMI would have its own board of directors, half appointed from each company, and Toyota would provide the president and chief executive officer. NUMMI would build a small car based on the Toyota Corolla to be sold as the Chevrolet Nova by GM. Chevrolet dealers were clamoring for an entry-level product, since they were the price leader brand, and in markets like California were being overwhelmed by the Japanese. More often than not, first-time buyers were choosing Japanese cars, which then also became the choice as second or third cars in households. Although they would have preferred a totally homegrown vehicle, the dealers welcomed NUMMI as a solution to their small-car problems.

But Roger Smith's public announcement of the venture was difficult for many Detroit hard-liners to swallow. It seemed like a blatant abdication of small-car development to the Japanese, especially since GM had earlier canceled plans to build its subcompact S-car, its designated import fighter, after data had shown it to be a huge money loser. Privately, Smith insisted that his strategy was to beat the Japanese by learning and incorporating all of their successful techniques, thus conquering them in the process. But to many critics both within and outside the company, NUMMI was a traitorous concept. They believed the only real solution to the Japanese threat was to cut it off at the borders through stricter trade barriers. Already, a self-imposed trade limit had been agreed to by MITI in 1981, but American industry was calling for more. And here was GM getting into bed with the enemy.

Smith was deeply hurt by the suggestion that he was being unpatriotic, but he knew GM didn't know how to build a profitable small car of its own—at least not at the moment. Perhaps to dispel this criticism, he made a dramatic surprise announcement shortly before the NUMMI deal was signed: General Motors would initiate its own futuristic experiment in small-car building. This as-yet-unnamed car, Smith promised, would make GM's collaboration a mere stopgap in the drive to vault over the Japanese.

So sudden and surprising was Smith's announcement about his

new program—which would later be named the Saturn Project, after the rockets that had propelled America's first spaceships—that the company's NUMMI negotiating team at Toyota was caught off guard. Jack Smith, who was heading the team, remembered his Japanese hosts asking him questions about the project and especially about Roger Smith's comment that NUMMI was merely a stopgap. What did this mean? they wondered. Jack Smith could not respond, since he had no information about the project, nor had he known the announcement was coming.

Although Roger Smith could give few details about the new project, since it was, at the time, only a collection of ideas thrown together by a "skunkworks" creative team at GM's Technical Center, the announcement heightened Smith's public image and, combined with NUMMI, gave him the reputation in some circles of being a visionary. GM's chairman seemed an unlikely visionary with his pudgy, elflike red cheeks and high, squeaky voice. But he dreamed of being the man who would make General Motors great again, and he saw his two-pronged import-fighting strategy of NUMMI and Saturn as part of a grand plan. All aglow from the largely positive press, Roger Smith could not foresee that neither NUMMI nor Saturn would transform GM, although both would reveal surprising sources for the company's problems. In the end, they were only side dishes to the company's main plate of woes.

The real flaw in Smith's vision was to think the wisdom of NUMMI (and later Saturn) would miraculously osmose throughout General Motors. Instead, during Smith's regime, it became yet another squandered opportunity for a company that no longer understood how it had to adapt in order to solve the problems many recognized.

Fremont, California—September 1984

STEPHEN BERA was a typical General Motors manager, a midwesterner who had worked for the company for twenty years. His expertise was production material control, and he'd been with Chevrolet, then the AC Spark Plug division, then central staffing—rising through the ranks, collecting his raises and bonuses with an eye to how much he could personally achieve and earn with the company before retirement. He was a capable manager, cut from the standard GM cloth—put in his time, collected his paycheck. Like most GM managers assigned to do a stint at NUMMI, he was anxious about working for Japanese management. The typical American picture of a Japanese plant was that it was an inhuman environment where people were treated like machines and forced to work long hours in sterile conditions. Bera's task was akin to a soldier being sent into enemy territory. He related that he and the other managers were told, "Go to the joint venture and bring back this 'magic' that exists in the Toyota Production System. So everyone went out there with just that in mind: 'Learn what you can. Learn your lessons well. You are going to help us alter the course of the company.' "

That's what Bera set out to do. But what he encountered changed his life.

"I went through a personality change out there," he admitted with amazement. "I felt better about working for Toyota. No more politics. No more doing things just for my own personal gain. The issue was, 'What's good for the company?' It was one hundred eighty degrees from everything I have ever done in my career."

The "magic" of NUMMI was very simply the Toyota Production System, dressed up in Western clothes, since Toyota knew California workers would not agree to exactly the same work habits that were routine in Japan. Its philosophy included seven fundamentals:

1. *Kaizen,* the never-ending search for perfection (continuous improvement)
2. *Kanban,* the reduction of costs through Just-in-Time
3. Development of full human potential
4. Building mutual trust
5. Developing team performance
6. Treating every employee as a partner
7. Providing a stable livelihood for all employees

At NUMMI there were just 4 factory job classifications, as opposed to as many as 183 in some GM plants. Employees worked in teams headed by fellow hourly workers trained at Toyota City. The team leader wasn't a boss, but more of an advisor, and the goal was for all members to eventually be trained to lead their teams.

Toyota management bent over backward to ease any fears workers might have about working for the Japanese. NUMMI's second president, Kan Higashi, who replaced Tatsuro Toyoda in NUMMI's second year, became so loved by employees that they cried heartfelt tears when he returned to Japan in 1989. Higashi had a deep and abiding respect for American workers. It wasn't a facade; it was real. During his tenure at NUMMI, he concentrated on empowering American workers by reinforcing their importance to the company. "The hourly people had a bitter experience because they had been fired from their [GM] jobs," he said later. "Our responsibility was to keep their livelihoods. At the beginning, I said, when these people retire, if they feel their days at NUMMI were very happy and productive, then the company will have been a real success. That is my most basic feeling. I was always looking at people individually. I heard many sad stories from their days at GM and I didn't want them to have the same experience. People had to work together and to make the company prosper. But we Japanese must be humble. We are being allowed to do business in another country and we must always be humble. So, for that reason, I tried to keep Japanese away from management positions. I had to have some Japanese in several positions, but later, I carefully replaced them with Americans.

"Today," he said proudly, "NUMMI feels like a local company. People have told me they are very happy there. But it is hard for Japanese companies to put Americans in key positions. They say, 'We can't put them in charge because they don't understand the Japanese language.' A fax couldn't go to the exact person because it would have to be translated first. I once gave a speech in Japan. I told them the most important thing was to send the fax in English, even if they had to use word pictures. Otherwise, the company would not become international."

Most of Higashi's attitudes were controversial at Toyota as well as GM. But NUMMI was a success in many ways, most importantly in forging a sense of community among all of the employees. Higashi understood human nature and was sympathetic to people whose lives had been devastated by Fremont's factory closing. He made sure workers were treated with the same respect as managers. There was no reserved parking and everyone stood in the same cafeteria lines. Small gestures, to be sure, but quite meaningful in a company whose managerial elite had always been allowed numerous privileges.

Although NUMMI was a success, the relationship between Toyota and General Motors management wasn't always smooth sailing. "Sometimes they were a good partner," said one Toyota manager. "But day to day they were a bad partner. There was such a strong tendency toward self-promotion. I was frustrated every time I had to go to Roger Smith about production, pricing or other matters. General Motors was most inefficient."

Most of the GM managers who worked at NUMMI were eager to inject its lessons into the main body of the company. And by the time they were repatriated—a process delayed by the fact that GM had no plan for making use of their newly acquired skills and knowledge—the press was filled with stories about the nonautomated miracle that had transformed GM's least-disciplined workers. But GM was in no mood to learn the lessons of NUMMI, especially the message that management, not labor, was responsible for most of the problems in the factories. When Stephen Bera completed his three-year stint, he returned to Detroit full of excitement, expecting to be assigned to put NUMMI methods and practices to work. But no such opportunity was offered. It was back to business as usual. Demoralized by GM's disinterest in using his new skills, Bera resigned from the company. (As an interesting side note, several NUMMI "graduates," including former NUMMI controller Bob Hendry and manager Mark Hogan, would later become members of Jack Smith's team; as would Lou Hughes, one of the original NUMMI negotiators.)

Before NUMMI demonstrated the opposite, Roger Smith believed automation, not people, was the answer. At the start of the decade, Smith viewed automation as the way to achieve higher quality and productivity so that GM could drive ahead of the competition. In 1980 he had crowed to the press that GM would employ fourteen thousand robots by the end of the decade. The company's great wealth enabled it to spend money other companies could only dream about. By the mid-1980s, when the company was perilously close to losing money in North America, Roger Smith declared, "Automation came along just in time to save us." But it was proving disastrous to the plants that depended on it.

GM's demonstration site for state-of-the-art automation was the newly built Hamtramck plant in eastern Detroit, which was equipped with all the latest high-tech equipment. Here, GM would build the newest Cadillacs.

The Hamtramck plant's sobering history might have been a precursor of the problems to come. In the late 1970s, responding to consistent problems with the quality of Cadillacs, which had left the marquee vulnerable to European competition, GM purchased a section in Detroit upon which to build a showcase automated factory. There it would assemble the new generation of smaller Cadillac Eldorados and Sevilles. The section, dubbed Poletown after the Polish immigrants who settled there in the late nineteenth century, was a close-knit immigrant community whose residents were outraged at being displaced by General Motors— even though they were well compensated for their homes and land. The resulting uproar was a public relations disaster for General Motors. Now the Hamtramck plant was up and running. But there were major problems throughout the system, and even though many people were aware of them, no one had the power to fix them. While Smith provided the money for automation and supported it completely, he clearly didn't understand it—nor did his engineering staff who encouraged him. With its 260 gleaming new robots for welding, assembling, and painting cars; its fifty automated guided vehicles to deliver parts to the assembly line; and a complement of cameras and computers to monitor, inspect, and control the process, the plant put stars in Smith's eyes. He believed it held the promise of a new era of efficiency and quality and would eventually become a model for all assembly plants.

What it became was a nightmare of inefficiency, producing poor-quality vehicles despite the heroic efforts of workers to correct mistakes before they were shipped to dealers. The Eldorados and Sevilles had once been among GM's most profitable cars, and

now they were major money losers. The only consolation to beleaguered employees was that the cars failed miserably with consumers, who saw them as too small and too expensive. So GM
never had to run the plant at full capacity.

The problem could be summed up simply: Robots couldn't
think. In that respect, they were too efficient. They obeyed the
commands as they heard them, and if the message was wrong,
they proceeded anyway, oblivious to the havoc they were creating. Unlike human beings, who had the flexibility to change direction if a problem occurred, robots went on their merry way,
no matter what the problem. Some robots weren't durable
enough to withstand the repetitive work of the assembly line, and
the software was inadequate. There was little coordination from
one workstation to another, so the factory was in a constant state
of chaos.

The legends of the maniac robots of Hamtramck were many:
There was the robot whose task it was to install windshields, but
instead was misdirected by computer command to drop them; the
unsupervised paint robots that sprayed everything in sight except
the cars; and the robots that systematically installed body parts
on the wrong cars. The problems were so great that humans often
had to work alongside their automated companions, repainting,
rewelding, and refinishing cars. Lines were stopped so frequently
(at a cost of $200 per downtime second) that one worker de-
scribed the process as being "like viewing a film in slow motion,
even when the assembly line was moving—which it often isn't."

Meanwhile, Toyota was preparing to use the lessons it had
learned at NUMMI about doing business in America in its first
wholly owned onshore plant. It would be as different from Hamtramck as night from day. It wasn't that the Japanese were disin-
terested in automation. They just believed it was only useful inso-
far as it could be incorporated into the rationale of the
production system. As always, Toyota was taking a cautious approach when it came to automation, and what it saw at GM gave
it good reason to tread carefully. When Roger Smith invited Eiji
Toyoda to take a tour of Hamtramck, the Toyota chairman found
it hard to hide his dismay. When Smith asked his opinion, Eiji

demurred, and he later told a colleague, "It would have been embarrassing to comment on it."

While GM executives were worshiping the false idol of automation, one of them, Lloyd Reuss, was stumbling into a different kind of trap. After a cursory look at the Toyota Production System as it operated in Toyota City, Reuss declared that it would be easy to duplicate. He visited the Toyota plants but didn't "see."

His naive vision was that General Motors could build its own version of Toyota City, which would be called Buick City. Reuss waxed eloquent about the plan for a GM car-building complex that would out-Japanese the Japanese. The site would be a renovated plant in Flint, Michigan; built in 1906, it would cost $350 million to renovate and equip with the latest technology.

Buick City, which opened in 1985 to great fanfare, was supposed to operate on a Just-in-Time system. Although today the cars made there rank among GM's best, for several years the Le Sabres assembled in Buick City were condemned as among the worst cars on the market, ranking near the bottom next to the notorious Yugo. They were plagued with problems: sloppy paint jobs, uneven fit and finish, windows that wouldn't stay up—the emblems of lousy quality. Automation chaos reigned inside, and the employee morale (never good because the work force was culled from rival UAW locals) quickly disintegrated. The people at Buick City and its suppliers had no idea how to make JIT work. Roads around the plant, which had not been widened to handle continuous two-way traffic, were clogged to the point of gridlock with delivery trucks. In its first two years the Le Sabre sold so poorly that there were constant layoffs. Reuss's Buick City was a disaster for many reasons. But the most obvious was that JIT parts delivery could only work if GM could predict its output and stick to it—including how many parts were needed per hour, how they would be delivered, and countless other details. It would take abandonment of some of the original theories, removal of many machines, and a singular commitment by the Flint workers and their new plant manager, J. T. Battenburg, to turn the plant around during the coming years.

Volkswagen was faring little better in understanding how to balance volume, quality, and cost. The Germans had a long-standing reputation as masters of mechanization. From the nineteenth century on, they were known for mechanical precision and excellence—not just with cars but also with products like bicycles, guns and artillery, and cameras. Most of the great books in mathematics, physics, and engineering were written in German. They were also the leaders in building huge industrial facilities such as power plants and steel mills. Volkswagen's origins were part of this genius; it was Hitler's dream that it would be the most technologically advanced mass producer of cars in the world. But like the Americans, German companies put most of the emphasis on the engineering of the cars and the machinery used to build them, and paid little attention to refining the system and getting the most out of their resources.

Volkswagen was a product of this tradition, although its unique history prevented it from laying important groundwork. When Nordhoff took over the operation after the war, he decided that the easiest and cheapest course of action would be to stick with the plant design created by Porsche and Hitler. The first Volkswagen plant, building its outdated little car, was hardly up to the standards of mass production being set by American carmakers, but Nordhoff never accepted that criticism. Fifteen years after going into production, he could claim in a speech to the Economic Club in Detroit, "Here in America, textbooks report on Henry Ford's five dollar days. In Germany, the workers of the four Volkswagen plants are among the best paid employees, working under the best conditions. The methods used at Volkswagen are similar to yours in many respects, and I am proud that we achieved the same performance as your industry."

His words had weight, since in 1962 VW was very profitable. The 1960s were VW's golden period, marked by soaring production and high profits. But the pathology of arrogance and complacency was already setting in.

By the late 1970s Volkswagen was in a similar position as General Motors—unfocused, investing heavily in automation, and ignoring the fact that it was so wedded to a faulty production concept—producing vast numbers of the same car—while the world began to demand more variety, even among smaller models. Its decision to purchase an unfinished Chrysler factory in Westmoreland, Pennsylvania, to assemble the Rabbit (Golf I), was a disaster from the start. It hired Jim McLernon from Chevrolet to run the plant, which opened in 1978. But someone had forgotten to do any real planning—or any research on what was involved in running a state-of-the-art plant in the United States. Although McLernon was American, the Germans gave him little autonomy to run the plant in the most efficient and effective way. Symbolic of the lack of localization was the fact that all official documents were written in German, and measurements in the plant were calculated by the metric system, even though Americans weren't trained to use that measure. Within weeks of opening, there was a labor strike, and things continued to go downhill from there— for nine tortuous years until Carl Hahn finally decided to close the plant and serve his shrunken U.S. sales base from the VW plant in Puebla, Mexico. He blamed the Rabbit's quality problems on substandard parts being shipped from U.S. suppliers, but that was only one of many failures. Even if the suppliers were shipping bad parts, one had to wonder who was minding the store that such a serious problem would remain unsolved for nine years. Besides, American "yuppies," the target audience for the Rabbit, simply didn't like the car. They had too many choices from the Japanese—lower priced cars with higher quality. Instead of responding to changing consumer tastes, VW retreated into its defensive posture, that Americans simply didn't appreciate sophisticated engineering. By the time Hahn closed the plant, it was losing $120 million a year.

Wolfsburg, Germany—November 1990

HALLE 54, the vast Volkswagen plant, was operating at full capacity. Parts of the cavernous interior had already been dismantled and rebuilt in preparation for assembly of the new Golf. Motorized vehicles carried guests along the path of the assembly line, stopping at a station where a robot was affixing a front bumper to the car. The station was supervised by a monitor that displayed the results of the work completed up until this point in the process. A white-coated worker sat staring at the monitor. During the twenty minutes the guests observed the robot, two out of three cars left the work area unfinished. The voice from the monitor kept repeating, "Exchange the screws" and "Redo the screwing." But the worker had developed his own way of taking care of the problem. He just walked over to the repair area that was separated from the robot station by a wire fence. He reached in and pushed a button. The cars moved on down the line, bugs and all. Asked why he didn't take care of the problem at his station, he replied, "Too busy. The night shift will have to repair the robot."

At the end of the line, the quality control workers were laboring furiously and sweating profusely. They really were too busy! The bumper supervisor wasn't the only one in the plant who passed along the bugs for others to fix.

This was easily the fattest production system in the world. There seemed to be no real concern about wasting materials, time, or labor. The work areas were a mess, with workers carefully stepping over broken windshields and moving around half-finished cars that were blocking access to every area.

The sad thing was, when Halle 54 opened in 1982, the massive automated plant, costing 2.1 billion German marks, was billed as the most advanced, highly automated system in the world. "Halle 54 is proof of technological lead, humane working conditions and solid company policy," bragged the releases accompanying its grand opening. In Halle 54, twelve hundred robots, affectionately called Robbies (and less affectionately called Iron Slaves), assisted 57,000 human workers in assembling the new Golf. The sheer size of the complex was (and is) staggering—forty-three miles of tracks inside, ten locomotives to move things into the factory, and four hundred bicycles to expedite worker movement. The factory covered an area the size of Monaco.

Early visitors to the plant were wowed by the sight of robots performing entire assembly tasks unaided. Here's one particularly vivid description:

"In the drive unit line 5, the engine which has just arrived incomplete is mechanically positioned. Scarcely has the correct position been achieved than a mechanical device takes a pulley and pushes it onto the crankshaft end. In a matter of seconds bolts are lifted and tightened. In the next stage a dainty Robby 'finger' takes—almost with tenderness—a V-belt from the stack and fits it over the pulleys."

It sounded wonderful and almost human: cute Robbies with precision action and tender loving care. The reality, however, was somewhat different. Although Halle 54 was widely talked about as innovative, brilliant, and futuristic, it was actually a catastrophe for the production of the Golf and the bottom line of the company. For one thing, VW relied on robots of its own design and manufacture, rather than purchasing more reliable and tested models from outside vendors. Like GM, it had a hard time accepting that someone else might be able to do it better. This practice also made it harder to get rid of poorly functioning robots and machinery. The in-house attitude (even when all evidence suggested otherwise) was "We made it, so it must be the best."

In *The Machine That Changed the World*, a book published in 1990, the results of a $5-million MIT study on the future of the automobile showed Volkswagen's Halle 54 to be a model of inefficiency. Daniel T. Jones, the European research director of the study, toured Halle 54 and observed that "the German plant was expending more effort to fix the problems it had just created than the Japanese plant required to make a nearly perfect car the first time. When we asked the white-coated gentlemen at the end of the line what they were doing, they said they were craftsmen. Well, Henry Ford got rid of that sort of thing in 1914." As recently as 1991, when this author toured the plant, there were still craftsmen touching up the sloppy work of the Robbies. And the unfinished Golfs piling up in the lots around the VW complex were visible testimony to the plant's inefficiency. White-coated men were still correcting robot mistakes—in one case applying window sealant after the robot failed to complete the task on every third window.

If General Motors was not paying enough attention to quality, Volkswagen was paying too much of the wrong kind of attention. The company didn't seem to grasp that quality had to exist in the context of other values. There was no question one could build a perfect car by hand, but it hardly suited the modern demand for mass production at low costs. Furthermore, contemporary thinking was shifting away from automation, and VW had yet to make the leap. Nor did they listen to the MIT researchers' warning that "only after having established a lean organization, does it make sense to think about automation technologies."

As the world's carmakers motored toward the next century, new pressures were changing the rules for everybody.

Toyota may have been the genius behind the best production system in the world, but nothing stays static forever. By the 1990s, as GM and Volkswagen grappled with their endemic manufacturing problems, Toyota was facing new challenges as well, and these were forcing the company to consider a radical change. Toyota projected that it would need eight thousand workers through 1995 to replace retirees and accommodate growth, but it anticipated hiring half that number. Its parts suppliers, especially secondary and tertiary companies, had even more difficulty recruiting, and relied more and more on illegal foreigners.

One problem has been how to attract the young Japanese workers who increasingly reject what they perceive as the "three Ks" of factory work: *kitsui* (difficult), *kitani* (dirty), and *kiben* (dangerous). Toyota's challenge is to enhance the image of the company and make the workplace more appealing. No matter how brilliant the system, human beings are forever changing their values and life-style preferences. Toyota had always prided itself on its ability to change with the times, but this was perhaps its greatest challenge ever: how to resurrect the factory as a positive career choice.

The gleaming new Kyushu plant, located on the southern island, seven hundred miles from Toyota City, was its first step toward that goal. Tadaaki Jagawa, vice president in charge of production and engineering, explained the challenge being met with the new plant: "Recently, young men have been saying they want to work with women in comfortable, air-conditioned places with background music. We plan to accept these demands as much as possible."

The Kyushu plant was indeed different. The decor was designed to soothe the eyes; the sound was gentle music. There was air conditioning and bright lights. Picture windows looked out on pastoral scenery. Men and women worked together—a phenomenal cultural change for a Japanese company. It wasn't your ordinary car plant. In addition to the setting, the plant employed technology designed to eliminate many of the stresses and strains that were the greatest complaint about factory work. The conveyor belt was built to minimize exertion. The innovative assembly line ran in a zigzag pattern; instead of workers adapting to the line, the line adapted to them. The illusion was that a factory is a pleasant place to work. Whether it would alleviate the labor shortage remained to be seen. Just in case this new manufacturing style failed to attract young workers, Toyota was preparing for the necessity of depending on fewer workers. The Tahara #4 plant at Toyohashi was highly automated in a flexible system and utilized only 411 workers per shift, as opposed to 3,000 in Hamtramck. In spite of Jagawa's belief that people, not machines, made the difference, flexible automation might ultimately be the solution to Toyota's labor shortage. "We must adapt vehicle design to accommodate automation," Jagawa said, promising that the company would learn from the experiment with automation at Tahara. But he cautioned against a reliance on automation at the expense of workers. "The purpose of technology," Jagawa added, "is to ease the work load on humans."

Also, from its experience at NUMMI, Toyota learned about warehousing. The central warehouse used for Kyushu will provide a coordinating point for supplies before they are delivered. Toyota was changing with the times.

Warren, Michigan—February 1993

INAKI LOPEZ was feeling good. Already his PICOS program had saved GM an estimated $7 billion. Inside the company, he was being hailed as the wave of the future. People clamored to join his team—remarkable when you consider that purchasing was once a remote outpost of sheer drudgery, and one of the least favored assignments in the company. It was becoming increasingly clear that Lopez was accomplishing something far more than changing supplier systems. He was organizing the genesis of a revolution that would eventually make its way into the guts of General Motors.

Lopez kept his "warriors" scrambling from morning until night. Having instituted PICOS, he was now absorbed with the work of 459 Creativity Teams, each one responsible for a different part of the system. "Every day, five teams come to my office at five o'clock to report on their progress," he said. "It is their job to find ways of reducing the number of parts and components we buy. For example, we determined that we were purchasing twenty-five different cigarette lighters. We needed only five, and we immediately implemented the change, saving $1.7 million for the company."

He smiled with satisfaction. Not bad for a day's work. Lopez's Creativity Teams included people from many areas of the company, and the engineers on the teams were given the authority to make the changes immediately.

His latest brainstorm was a concept he dubbed Plateau 6, the "ten man-hour car," which called for suppliers to do actual assembly on the line. They would truck their modules to the plants and install them as cars went down the line. When GM's engineers heard of the concept, they were stunned. "It seemed completely off the wall," admitted one. But within two months, the doubting engineers had figured out a way it could be done.

As successful as Lopez had been, he saw it as only the beginning. Eyes gleaming with missionary fervor, he said, "I will go to my farm in December and squeeze out my brain cells so that I can see what I can do in 1994." He added, "The Toyota approach cannot solve GM's problems. For the West to meet the Japanese challenge and overcome it, the West has to be prepared to create an entirely new approach that allows companies to make quantum leaps. Otherwise, we will always be learning from them and trailing behind."

Lopez was making an impact on the organization that was both material and emotional. His staff, many of them Spaniards who followed him like a cult leader, viewed him as an organizational savior. A stream of magazine and newspaper articles heralded him as a great revolutionary force.

But the fervor surrounding Lopez made many of GM's executives uneasy. Some worried that if he gained more power in the organization—especially in the manufacturing areas—his techniques might destroy the systematic process of change. He wasn't necessarily sensitive to factory conditions or union issues. And what some saw as his wonderful eccentricity and unconventionality, others referred to as "Lopez's personality problem."

Although the history of the auto industry had demonstrated many times that single individuals could make a great impact, Lopez's critics wondered if the messianic fervor surrounding him was healthy. They watched with alarm as his influence grew.

But across the ocean, one man was observing Lopez with special interest. Ferdinand Piech, frustrated by VW's spiraling costs and the resistance of the supervisory board to his proposed changes, was looking for a way to make a dramatic impact. He was impressed by the unconventional Spaniard.

It's not a moon shot.

People have known how to build cars for a century. A guy with a collection of parts, a toolbox, and an empty garage can build a car.

But a car is more than the sum of its parts, and building a car is more than assembling them. It is a living, breathing system whose complexity extends beyond the mechanical task of fitting together elements or screwing in bolts.

Inaki Lopez is fond of saying that lean production is born of the same principles as lean bodies. Lou Hughes would agree with him.

For many years, Hughes was a determined bean counter toiling away in the corporate halls of General Motors. Like many of his colleagues, he believed that the success or failure of a company was based on its numbers. This was the standard GM philosophy.

But in 1982 Hughes experienced a religious conversion. As a member of GM's NUMMI negotiating team, he accompanied Jack Smith to Toyota City. His task was to make sure the numbers added up. Instead, he observed the Toyota Production System and was enlightened. Hughes would become one of the few General Motors executives who made the shift from finance to operations, going on to head Opel, then become executive vice-president of international operations. Since his first visit to

Toyota City, Hughes never again downplayed the importance of the production process. In fact, he insisted that both he and his staff members regularly spend a few weeks on the assembly line so they would never lose sight of the company's purpose.

"Lean production is like the human body," he would say, echoing the opinion of Lopez and others. "If you have a toothache, a tiny nerve in one tooth can get your entire system out of whack. It is the same thing with lean production. It is a sensitive system and you have to have all the elements operating—people, equipment, systems and materials—and you can't move unless they are all working."

It's hard to believe that for most of the century, General Motors didn't know this. Neither did Volkswagen. Toyota did and that's what gave it the edge. But the auto world was about to change again, and even the Toyota Production System would have to undergo a new revolution. It could no longer accommodate the flood of new products in their many varieties, the greater engineering complexity of Toyota, or the pressures of a four-year new-product cycle. Like the roads and highways around Toyota City, clogged to the point of gridlock by hundreds of trucks making Just-in-Time deliveries, the system had outgrown itself. All systems eventually do.

EIGHT

Up and Down
the Line

The transformation required will be a change of state, metamorphosis, not mere patchwork on the present system of management.

—W. Edwards Deming

HE WAS KNOWN only as Louie, and he worked as a welder in GM's truck and bus division in Flint, Michigan. Ben Hamper immortalized Louie in his book *Rivethead: Tales from the Assembly Line,* a chronicle of Hamper's checkered career as a GM worker. About Louie, Hamper said: "Louie had a great little racket goin' for himself. He peddled half pints of Canadian Club and Black Velvet up and down the line in the Cab Shop area. He charged three bucks a bottle, almost double the store rate, but who was gonna argue? The booze was in the door, you didn't have to wait for it, and Louie delivered right to your bench.

"Shoprat alcohol consumption," Hamper went on, "was always a hot debate with those who just didn't understand the way things worked inside a General Motors plant. While not everyone boozed on a daily basis, alcohol was a central part of many of our lives. It was a crutch not unlike the twenty cups of coffee millions of other Americans depend on to whisk them through their workday. We drank our fair share of coffee, but the factory environment seemed to lend itself toward something that was a great deal more potent and rejuvenating."

This was the classic portrait of the American factory worker: stunned by a heavy brew of boredom, alcohol, and drugs; working in a mindless haze waiting for the shift horn to signal the end of another soul-deadening day. Hamper also described in vivid detail a scheme that allowed approximately half the workers on his line to sit back and do nothing for several hours during their shifts. It was on these "breaks" that he began to write his book.

Ben Hamper's stories of life in the underworld of GM's factories was relentlessly depressing, and with every turn of the page it seemed to support the negative stereotype of America's blue-collar workers. In Hamper's world, life was very clearly divided between the factory grunts who despised their jobs (and therefore had to escape into drink, drugs, and hooky) and the white-collar supervisors who played a daily game of cat and mouse, cracking the whip whenever they caught one of the line workers goofing off. The managers in Hamper's scenario were idiotic mouthers of a company line that they were unable to justify. But they were rigid and authoritarian in the way they used their power to control the blue-collar workers. That in itself wasn't so surprising. Expressions of contempt for the "common" laborer have a long precedent, and they rise above individual cultures to form a universal elitism that pervades all industry. Perhaps this elitism is merely an acknowledgment of what every laborer knows so well: Working in a factory is a hard, hot, heavy job, no matter how many worker-friendly programs are devised. It doesn't matter if you're in an American, German, or Japanese factory, blue- and white-collar workers never live in blissful harmony. And blue-collar workers have little real control over their fate or environment.

Yet the real issues of what is commonly called human resources transcend the simplistic notions of blue and white frictions or good and bad workers. It might be said that there is no such thing as a bad worker—just a bad company organization. In the latter part of this century, as the great global car companies struggle to clean house at the top, the issue always comes down to the worker. No company can be successful, regardless of how many brilliant systems it devises, unless it has a strong, well-articulated philosophy driving its people. Today, our three car companies, each in its own way, face a people crisis. The Western model is to codify the behavior of both groups through complex contracts that grant rights and responsibilities. The Japanese have no contracts as such, but there is a cultural rubric of conformity.

GM's long history of labor-management frictions will take more than good intentions to resolve. For one thing, the company must stop blaming middle managers for the bureaucratic paralysis of the organization, which was instituted and maintained by the executive class. Toyota's fabled management genius, often misunderstood, is not based on motivation and individual achievement, but rather on a social structure that includes obligation to one's peer group, superiors, and company. To its credit, this system has succeeded in creating the most productive factories in the world. But it does not seem to operate so efficiently in the overstaffed offices, where lifetime employment is promised in exchange for subliminating individual ambition to the will of the company. Volkswagen's social elitism has rewarded workers with a generous standard of living, but little sense of community or connection to the company. Codetermination laws gave labor representation on the supervisory board, which bought peace but not a shared sense of destiny.

In recent years the slogan "People: a Company's Most Valuable Resource" has been the popular theme of the new management movement, and most companies, East and West, pay lip service to the ideal. But remarkably little has changed in the long-standing policies and attitudes that govern large work forces. The essential cultural shifts that truly transform workplaces are not so easy to comprehend and even harder to put into practice, as businesses grow larger and more cemented in their ways. Unfortunately, it usually takes a serious crisis to shake them loose.

For many years General Motors has had a schizophrenic relationship with its workers. It's been like a dysfunctional parent that can't decide whether to hug or hit its child. Once so benevolent it was nicknamed Generous Motors and Mother Motors, the company fostered trust that there would always be jobs and benefits for all loyal workers. To some degree, GM and the UAW had an incestuous relationship. GM negotiated generous contracts with labor, then immediately gave the same benefits to its white-collar workers. The extra cost was passed on to consumers. Such benevolence created a false sense of security among workers that was brutally shattered when times got tough and both white- and blue-collar workers had to be laid off.

Among blue-collar workers whose ranks have been slashed repeatedly since the 1970s in a yo-yo pattern of layoff, rehire, layoff, rehire, it seemed the company had no direction, much less concern for their welfare. From the early post-oil-crisis layoffs of 1974 to the latest round of factory closings in 1991 and 1992, workers were left feeling betrayed by the company, especially when they had been promised jobs in exchange for their cooperation on new programs.

During the 1980s progressive union leaders like Donald Ephlin, head of the UAW at GM, encouraged the idea that labor and management must discontinue their traditional adversarial relationship and become partners in building a new era of growth and efficiency. Ephlin was a controversial figure, a rare bird among UAW regulars who were fundamentally distrustful of the motivations of management. History had given them no reason to believe that GM would look after their best interests. But Roger Smith, in his "visionary" mode, urged Ephlin on. Working closely with Smith and his executives, Ephlin was the driving force behind Quality Network, a joint management-UAW program that was designed to build a spirit of teamwork between the two. It was to become GM's version of a more humane workplace and shared destiny.

Roger Smith waxed eloquent about the wonderful world ahead when labor and management would lay down their weapons and work as one. He said this kind of cooperation would make GM great again. His implied promise was that if labor supported the long-term goals and programs of the company, the workers would benefit through better working conditions and job security. The UAW membership was initially fearful of getting too cozy with the people who had the power to hire and fire, but

Ephlin and other backers of Quality Network argued with compelling logic about the reasons for change. "Management and labor must face up to the challenge," he said, "to recognize that we have to change the way we do business because we are suffering and losing our industrial base to tough competition." Quality Network was established with much fanfare in 1988. At first, it seemed like a cultural revolution had occurred at General Motors.

But the promise of Quality Network has yet to be fully realized. Ephlin retired before he saw his vision compromised at the hands of GM corporate management. His strong belief that job security could only be guaranteed by a sound, profitable company led Ephlin to stake his reputation on arguing that GM could not afford all-encompassing income protection. Ironically, it was management—specifically, Bob Stempel—that caved in on the very protections Ephlin opposed in 1990. In the coming years it became clear that GM's commitment to labor was only skin-deep.

A good example is what occurred at the Tarrytown, New York, plant. Tarrytown was a model of union-management cooperation. "We cooperated with the company to cut costs," said a Tarrytown worker. "We organized into teams for efficiency, we worked hard, we made concessions. We were told if we did all of this, it would be an investment in our future. We think we've got one of the best operations in the country, but what good did it do us?"

Not much, considering the vehicle Tarrytown was assigned to build. It was a poorly designed and engineered plastic van. No matter how well motivated the workers were, they couldn't do much to improve sales. The problem was the vehicle itself. GM's promises failed because the company didn't grasp that employee cooperation couldn't compensate for a poorly designed van that people didn't want to buy.

When Bob Stempel announced in early 1992 that Tarrytown would be among the plants scheduled for closing, there was stunned disbelief among the workers, followed by outrage. It was at least the fourth time in GM's recent history that a particularly motivated group of workers tried to save their jobs by doing exactly what management asked, only to see the company fail them.

It wasn't only blue-collar workers who suffered from GM's careless management philosophy. White-collar workers experienced a different kind of indignity. What seemed on the face of it to be a company filled with opportunity was really a Faustian bargain for the young, well-educated managers who came to work for General Motors. They were "paid off" with high salaries and good benefits as long as they toed the company line. If a manager wanted to move at a steady pace up the corporate escalator, he soon learned that he shouldn't make waves or show any creative bent whatsoever. It was well known that the way to get on the fast track (known in GM lingo as HI-POT, for high-potential employee) was to be loyal to company policies—never mind the cost. A retired GM executive described with disgust how it was: "The whole system stinks once you're in it," he said. "You continue to want to make vertical decisions: 'What is it that I should decide based on what is good for the company? I want to get promoted.'

"I can go through a litany of those clowns. They go from this plant to that complex and then, all of a sudden, they've got plaques all over their walls that say how great they've done—but the plant's falling apart and the division's falling apart."

After GM reorganized in 1984, with the intention of flattening the organization and pushing decision making down to the levels where people actually confronted the problems, things only grew worse. The reorganization was so ineffective that the end result was actually to increase layers of authority rather than do away with them. It was both less efficient and demoralizing.

"Unless you're working on the Fourteenth Floor, you have about a zillion bosses," grumbled a plant manager in Flint. "Every small thing requires approval up the line. They have thirteen thousand checkers in this company to make sure things are done right. Hell, they have checkers to check the checkers. It's madness."

In the late 1980s the company halfheartedly started a program called Leadership Now, meant to train executives to be better managers of their people and stronger leaders. The est-like seminars excited many people initially, but ultimately proved futile. One executive recalled how useless they were in a company that otherwise was resistant to change. "You go in there and sit around for a few days," he said. "You get all touchy-feely and talk about how to be a caring, wonderful manager. Then, on Monday, you go back to work and the same bloated bureaucracy is there and the same people are in charge. They haven't changed, so how can they expect you to change?"

By 1990 GM was caving in on itself. Although the company still paid lip service to Quality Network and other improvement programs, they lacked credibility. If you were a manager, you did your job and hoped Stempel or Reuss or some other important person considered you a part of the team. If you were a blue-collar worker, you prayed that by some miracle your factory would stay in business until the kids left home and the mortgage was paid off.

Jack Smith walked into this environment like a breath of fresh air and immediately began to make a difference. People who had spent their entire careers zipping their lips against any critical words now found that the expectations were reversed. The new Smith wanted to know GM's problems. He wanted criticism, if it was constructive. He wanted to hear ideas, and he wanted to hear worst-case scenarios, not just good news.

Within six months he had slashed the office staff—including the checkers checking checkers—from 13,000 to 2,500, reassigning people to operating divisions. He closed the executive dining room, and brought an openness to the workplace. Unlike his predecessors who retreated into their offices, Smith became a visible and accessible presence, wearing sports shirts and sweaters to strategy board meetings.

It was a hopeful time. But Jack Smith knew that it wasn't enough to change the company's management style or physical organization. He also had to do damage control with the UAW and try to stop the hemorrhage of money and market share. Even so, it was a beginning.

Wolfsburg, Germany—November 1991

A VISITOR to Halle 54 in Wolfsburg, Germany, on a chilly Thursday in late November, was surprised to see that sections of the plant were quiet and dark—as though it was a holiday. Considering that the new Golf had just been launched and she'd been told that orders were piling up faster than cars could be built, she had expected to walk in on a scene bursting with energy and urgency. When she asked her management escort to explain what was going on, he said with some embarrassment, "We're missing about one-third of our workers today."

"Why?" she wondered. Was there an epidemic? A work stoppage?

He assured her that nothing was wrong. It was business as usual. "They just decided to take a long weekend. Yesterday was *Buss- und Bettag,* a Protestant holiday in Lower Saxony when people repent their sins."

When she returned for a visit to Wolfsburg the next year, in early July, she was warned that she'd better make plans to get out of town early on Friday. After noon, the traffic jams caused by white- and blue-collar workers leaving for their annual three-week holidays would make traveling a nightmare.

The visitor was left to wonder: Why are German workers always on vacation? It wasn't an idle question. Even Chancellor Helmut Kohl was calling Germany "the holiday republic."

If GM's blue-collar workers are continually waiting for the axe to fall, no such concerns trouble their VW counterparts, who may be one of the most coddled work forces in the world.

After World War II, with Germany in chaos, government, management, and labor collaborated to rebuild the shattered economy. The idea of "codetermination"—management and labor sharing the responsibility and benefits of a new era—led to Germany's strong and influential labor unions. Working together, they created the Wirtschaftswunder—the "Economic Miracle" of the 1950s and '60s. In 1974 Parliament passed a law that institutionalized labor representation on the supervisory boards of German companies. Labor's influence in corporate governance, along with the size of IG Metall, which has organized most of Germany's automakers and industrial companies, has given IG Metall power beyond that of the UAW in the United States or the company-based unions in Japan.

The IG Metall representatives who serve on supervisory boards have great influence over corporate decisions—and much of it is self-serving. For example, in order to get labor's approval for the investments he wanted to make outside of Germany, Carl Hahn had to meet their terms. The SEAT and Skoda deals were approved only after VW promised there would be no layoffs in Germany as a result of any production shifted to factories in Spain or the Czech Republic. That agreement protected the workers, at least in the short term, but it shielded them from the reality that VW could no longer afford the labor practices—high wages and compensation, and 20 percent absenteeism—that met the demands of labor.

Now German unions are pressuring the government and companies to bring wages in eastern Germany up to western levels by the middle of the decade. Already, about 500,000 former East Germans have lost their jobs as a result of privatization, and more would lose their jobs if wages were forced up too quickly. Eastern Germany's industrial base is archaic and requires massive investment. By artificially pushing up wages without the justification of more efficiency, unemployment will only get worse.

In the beginning, German reunification brought a massive stimulus to the economy. Car sales soared as former East Germans replaced their old Trabants and Wartburgs with Volkswagens and Opels. For a time, German companies enjoyed the prosperity generated by the need to update everything in the former Communist state. Buoyed by the signs of vitality, industry lost sight of the truth: High costs and rigid employment practices were causing Germany to lose its attraction as a place to manufacture. To date, the former East Germany has attracted few major foreign industrial investors, and Germany's luxury-car companies are beginning to recognize that they cannot serve world markets if production is centered in Germany. BMW, the company that thrived on the notion that its cars could only be built by "elves in the Black Forest," stunned Germany in 1992 by announcing it would assemble cars in South Carolina. In 1993, Mercedes also admitted that Americans could assemble its highly engineered models. Volkswagen, already a multinational, indicated that it had no choice but to consider building Audis in North America.

In 1991, movie-goers in German theaters were treated to a cartoon sponsored by the employers' federation. The cartoon was an evolutionary tale, showing a creature evolving as a fish, reptile, ape, caveman, peasant, and, finally, a carpenter. The carpenter, carrying his saw, moved steadily up a red line, showing the growth years after World War II. At 1990 the red line leveled off and the carpenter sat down and started to saw off the piece he was sitting on. Audiences laughed, but it wasn't really so funny. It was a parable for the country's malaise.

At Volkswagen, the costs keep rising. Management blames labor for insisting on pay increases and a shorter workweek when the company is being challenged in its own backyard by the likes of Opel as well as by the threat of a steady movement into its territory by the Japanese. Labor blames management for poor investments and planning. "During the last decade there has been a shift in management philosophy toward U.S.-oriented short-term management thinking," complains Gerhard Uhl of IG Metall. "Management primarily focuses on their own careers and their own well-being and less on the company and the well-being of the working community."

Management counters that the 5 percent wage increase and thirty-five-hour workweek won by the unions in 1992 ignored the necessity of cutting costs to make companies more competitive with nations that paid less to workers who, in spite of less education, were nearly as productive as the Germans.

In truth, both sides are to blame, and the rigidity of the system prevents realistic discussions of how business and labor might adapt to their changing environment. The spirit of *Wunderjahre* —working together for the good of the company and the nation —has long ago deteriorated into egocentrism: every worker for him- or herself. VW's workers can take five-day weekends with a clear conscience, even as unfinished cars pile up in the factories, because they have little motivation to do otherwise. They earn their full salaries and the company always seems to have enough people on hand to build what it needs.

This attitude has been partially shaped by a deeply embedded elitism which gives the laborer little status or glory. Blue-collar workers may be well paid, but they are at the bottom of Germany's rigid social hierarchy. Once a factory worker, always a factory worker.

The system is inflexible, with the length and type of one's education permanently locking one into a role. In German society it is almost inconceivable that one would change professions or accept work that is not on a par with one's education or credentials. A trained autoworker who has been through nine or ten years of technical school plus three years of apprenticeship to become a certified machinist or mechanic would sooner be unemployed than accept a job as a construction worker repairing roads or a factory worker beneath the appropriate level. Within auto factories, seniority and classifications make it difficult to move people around. Even welfare recipients are allowed to turn down jobs that are deemed "ethically unbearable." In Germany one's identity and worth are wrapped up in one's status. The entire nation permanently has its nose up in the air.

There is an uneasy aura surrounding Germany's elitism, especially in light of the return of neo-Nazism and the violence against guest workers from Turkey and asylum seekers from Africa and former Communist countries. After World War II, foreigners were accepted—in part because Germany needed laborers to support its growing economy, and in part to assuage the guilt of its racist past. Culturally, these people retained their own identities, living in isolation from their German neighbors. And as the nation prospered and the new generation grew up, there was less tolerance. The old prejudices began to reassert themselves. Today, many German factories are manned by foreign workers who are prohibited from becoming citizens, even if their families have lived in the country for generations, and they have no memory or connection to the place of their ancestors' birth. Citizenship is limited to those who can prove German ancestry.

The lack of motivation has given rise to severe alcohol and drug abuse among factory workers. A VW labor official admitted there wasn't a drug in existence that couldn't be purchased on the shop floor or in the bathrooms, which have become regular drug dens. Alarmed, the labor council has responded with on-site drug counseling.

Owing to its history and its emphasis on production, machinery, and work rules to govern behavior in the factory, Volkswagen never developed an integrated management philosophy that went beyond "build more cars." Now it is trying to play catch-up, but its efforts are often disjointed and ineffective. Volkswagen has been no more successful than General Motors in implementing JIT. On at least one occasion, the company had to fly engines to Wolfsburg from Kassel because of production problems in the engine plant. When Carl Hahn was chairman, he often complained about line stoppages, but seemed powerless to do anything about them. Like GM, Volkswagen had a very naive notion of JIT. Another example was that in the waning days of Hahn's tenure, the company announced that it would begin a program of *kaizen*—borrowing the concept of continuous improvement from the Japanese. A *kaizen* room was set up in a small cubicle near the cafeteria in Halle 54, and this immediately touched off arguments about how the program would be executed and who would be in charge. The production, design, and procurement departments feared that jobs would be eliminated or delegated elsewhere. The various fiefdoms within VW had little motivation to see *kaizen* work.

The company took its first baby step toward *kaizen* when it set up a department for improvement proposals. At first, employees who submitted proposals for the company received pocket calculators. Goeudevert argued that fifty marks should be paid for each suggestion, but that was rejected because it was quickly seen that there was no objective way of evaluating the worthiness of the suggestions.

Kaizen became another good idea that the organization could not implement because it did not know how to adapt. Intuitively, everyone recognized its value, but no one knew what to do with it.

. . . .

"Toyota has great factories and lousy offices" is the verdict of a company critic who charges that Toyota's management philosophy is in desperate need of a contemporary update. "Make no mistake about it," he grants, "Toyota's ability to build efficient factories and develop a lean production system has revolutionized manufacturing throughout the world. But excellence in systems does not necessarily translate to excellence in management or decision making."

It was easy to put blinders on during Toyota's decades of stunning growth. But today, the company is at a crossroads, grappling with multiple challenges at home and abroad. The company that has gift-wrapped its production system for the world struggles with how to manage in a new era where nothing will be as easy. It's an open question whether Toyota has the will as well as the managers.

That this would even be an issue comes as a surprise to many people. During the 1980s the Western world engaged in a feverish love affair with the idea of Japanese-style management. There was a romantic notion that the Japanese had harnessed something almost spiritual in their work life—a quality that was uplifting and quite different from the individualistic styles and motivations found in Western companies. But gradually it has come to light that the stereotype of the good Japanese workplace vs. the bad Western workplace is a glorified version of reality. In his book *The Japanese Management Mystique* Jon Woronoff challenges the myth:

> There is a bizarre contest between an idealized and expurgated Japanese system and a debased and unflattering caricature of the Western system. The Japanese treasured the individual worker and sought his participation; Western managers treated workers like objects and just gave orders. Japan offered job security and even lifetime employment; in the West, companies engaged in hire and fire. Japanese workers donned neat uniforms and engaged in quality control; Americans wore greasy jeans and left Coke bottles in the auto frames.

Viewed through a truer prism, Japanese companies are revealed as having some serious problems with human resources. In 1982 Kamata Satoshi, a Japanese journalist, went to work for Toyota and kept a diary of his experiences which he later published in a controversial book called *The Auto Factory of Despair*. Contrary to popular belief, Satoshi reported, Toyota workers were likely to feel a sense of "despair" because of their job routines and also because the company treated them like "human transfer machines." Satoshi vividly described the grueling routine: Workers spent eight to ten hours a day in tiny spaces, were given only short breaks, and were made to work at a machinelike pace. Supervisors were prone to speed up the lines, assign extra tasks, and regularly keep workers on for overtime. Satoshi painted a picture of exhausted workers who suffered frequent injuries because their concentration was low. The turnover rate was exceptionally high, and, sadly, some took their leave through the drastic measure of suicide.

Satoshi's description may have been somewhat exaggerated. Nevertheless, it was growing apparent that Taiichi Ohno's brilliant production system masked some troubling company policies. What is little known is that when Ohno introduced the system in the 1950s, he encountered loud resistance from the still-strident labor unions. At the time, workers had been trained to operate one machine and to perform work tasks in a less regimented way. They resisted what they viewed as the extra burden of performing many tasks at a faster rate for more hours every week. But Ohno, who was closely allied with union leaders (who were actually a part of management), was able to gain approval for his plan, and dissidents were fired. Ohno later admitted, "Had I faced the Japan National Railways Union or an American union, I might have been murdered."

Even so, the times were different then. Virtually all of the workers saw themselves as being privileged to work in a factory instead of the even-more grueling and less rewarding life on the farm. Japan was just beginning to rebuild itself from the war, and workers were more willing to swallow their dissatisfaction in exchange for jobs that promised good pay and guaranteed lifetime employment. Over time, the company unions in the auto industry became part of the consensus structure of management. When occasional militants would try to organize, management simply set up opposing company-sponsored unions and encouraged workers to join. The overriding work style in Toyota's factories remains unchanged from the fifties, even as the new generation demands a change. The difficult/dirty/dangerous conditions of blue-collar work are being shunned by young people who have been raised in times of abundance. They do not share the sacrifice mentality of their parents and grandparents, who suffered the deprivation of the war and its aftermath. They want better, more balanced—even fun—lives, and the automobile factories do not offer it, even with the swimming pools, athletic fields, and comfortable dormitories that Toyota has provided for them.

It is not surprising that Toyota's workers would begin to demand change. This is part of a process that occurs in all companies as they mature; a disease invades the system, turning the passionate search for opportunity and perfection into layers of increasingly inefficient bureaucracy. Shoichiro Toyoda has tried hard to overcome what he calls "big company disease," that cancer of complacency that afflicts large businesses. In 1987 the company commemorated its fiftieth anniversary by sponsoring an essay contest for employees, and the results showed that at least some workers were troubled by Toyota's future. The theme of the contest was "The New Challenge Facing the 21st Century." One entry was startlingly direct. It was a drawing of a small girl standing beside a large dinosaur. Its caption read, "Show me the 21st Century, the new challenge that threatens survival." The dinosaur represented Toyota and the message was clear: Toyota risked growing extinct.

During the 1980s, Shoichiro spoke often of the need to flatten Toyota's bureaucracy, and he announced a major reorganization in the final years of his presidency—consolidating departments and eliminating the title of *kacho,* or section chief. But bureaucracies are not so easily flattened. Even though the *kacho* title was gone, it still appears on name cards so that counterparts in other companies can understand the rank of the person with whom they are dealing. Inside the company, everyone knows who the section chief is, even though he is no longer referred to by that title. Form prevailed over substance, and nothing really changed.

For meaningful reorganization to take place, the underlying attitudes and values of a company must change, and this was not successful at Toyota. The insidious bureaucracy continued to operate after Shoichiro's reorganization because the corporate dynamics had not evolved. For one thing, Toyota had ceased to attract the free-spirited thinkers of its past—men like Eiji Toyoda, Ohno, and Ishida—who could infuse new ideas. The company was filled with the same kind of analyzers and information gatherers as GM—rigid bureaucrats who could not fathom a need for change. Here is one example: Shoichiro worried that decision making was too long, tortuous, and time-consuming. *Ringishi*, memos circulated throughout the company to gain consensus on a proposal, involved getting numerous personal *hanko* (comparable to signatures) on a document. The more important the issue, the greater the number of *hanko*. After the reorganization, only three or four *hanko* were required for acceptance. But as one executive described it, "The organization was not changed. The papers with three *hanko* were passed on to top management, but the actual papers—with a dozen or more *hanko*—were hidden." In other words, the same bureaucracy was in full swing; only the pretense of flattening remained.

While upper management has grown more sluggish in its bureaucracy, Toyota's white-collar managers are finding that the intense drive for continuous improvement is beginning to take its toll. The good ideas of simpler times have grown into monsters. Take the policy of encouraging employee suggestions. On the face of it, this is a positive, creative way to give workers a feeling that they share in the company's direction. But consider this: In one year, Toyota received 1,906 million suggestions—an average of 39 per employee. And 95 percent of them were adopted! That's more than 1.8 million new practices put into effect during one year. Even if most of the suggestions were small, one-step tasks, it's still a lot of change. Many of the suggestions are meaningless, made in response to heavy pressure to participate. When making changes becomes an end in itself, without a cohesive governing principle, it leads nowhere and creates unbearable pressure on the people who have to follow through on the suggestions.

White-collar workers are feeling the burdens of the intense pressure to perform on the job and in the after-hours ritual partying with clients and business associates. Twelve-hour business days, including partying, and long hours of commuting have started to take their toll.

Recently, there has been much publicity about increased incidents of *karoshi*—sudden death from overwork—among salaried workers in Japan. It is estimated that more than 10,000 people die from *karoshi* every year. The families of some have successfully won lawsuits against companies, but the workaholic ethic is alive and well. A popular caffeine-and-vitamin drink is regularly sucked down by corporate climbers forced to devote every waking hour to their jobs. One brand, called Regain, asks in its advertising jingle, "Can you fight twenty-four hours, Japanese businessman?" For a time, the Regain jingle hit the top of the pop charts.

A new paranoia has risen among Japan's salaried men because of the recognition that there are too many of them. The more efficient factories and bureaucracies have created a surplus of white-collar workers. In Western companies, such a surplus would be handled through early retirements or layoffs. In Japan, where workers are guaranteed employment for life, the fear of being laid off is supplanted by the equally dreaded prospect of becoming what is known as a window sitter. Window sitters are employees, usually in their late forties, who are deemed no longer useful to the company. They are kept on the payroll and report for work every day, but there is nothing for them to do. In a culture that values productivity above all, it is a deeply humiliating loss of face to be branded a window sitter—one that stigmatizes the entire family and affects social status. Most try to create work for themselves—reading and writing reports that nobody else reads, or even performing odd jobs around the premises. Some are given meaningless titles and functions as a way of helping them save face. But it doesn't really work. Everyone knows the truth. If the driven white-collar class is stressed to the limit from overwork, window sitters are equally stressed from underwork. Some cannot stand the embarrassment and retire early.

Supporting window sitters is costly for Japanese companies, especially as the population ages and there are more of them. Greater efficiency through computerization and other technology will deepen the crisis, since even fewer people will be needed to work in the offices. There are signs that lifetime employment may be in jeopardy, especially with current conditions, including a slower rate of economic growth and investments in foreign markets. The traditional compact between management and worker —security in exchange for loyalty—could become a thing of the past.

Equally problematic as companies move out of Japan is the fact that their management culture is so different from that of their hosts. NUMMI was an exception because of its carefully crafted agreement that shared management and responsibility between GM and Toyota. It also benefited from the early efforts of both groups of managers to create a hybrid of the two cultures. But in the normal course of events, Japanese companies risk problems when they enter foreign countries, in particular, those in the West.

In an American company, good managers are expected to think independently and exercise a degree of individual initiative to get ahead. In conformist Japan, different qualities are valued. Workers are trained to be good cooperative members not just of a group but of the entire community represented by the company. For example, the corporate culture of Toyota is vastly different from Nissan, and anyone who has spent a few years in either company would find adapting to the other's ways as difficult as going to work for a foreign company.

The Japanese are encouraged to be generalists, not specialists. In fact, too much personal ambition is frowned upon. Managers who have lived abroad have a difficult time being assimilated back into the very organization that ordered them overseas. They are not valued for the unique experience they had, and are often transferred out of their main companies into its subsidiaries.

Such was the fate of Kan Higashi, the former president of NUMMI. He was not rewarded for his success in America. Nor was he given a position that would have utilized his understanding of Western ways. After six years in America, he briefly worked in Toyota City, then was made EVP of a newly formed Toyota-owned mobile-telephone company in Tokyo. Although it was an important job, it is always more prestigious to work for a large company than for a small one, and for an old company instead of a new one.

General Motors, Volkswagen, and Toyota all suffer from the unique problems inherent in their respective corporate cultures— as well as from the broader traditions of their home countries. Attitudes, behavior, and policies that have evolved over decades are difficult to change.

As General Motors became arrogant and complacent, it lost touch with its customers and likewise its employees. It could not help, therefore, making poor use of them. It promoted managers whether they achieved results or not (witness Lloyd Reuss), and didn't give blue-collar workers the training, equipment, or systems that would allow them to build quality vehicles at competitive costs. GM's blue-collar workers have shown they can be motivated and productive, given the right environment, tools, and management.

Volkswagen is like GM in its arrogance and complacence. It's too bad that VW did not take a lesson earlier from GM and its decline to see the mirror image of itself a decade later. But VW, in its rigidity and overconfidence, scoffed at the idea that it could be compared to GM. After all, GM did not have its engineering genius or factories staffed with academic and technically credentialed workers.

But VW was operating in the same vacuum as GM, ignoring the reality all around it. Despite the growing signs of stress and malaise, it continued to acquiesce to the demands of labor, without exerting financial controls or listening to the desires of a diverse group of consumers—beyond the middle-aged men with secondary-school diplomas who had always been its most loyal customers. All criticism was dismissed with the certainty that people would buy its cars at whatever price because they were the best of their kind.

Toyota's blue-collar workers are among the most productive in the world, supported by an organization and systems that utilize their capabilities and energy to the fullest. However, while Toyota has been functionally brilliant in the factory, it is less so in its offices. White-collar workers spend long hours at small desks, locked in a management system that does not encourage or develop individual potential. Until now, the system was not questioned, since people gladly traded personal growth for the security and prestige that came with working for Toyota. But Japan and Toyota face challenges to their principles.

It is ironic that as bureaucratized as the three companies have become, all were created by independent thinkers. Toyota became great because it encouraged the creative contributions of many people who today would no doubt find themselves stifled by its environment. Must Toyota face a crisis as severe as those of GM and VW in order to change?

General Motors has had one advantage not shared by Toyota and Volkswagen—the opportunity to learn new ideas and methods from the foreign companies who set up operations on its shores. While many Americans greeted the arrival of Japanese transplant factories first with cynicism, then with fear, these factories have demonstrated the appeal of the United States as a manufacturing area, and they have been great teachers for U.S. companies. Overall, Americans are more flexible and open to accepting new ideas. Unlike either Germany or Japan, they welcome outsiders and can adapt methods that differ from their own —even though this adaptation often comes gradually and is not without pain. Since Germany and Japan have no such transplants in their midst, they have not had the opportunity to see different ideas in practice or to experience firsthand the power of a formidable foreign competitor in their backyards.

Georgetown, Kentucky—December 1992

THE QUIET TREE-LINED STREETS and old southern mansions stand as reminders of a gentle, bucolic time. Amid a lush landscape of rolling hills and emerald-green horse farms, Toyota chose to build its first American assembly plant in 1985.

The announcement that Kentucky had won the "sweepstakes" (several states had been in hot competition for the chance to host Toyota) was greeted by the residents with equal amounts of relief and fear. As one of the poorest states in the nation, Kentucky was desperate for jobs. The local newspaper, the *Georgetown News and Times,* heralded the announcement with a deep headline: "Toyota, a Big Yes; Oh, What a Feeling!" But many felt uncertain whether the arrival of the Japanese signaled a net gain or loss. This was not an internationally sophisticated area where people were accustomed to "foreigners." There was an inborn suspicion of outsiders of any kind, including Americans from the urban centers to the north.

But necessity eases a host of fears, and this struggling state surely needed the jobs and commerce that accompany a thriving auto assembly plant.

For those who wondered, in 1985, what it would be like to work for the Japanese, the jury was still out. On the hopeful side were the glowing stories out of NUMMI, whose successful operation and satisfied workers had become legendary. Honda had experienced a few rough patches, but generally seemed to be settling nicely in rural Ohio.

A troublesome undercurrent with Japanese transplants was the ever-present suspicion of racism against blacks. Although no overt signs of racism could be observed, there were other clues. Japanese factories were usually set up far away from urban areas, in rural towns inhabited by few minorities. The companies argued that they based their choices on economics, but civil rights groups continued to be concerned, especially when the antiurban prejudice seemed blatant. Honda's plant in Marysville, Ohio, was a case in point. When Honda opened the plant, it announced it would only accept applicants from within a thirty-mile radius. The prescribed distance happened to be a scant five miles short of Columbus, a black population center. There were virtually no blacks in Marysville, a classic Middle America rural setting. Critics charged that Honda set the distance at thirty, not forty or fifty, miles so it could avoid having to hire blacks. And indeed, less than 3 percent of the workers at Honda's plant are black, though the percentage has risen since Honda settled a lawsuit and has since increased minority hiring.

In Kentucky many criticisms were voiced before the plant was even open. One was the phenomenal sum the state paid to win the plant in the first place. At $125 million in financial incentives it was the largest ever offered by a state. Governor Martha Lane

Collins defended the incentives, saying that the arrival of a Toyota plant automatically implied the arrival of many other related component companies to effectively manage Toyota's Just-in-Time system. But the fat give-back didn't sit too well with the conservatives in the state who felt hoodwinked by the Japanese.

The UAW was worried, too. At first they assumed that the Kentucky plant would be a union-friendly operation. Why not? Toyota had already experienced the benefits of cooperation with the union in NUMMI. But from the start the Toyota operation in Kentucky resisted the UAW's efforts to organize, saying it was up to the work force to decide if they wanted a union. It was a blow the union could barely afford, and it seemed to be a growing trend among transplant operations.

With controversy swirling around Toyota, the weary unemployed lined up, 100,000 strong, to apply for 3,000 jobs. All that really mattered was work; they were willing to swallow their doubts. For many who had heard about the job security and glorified partnership between management and workers in Japan, it seemed like the chance of a lifetime. Many who applied were college graduates, and those workers who had experience in other factories figured they had an edge. As one hopeful applicant explained the usual process, "You wrote down what work you had done before, and that was the end of it. If you knew somebody who worked in the plant and he put in a good word for you, that helped."

But applicants to the Toyota plant, who were used to a lottery-style application process, were in for a shock. Each candidate was evaluated with the care usually reserved for management positions. First, there came a battery of tests—reading, math, manual dexterity, technical knowledge, and "job fitness." Lengthy psychological quizzes followed, in order to uncover those with unacceptable attitudes. A sample true-or-false question: "It is important for workers to work past quitting time to get the job done when necessary." It didn't take a rocket scientist to read the message Toyota was telegraphing with such questions.

If an applicant passed the tests, the next stage was working on a mock production line to check speed and skill with technical tasks. Then it was on to the doctor's office for a physical and a drug test.

UAW officials watched the process from the outside with skepticism. "I know what those tests are really for," one said angrily. "They're to eliminate anyone who might have a mind of his own. Anyone who might sympathize with the unions."

Toyota management scoffed at the idea. They were bending over backward to make certain everything was done fairly and with sensitivity. Those who looked hard to see the famous Japanese prejudices at work could find no fault with the hiring process. Toyota even worked with the Urban League to assure the appropriate number of minorities. Only occasionally did Japanese prejudices leak out—such as the comment by one of Toyota's trainers that he feared American hands were too big to perform intricate assembly tasks.

Toyota placed the kind of emphasis on worker selection and workplace atmosphere that went far beyond anything seen in their home-based plants, since conformity in Japan made selection easier. Peer pressure would eventually dull anyone with a strong will to be different. Americans were by nature more independent. Toyota chose those that could adapt most easily to its ways.

There was good motivation to do so. Wages were among the best in the country, in spite of its being a nonunion operation. The work environment was clean, pleasant, and low-key. American music, selected by the workers, blared from loudspeakers. It seemed in every way an "American" company—only better. A 1992 study published by the Center for Business and Economic Research, College of Business and Economics, at the University of Kentucky, gave Toyota's operation high marks—especially in reviving the local economy. It was estimated that between the payroll and supporting expenditures, Toyota invested $574.5 million in the local economy in 1992. If indirect effects were added—such as spending by employees, purchasing from suppliers, and other related costs—the number almost doubled. When Toyota announced its plan in 1985, its projected capital investment was $800 million. Since that time, the company had added a power train plant and a second assembly plant, bringing total expenditures to nearly $2 billion.

Seven years after Toyota executives first experienced "My Old Kentucky Home" being played at the Kentucky Derby, the company is considered a welcome resident and neighbor. But it is by no means an independent domestic operation. Toyota outposts are umbilically tied to Toyota City, and the key players in Kentucky, including many production engineers, remain Japanese. Although Toyota has promised that within a few years, most of the management will be American, it is clear that there are many positions that will be permanently staffed by Japanese. As in many Japanese operations in the United States, white-collar jobs are limited to certain departments, and rarely are of high status.

Today, General Motors is replicating the style of a Japanese transplant in East Germany. Its newly built Eisenach factory is the most modern in East Germany, and GM has been very selective in its hiring of only a fraction of the previous work force. Since none of the workers had prior knowledge of lean manufacturing or even modern production equipment, they were free of prejudice and willing to learn. Because the factory did not employ surplus workers, they were relieved of the fear of layoffs. In many respects, Eisenach is a testimony to what Americans have learned from the experience of having Japanese transplants in their midst.

NUMMI remains the rare example of American-Japanese collaboration to the benefit of both. Its origins were never "them versus us." The UAW was a full and respected partner. The fifty-fifty ownership agreement awarded top jobs and management responsibility to Toyota, but GM people were everywhere. GM belatedly learned from NUMMI, and today many NUMMI alumni have key roles in the company's revival.

Toyota, meanwhile, has learned to adapt its systems to a more American way of doing business. Its experience at NUMMI paved the way for Kentucky, alerting the company to the pitfalls of doing business in America.

The UAW has learned that it is possible to become a participant in improving productivity without compromising its responsibilities to its members.

John Krafcik, who spent time at NUMMI as a quality-control engineer, later wrote in a report on the contributions of NUMMI that what was evolving was "a hybrid work force which may well be (to borrow GM's Nova advertising slogan) 'the best of both worlds.' " Nova was built at NUMMI.

Volkswagen has operated assembly plants in Brazil, Mexico, and elsewhere for decades. But it has rarely enjoyed a peaceful coexistence between management and labor. Perhaps in desperately poor countries, Volkswagen thought workers would be satisfied with any conditions. But after years of experiencing German-style management in VW's Puebla, Mexico, plant (which was producing poor-quality cars at relatively high costs), the workers finally rebelled.

When VW announced it was planning to institute Japanese production techniques, it won the support of the main body of labor, but ignored the protests from a smaller but powerful faction. Nobody bothered to find out the implications of displeasing this group, and Volkswagen managers were stunned as the plant erupted into violence and all work ground to a halt. The police finally had to be summoned to force the workers out, and VW had to close the plant.

Volkswagen petitioned the Mexican labor tribunal for permission to cancel its agreement with the union. Eventually, the petition was accepted and the workers came back without the unions.

But the episode underscored that Volkswagen lacked the fundamental knowledge of the labor practices that led to the disruption —in spite of many years as Mexico's largest automobile producer.

Another example of cultural isolation is evident in a story told by a VW dealer on the East Coast. He complained to a VW executive that the Fox, a small car imported from Brazil, needed an automatic transmission to attract customers who couldn't drive a stick shift. He also suggested that the Passat, a larger model, needed a V-6 engine and power windows and seats to justify its high price. He was told, "VW makes engineering decisions, not marketing decisions. We let the market come to us." This arrogance about the superiority of the product has been conveyed into an excuse for poor sales. It's not the company's fault. It's the customer's.

While General Motors actually benefited from foreign transplants, Volkswagen never had a respected rival use German workers to teach it that things could be done differently. Even if there had been such a teacher, it's doubtful anyone would have listened as long as the factories could keep churning out Golfs and there was enough cash in the bank.

Warren, Michigan—February 1993

JACK SMITH sat in his office at the GM Technical Center, shirt sleeves rolled up, seeming more relaxed than the weight of his responsibilities might warrant. On this day he was thinking about PICOS, Inaki Lopez's program that had in only a few months revolutionized a purchasing strategy that slashed supplier prices. But saving GM $7 billion was only part of Lopez's target. Smith was also excited about how his leadership and passion had transformed an army of bureaucrats into front-line warriors. And, unlike anyone before him, Lopez had achieved this in a relatively short time. For Lopez, it was simple: "Identify a problem and a goal, then figure out how to get it done. Ignore all internal barriers that say you can't do it."

"What Lopez did," Smith said, "was take a group of purchasing agents—people who were out of the mainstream of the company; people whom Roger Smith would have called 'the frozen middle'—and transformed them into motivated, hardworking, successful contributors. Lopez taught them they were important to the transformation of General Motors. He showed them how to change. Now he has people trying to join his department, when a few years ago they couldn't wait to get out. No one would have believed you could use the purchasing staff as the change agents for the company."

Now that Lopez had proved what he could do with purchasing, Smith was considering how he could best use the PICOS system throughout GM. "GM can get more out of PICOS," he said. "It is a way of attacking the problem of costs. The biggest problem we have internally is that by getting more productive, we free up a lot of people. What do we do with them under our contract with the union? Now that we have reduced our job banks by fifteen thousand, that problem is less severe, and Lopez is trying to bring work inside so we can use some of these workers who are freed up after we transform an operation."

Smith inherited some major union problems that he was struggling to understand and address. "I realize how badly GM managed the relationship [with the UAW] in the past," he admitted frankly. "Everything was boiling over when I came into the job. The UAW had not been informed ahead of time which plants would be closed under the Stempel-Reuss program announced in February. They should have been told ahead of time, as a courtesy, at least." When Smith took over, he immediately learned how frustrated the company's UAW representative, Steve Yokich, was. "He had no place to turn to get answers about what was happening inside GM."

Contrary to early suspicions, Smith believed the UAW was encouraged about some aspects of Lopez's efficiency drive. "They like Inaki because he wants to bring work inside and wants to make GM competitive," he said. But before a fully trusting relationship could be established between GM management and the UAW, some old hostilities had to be mended.

When Smith and Yokich first sat down to talk, Smith immediately saw "there was no trust between us whatsoever. As we talked, I realized that small things that had been impediments between us started to get solved—not major issues, just a few things here and there. It was as if both sides were testing one step at a time to see if things really had changed. The more we talked, the more I realized that we had done a lot of things wrong. One of the things that shocked me was how badly we implemented the last contract. It was humiliating to learn this. In GM, the contract was negotiated by finance people and central labor staff, but not by operating people. As it turned out, many didn't read the contract or understand how it affected them, so they didn't realize where they violated it. I have started a Labor Strategy Council so that we don't have another mess like this in the future. Our operating people are going to know what the contract says and how they have to operate under it. I can assure you that the UAW knows it page by page and holds us to every provision."

It all seemed so obvious. But after years of neglect, General Motors was starting to learn the old lessons from scratch.

NINE

Shrinking Highways

We are presented with a rare historical moment in which the threat of worldwide conflict seems remote and the transformations of economies and technology are blurring the lines between nations.

—ROBERT REICH, *The Work of Nations*

THE ENDLESS OPEN HIGHWAYS of the civilized world once beckoned travelers with the promise of personal freedom unlike any previously known. In the private cocoon of the automobile, people could escape the cluttered ancient cities of Europe, the teeming, overpopulated coastal metropolis of Japan, and the smokestack dreariness of industrial America.

The automobile has been so much a part of American culture in this century that it is hard to recall a time when a visit to a neighboring town fifteen miles away was a full day's trip by horse-drawn carriage, when the most pressing environmental problem was the deep piles of horse manure filling city streets, when people could live entire lifetimes without meeting anyone who wasn't within walking distance of their homes.

Many odes have been written to the glory of the car; many a

young man or woman has felt the swell of possibility contained in the faint jingle of ignition keys in the pocket.

But only one hundred years after this wonderful invention first tantalized the citizens of the world, the freedom is being curtailed. Both metaphorically and literally, the brakes are on for drivers and carmakers.

Cars creep along the California freeways, the gray haze of exhaust blocking out the sun. From necessity, cars have become traveling offices equipped with phones, fax machines, and even televisions. The roads and bridges of the Northeast and Midwest are crumbling beneath the weight of millions of vehicles traveling daily over their fragile, weather-beaten surfaces. Speed limits are irrelevant on most urban highways, where rush hours turn roads into parking lots for several hours each day, as frazzled drivers try to calm their nerves by listening to books on tape or meditation music.

The German autobahns were once roads unencumbered by any limit to speed, the ultimate symbol of German engineering prowess and vehicle performance. While the East German wall was standing, Wolfsburg was in the northeast corner of the country, and the road to West Germany's major cities was swift and open. Today, the autobahn near Wolfsburg is the direct route into eastern Germany and Berlin. Instead of flying down the roads at speeds of up to 180 kph, cars now crawl around large trucks hauling goods into and out of areas that were formerly closed to western commerce.

In Japan consumers can purchase vehicles that are equipped with refrigerators and outfitted to look like living rooms. Motorists have come to expect heavy traffic wherever they go. Weekends out of Tokyo to resort areas like Hakone require an allotment of five hours for a drive that would take less than two hours at a normal speed.

In *Carpool: A Novel of Suburban Frustration* Jenny Meade places "carpool fatigue" among the most severe modern ailments. She describes it as being "like shell shock, only you don't get veterans' benefits; they just fill up your tank and send you back to the front." Meade seems to mean it when she adds, "if Henry Ford were alive, I would strangle him."

Naturally, there is an anticar movement. In May 1992 the second International Conference for Auto Free Cities attracted more than fifteen hundred people, most of whom brought along serious proposals to rid the world of cars. One of the participants, a Wayne State University professor named Ralph Slovenko, has long been laughed at in Detroit circles as the nutty professor of Armageddon (or, as he would say, "Autogeddon"). But Professor Slovenko is a pretty serious guy. He believes that cars have wrecked the world. "When you're in a hole, stop digging," he says, although he admits that it would probably take "World War III, the bombing of our cities" to get rid of cars.

Even the psychiatrists are getting into the act. A cottage industry of therapists has sprung up to deal with auto-related malaises. The *Journal of Psychiatry and Law* notes that "bumper-to-bumper traffic causes irritation and frustration, which gives rise to hostility, either on the roadway or upon arriving at work or at home." One psychiatrist said that his patients are so disturbed by traffic that they often spend most of their $200-an-hour sessions talking about commuting problems.

But while things grind to a halt on our roadways, the world's carmakers continue to predict more and more growth. The conventional wisdom of carmaking, as old as Alfred Sloan, is that markets are not saturated until there is at least one car per person, even though the true measure of the utility of the car may be density per mile of road. Automakers like to argue that this goal is a long way from being reached, especially in third-world and newly industrialized nations. Toyota talks openly of a 50-million-car market in China, even as its own island is running out of space for cars. One wonders where in a nation without a passable road system those cars would travel. Infrastructure must come before car demand.

Recently, the twelve thousand employees of Yanase & Company, Japan's largest import car dealer, were ordered to take the train to work, and its seventy-six-year-old chairman, Jiro Yanase, has asked Toyota and Nissan to do the same. His point: The best way to boost car sales is to make driving a car more appealing. And one way to do that is to ease the congestion that tangles every highway in Japan. Yanase means business. "We check the car parks every day to make sure that no unauthorized employees have driven in," said a manager. "If they break the rule once, they will be given a warning. If they break it again and again, they will be admonished, and their salary may be cut."

Amsterdam has declared its intention of becoming the first major city to ban cars from its Old World, canal-ringed center. The congestion of 67,000 cars a day converging on its center has finally caused an urban nervous breakdown. Wider sidewalks and bicycle lanes will squeeze cars out. Huge parking fees and towing fines will offer further discouragement. "For years, the city was forced to adapt to cars," said an official. "Cars will now have to adapt to the city."

As a practical matter, the true measure of a market's saturation may not be the number of cars per person but the number of cars per mile of road. When road congestion becomes so oppressive that a car can't be used for speed and efficiency, its value diminishes. This is a particularly pressing issue for the world's major carmakers, which all confront saturation in their home markets and must look elsewhere for growth.

This used to be easier when carmakers could freely export cars to many markets or transfer obsolete tooling to places like Latin America for production of cars that were outdated in their home markets. But countries that once tolerated this situation now demand local assembly of modern cars.

As automobiles grow more uniform across all markets, and nations demand a stake in the development of their home markets, new challenges emerge for international companies.

Large car companies are already internationally diversified to the extent that they have models suitable for all. For example, although GM is known in the United States for its large cars, its Opel models, developed and produced in Europe, are internationally acceptable. Recognizing the difference between the United States and elsewhere, where higher gasoline prices dictate smaller, cheaper cars, GM has given Opel responsibility for developing markets outside of North America. Today, among the company's most efficient operations are the GM plant in Brazil and the new small assembly plant in Hungary, where workers are passionately embracing capitalism.

During the 1960s Volkswagen began venturing abroad on a selective basis, mainly in Latin America, with mixed results. Under Carl Hahn it expanded into Asia and eastern Europe. VW's small cars have been as popular in some foreign markets as they are in Germany. In fact, the government of Brazil has recently voiced its desire to begin building the Beetle (they call it Fusco) again. In Mexico, Volkswagen is the number one brand, with a higher market share than VW has in Germany.

Toyota may be the most reluctant, yet successful, investor in foreign markets. Not only does the company's broad product range mean that it has something for every market, rich or poor, it has also demonstrated a deliberate and determined pursuit of sales around the world. Toyota's strategy is very simple: export from highly efficient plants in Japan to every market possible, until trade barriers to exports are erected. When that happens, begin local production in foreign markets, but maintain a functional link to Toyota City. No other automaker in the world has such an effective internal organization to support this type of varied and far-flung network of assembly operations, which range from wholly owned to joint ventures to minority interests. Toyota has many kinds of foreign production arrangements, the largest of which is its multibillion-dollar operation in Georgetown, Kentucky, and the smallest of which is the CKD plants owned jointly with local partners in numerous Asia-Pacific countries, where Toyota has been especially active. A car made in one of these countries—Thailand, for example—is no longer Japanese, and therefore not subject to quotas in the West.

These companies and others will increasingly collide with each other—not in their home markets, but in foreign markets where none of them hold claim to any special privilege. Eventually, they may also be forced to adopt less savage expansion policies. They risk what economist Sylvia Ostry calls "system friction"—too many countries employing the same systems and technology to produce an excess of the same kinds of products for markets that are not growing fast enough to accommodate them all.

This is an unprecedented dynamic. It is one thing for GM and Volkswagen to battle for dominance in Europe, or for Toyota and GM to fight for American market share. It is an entirely different matter when the big companies face off in unfamiliar territories like China or Indonesia. These endeavors require sensitivity to what is good for local economies and people and the more challenging task of identifying consumer needs and interests. It is far more difficult to operate subsidiaries when the key players may not be native, but the host country wants automotive investment —seeing it as an important source of hard currency through exports, a means for acquiring technology and jobs. Furthermore, while most economists believe that if worldwide growth exceeds 4 or 5 percent, there will be enough job creation to encourage a free-trade mentality, the sluggish growth rate predicted for the 1990s will mean more governments choosing managed trade to protect their own jobs.

Nations are fond of their long-held assumptions about staying competitive, being number one, and winning the economic war. But today's carmakers, along with other industries, are being forced to create new criteria for success.

The old rules of industrial gamesmanship are like dinosaurs whose carcasses block the path to change. The new rules are less clear. But as Robert Reich points out in *The Work of Nations*:

> History rarely proceeds in a direct line. . . . Those who project that today's steady improvement (or deterioration) over yesterday's will become even more pronounced tomorrow often end up embarrassed when the future finally arrives. In the intervening moments, there will occur an earthquake, a potent idea, a revolution, a sudden loss of business confidence, a scientific discovery—reversing the seemingly most intransigent of trends and causing people to wonder how they could ever have been deluded into believing that any other outcome was ever remotely possible.

The fact that these words were penned by America's new secretary of labor is in itself a striking example of how much we are changing.

All companies must choose between passive change (being dragged into the future by circumstances) and active change (directing the course of events). In the past, GM, Toyota, and Volkswagen have had their share of both experiences. Sometimes it's been a combination of the two—the ability to make lemonade out of lemons. This was certainly the case with the Toyota Production System, which was developed because Toyota was too poor to waste resources. It was also behind the Beetle, which existed because Volkswagen couldn't afford to design anything better.

In the global economy, competition exists not just between companies, but between entire socioeconomic systems. They set the all-important context that shapes the actions and fortunes of individual firms. During the next few years the company that will become strongest internationally will be the one that holds the most progressive policies of growth and development, as well as the one most attuned to broader issues of social responsibility and the car's place in society.

New Hampshire—January 1992

ON A BITTER COLD DAY in New Hampshire, with the snow packed in icy mounds around the platform, Paul Tsongas raised his small frame to its full height and bellowed: "If you have a choice between a [Chrysler] Jeep and an Isuzu, buy the Jeep."

The 1992 U.S. presidential campaign was in full swing, and the most popular demogogic theme of its primaries—uttered by liberals like Tsongas and Tom Harkin, as well as by ultraconservatives like Pat Buchanan—was isolationism and protectionism. It always got a rise out of audiences, especially since George Bush's recent trip to Japan had been such a flop.

Just that week, the Los Angeles County Transportation Commission canceled a $121-million contract with Sumitomo Corporation to build railcars. The backlash had begun.

But often it was more a gut issue than a bread-and-butter issue. What Tsongas may not have realized was that GM owned 34 percent of Isuzu, and the "foreign" truck he was encouraging people not to buy was assembled in a factory in Indiana. Sometimes the most strident protectionists seemed to contradict their words with their actions. For example, even as Lee Iacocca was delivering firebrand stump speeches decrying the evils of Asian imports, Chrysler was importing Asian cars and components and selling them in the United States as American-made Plymouths and Dodges.

It's not so simple anymore. In spite of the vast cultural differences that make the United States, Germany, and Japan clumsy partners in the dance of global industrial growth, there's no way to step back into the world we once had.

Just look at how interrelated GM, Toyota, and Volkswagen already are with a host of countries and companies across the world. The following is only a portion of their connected interests: GM owns Opel in Germany, owns 34 percent of Isuzu and 3 percent of Suzuki, jointly owns Holden in Australia with Toyota, has many successful operations throughout Latin America, and jointly produces cars with Toyota at NUMMI. Toyota also holds a share in Daihatsu, assembles trucks in China, markets Volkswagens and Audis in Japan, has VW produce its trucks in Germany, has its own assembly plants in the United States and Great Britain, and has dozens of small, jointly owned CKD plants around the world. Volkswagen, in addition to its operations in Spain, Mexico, and Czechoslovakia, builds Golfs and Jettas in China, is engaged in a joint venture with Ford to build minivans in Portugal, jointly owns Autolatina with Ford in Brazil, assembles vans in Taiwan, and will produce a car in Spain with Suzuki.

The world suddenly seems very small. Sales of NUMMI cars are going to affect GM's profits, just as sales at Autolatina affect VW's, and the old issues of trade restrictions and protectionism may be a case of biting the hand that feeds you.

Sometimes, in the rush to close their borders to imports, countries inadvertently open them up to even more threatening specters. When American carmakers clamored for stricter trade limits for Japanese vehicle imports, the response of Japanese companies was to open up ten assembly plants in the United States, followed by hundreds of related Japanese component companies. The end result: excess capacity in the United States and a net loss of U.S. jobs—despite the thousands employed by Japanese companies. Japanese transplants have higher productivity and lower local control than American factories, and this reduces the number of employees needed.

Not surprising, the Japanese seem the most interested in open markets and free trade, even as their home market is difficult to penetrate. Japanese consumers are intensely nationalistic in their car-buying behavior. Foreign producers of mass-market cars believe that the cost of setting up dealer networks would be prohibitive because of Japan's high real estate prices and the likelihood of long-term losses before any of them could realistically expect a big payback.

The face that corporate Japan presents to the world is one of supportive internationalism as it tantalizes struggling markets with the promise of investments. One must always read between the lines. For example, Shoichiro Toyoda told European automakers at the World Automotive Forum: "All of us at Toyota have profound respect for the history and tradition of European culture and European technology. We are determined to adapt our cars to European needs and circumstances in the best spirit of the European automotive tradition. And we know that the best way to do that is with an integrated local presence. That is why we are moving to develop cars here, to produce a lot of them here, and to buy parts and materials for them here. In the process, we are blending Toyota's way of doing things with European traditions and values."

Translation: "We want to come into your market and build our cars here. We will employ your people and operate European-style facilities, but they will be managed from Japan. We will buy parts and materials locally, but some of those 'locals' will be Japanese companies that follow us. We respect your culture, but we will do things our way because we believe it is better."

This is exaggerated, but the point is sound. Europeans are suspicious of such statements from the Japanese, and, watching what happened in America, they have reason to be. Deep down, they fear that the Japanese are only interested in one thing: global domination—war behind the mask of brotherhood. As Volkswagen executive Dr. Peter Frerk said caustically, "Dr. Toyoda is such a nice guy—always smiling, always polite. And this culture, this self-restriction! They are not like the industrial leaders of the West traveling around in Gulfstream 4s. Rather, they are a system striving for dominance. And they cannot do this by themselves because this shogun class has emerged into a full-blown trade success. They had the good fortune to avoid the Enlightenment two hundred years ago. They don't have Constitutional Fathers, or Montesquieu, or Rousseau, or Kant, or Voltaire. How wonderful for them that two hundred years later, they are a closed group undisturbed by individuality. No true unions, no true journalists—an entire transparent society among themselves, closed to immigration. There is no multiethnic and multicultural approach. They are only striving for dominance."

In a speech before the EC-Japan conference in November 1991, Frerk warned that "the Europeans are not prepared to abandon some specific cultural identity which we have achieved. Instead, our Japanese colleagues will be asked whether they are inclined to conform to a greater extent with the habits and practices of their European host countries, even if it were to lower slightly productivity by comparison to some practices used in Japan." Frerk said he was concerned by the elite hiring principles employed by Japanese transplants in Great Britain, where only four hundred jobs were awarded from nineteen thousand applicants and only twenty-two foremen selected from four thousand applicants. "It will not be possible to have an important industry exclusively recruit such selected volunteers in the future," he said. "In a globalized future automotive industry, we Europeans would regard it as socially somewhat irresponsible to accept only the very best recruits in all places. Our work force is not made up of select volunteers."

The German people have harbored ill feelings about the Japanese since the 1970s when Japanese exports severely disabled Germany's camera, television, and motorcycle industries and put many companies out of business. Alarmed by the trend, then Minister of Economics Otto Graf Lambsdorff visited Japan to see what they were doing that was so special. He returned saying the Japanese were very hardworking and didn't demand high salaries —and this was the secret of their competitive edge. His remarks infuriated German workers, who felt it was a direct attack on their work ethic and standard of living. The Japanese were viewed by some as "the yellow enemy."

At the time, the fear did not spread into the auto industry. Japanese cars were dismissed as being cheap and of low status.

(In the late 1970s a German banker told this author, "In Germany, only the Turks drive Japanese cars.") This image persisted well into the 1980s. In the first half of the decade, the dollar was so strong and there was so much money that German carmakers —especially luxury producers like Mercedes and BMW—grew increasingly arrogant. Somehow they felt they were exempt from the onslaught that had afflicted other industries. Leaders like Carl Hahn could afford to be magnanimous about free trade. Why worry when there is no real threat?

But Japanese carmakers were quietly making inroads throughout Europe. They began by concentrating their efforts in countries where there was no national car industry—and they were successful. As Japan's share of market grew to 30 percent or more in countries like Switzerland, Ireland, Finland, and Denmark, the threat became more real and European carmakers (especially the French and then the Germans) belatedly began to press for trade restrictions.

Before Toyota launched Lexus, the reaction from Mercedes and BMW was pure scorn. How could a Japanese luxury car hope to compete? Eberhard von Kunheim, chairman of BMW, wondered why Toyota's luxury car could be purchased much cheaper than a BMW. BMW's engineers took Lexus apart and concluded that it was a well-built car—so well built, in fact, that there was no way Toyota could make a profit at the advertised price. For the first time, German automakers accused the Japanese of dumping.

But the problems seemed to be not with the Japanese, but with German automakers who had allowed themselves to become lazy, arrogant, and isolated from their consumers and the competition. By 1990 it dawned on the Germans that the world had changed and Toyota had done what they thought was impossible. If the Lexus could outsell Mercedes in the United States, why shouldn't the cheaper, mass-produced Toyotas erode VW's position elsewhere?

Today, the Japanese refer to "fortress Europe," and claim that when the Europeans place limits on free trade, they deny consumers a full range of products. But the huge trade deficit between the Common Market and Japan, and the United States and Japan, made it difficult for the Japanese to do anything except go along with the negotiated limits. Although they have repeatedly shown themselves to be good negotiators, the Japanese had no way to bargain away the appreciation of the yen against the dollar or European currencies—which has pushed up their prices and is forcing them to move even more production out of Japan.

The debate between Japanese and European manufacturers is not unlike the twenty-year argument that has gone on between the United States and Japan. And the fallout is often the same. At the World Economic Summit in January 1993, Ferdinand Piech grew so heated that he waved his finger in Shoichiro Toyoda's face and harrangued him about Japan's closed market. It must have been a shock for Shoichiro, who was accustomed to the cordial and dignified manner of Carl Hahn.

Volkswagen, and Germany in general, must tread carefully with the Japanese. It cannot afford to be seen as overly protectionist, even with its most aggressive competition, because it, too, depends so heavily on exports.

General Motors has experienced virtually no prejudice against its presence in Europe. The doors are wide open. The reason is simple, says one Volkswagen manager. "GM is completely integrated into the industrial base of the host community. Management is a mixture of native and American, and it tends to be 'multinational European,' which is a new species."

General Motors and Ford have long been a part of the German industrial landscape. Both have been completely integrated into the economy since the 1930s. Although the European auto companies try to exclude them from some meetings, the public generally views them as German/European companies.

Ironically, Japanese consumers have always been filled with admiration for German cars. During the years of the "bubble economy" (1986–90), when Japan created a lot of paper millionaires from stock and real estate speculation, there was a surge of high-ticket German car purchases. Young people bought BMWs as a status symbol. They were especially popular in Tokyo, where European fads thrived: It became fashionable to wear French or Italian designer ties, carry Louis Vuitton briefcases, and drive BMWs. (Unfortunately, Mercedes ran up against an image problem when it became the favored brand of the *yakuza*—Japanese

Mafia—whose dark-windowed Mercedes cars prowled the streets of some of Tokyo's seedier districts.)

Perhaps it was the high regard of the Japanese for German engineering and products that made it so hard for German automakers to see the Japanese threat coming. By 1991, as German car sales began to fall in Japan, Japanese car sales rose in Germany.

While European and American auto companies would like to keep restrictive trade barriers in place until they become fully competitive, the truth is that each of the new Big Three faces internal challenges that would still be there even if the barriers were removed.

We can see this clearly when we examine in more detail the status of Japanese transplants in the United States. Japanese automakers now have ten transplant operations in the United States capable of producing more than 2 million vehicles. U.S. automakers might grumble that it was disloyal for state governments to court these transplants so vigorously, but the fact remains, these transplants have become important contributors to their local economies. Furthermore, their strong competitive presence has forced American automakers to make enormous improvements in car quality, productivity, and customer service. They may be a competitive threat, but they have also been a catalyst for change. European producers may suffer today from their lack of role models to stimulate the corrective actions that have been taken in the United States. Honda, Nissan, and Toyota are relatively recent migrants to Great Britain and are still adjusting to their new surroundings. Italy, France, Spain, and Great Britain, four of the five largest markets in Europe, had severe limits on the Japanese until January, 1993, when a period of gradual market openness began. But as a group, European automakers are behind the United States on key competitive points such as product diversification and affordable costs.

They also have internal structural issues that complicate their options. Consider that a market not much larger than the United States supports six mass producers (VW, Fiat, GM, Ford, Renault, and Peugeot) and numerous specialty manufacturers (including Saab, Volvo, Mercedes, BMW, Rolls-Royce, and Jaguar).

Every one of these auto companies, with the exception of GM and Ford, has a decidedly nationalistic view of itself. But now, as vehicle standards throughout the Common Market are standardized, national companies will aggressively pursue each other's customers. In doing so, they will find heavy competition from the Americans. GM and Ford-Europe both have significant advantages as pan-European companies with factories located throughout the continent, more or less indifferent to nationality. Their cost structures are better, they may be more sensitive to consumers throughout Europe, and they have no obligation to support local suppliers if they are not competitive (as Inaki Lopez demonstrated). The greatest pressure on European carmakers may not be from the Japanese, but from each other and from Americans with European operations. As all of them try to lower costs in an attempt to compete, the fervor for keeping the Japanese out may become a moot point. The status quo will be shaken, no matter what.

Japanese carmakers face little competition from outsiders in their home markets, but they are entering a low-growth, strong-yen period which will place them in a very non-*kyosei* battle for share with one another at home and in major markets abroad. Increasingly, the Japanese are finding the major profitable export markets restricted or unprofitable. And even investors with long-term goals must make a profit eventually. Smaller companies like Mazda always relied more heavily on exports and will be shaken by current trends because they may be financially too weak to undertake investments needed to sidestep a stagnant home market and declining profits on exports.

The realities at home are brutal: excess capacity, a blue-collar labor shortage, and higher break-even points—to name a few. How will the smaller Japanese car companies survive?

Clearly, were it not for *kyosei,* Toyota might be strong enough to put all of its Japanese rivals out of business. Fortunately for its domestic rivals, it would be socially unthinkable for the company to do that. It is even conceivable that Toyota might become the rescuer of Japanese auto companies.

But even as opportunities to thrive through exports lessen, it becomes clear that what the world is demanding is not the old ship-and-sell mentality, but a new era of capital investments in local assembly plants. Development, not trade, has become the most pressing challenge for the global carmakers. The real expansion is occurring in virgin territories: Latin America, Mexico, eastern Europe, and the Far East. The greatest clash will take place outside the companies' home territories. And if the giant auto companies think they can invade undeveloped markets and treat them like banana republics, they are kidding themselves.

Volkswagen's primary interest in Skoda, despite Carl Hahn's glowing rhetoric about eastern European revival, was to cut its overall costs by producing cars in a cheaper labor market. But the Czechs had big stars in their eyes. They looked at Volkswagen, coming from a country where workers were paid fantastic salaries—even when they were sick or on vacation!—and their expectations skyrocketed. Volkswagen's promise of good pay and guaranteed employment was quite appealing. So was its commitment to shore up the Czechoslovakian economy. But two years after the takeover, car sales are down by almost half (in part due to the flood of good used cars being shipped from Western Europe), the operation is bleeding money, and VW is already talking about short shifts and sacrifice. On a positive note, there have been some drastic improvements in quality. No longer do cars have windows that can't be cranked down or ill-fitting doors. Wage increases have made Skoda workers some of the highest paid in Czechoslovakia. But VW's own financial trouble could weaken its commitment to Skoda, and most certainly lengthen the time over which it fulfills its promise.

Many Skoda workers, who were made to feel a part of Volkswagen in the beginning, are embittered by the fact that Wolfsburg workers still make as much in a day as they earn in a month. Meanwhile, the VW director haggles with the Czech government for reductions in taxes and duty-free shipment of goods from Germany. Always in these conversations, there is a hint of the threat that if things become too costly, Volkswagen may decide it has made a mistake.

Skoda might be another example of how carelessly Volkswagen moves into undeveloped markets. When the venture was decided, Hahn made a big point about how a Czech enterprise would be successful and easily managed because culturally the Czechs had so much in common with Germans. But any common heritage the two countries shared was long ago, before World War II and communism. "Culture" isn't a static, never-changing reality. People's attitudes and behaviors are shaped by their experiences, and the Skoda workers are in no way similar to Wolfsburg in that respect. One need not go as far as Prague to learn that. When VW invested in East Germany, it showed that a forty-year separation of homogeneous people under separate political and economic systems had created two different work ethics. The primary style of VW managers at Skoda is to be autocratic and demanding. While in the years ahead it may prove to be a successful venture, there is little warmth between the two companies now. The prevailing question: Does VW just want cheap labor in order to improve its manufacturing cost base, or is it committed to larger social and economic goals in eastern Europe, which "statesman" Hahn emphasized while wooing Skoda?

Now VW may be embarking on a form of whiplashing as it prepares to open the new Mosel factory in eastern Germany in 1996 to replace the crumbling Trabant plant, which it took over after reunification. Although IG Metall secured an agreement that labor there would not replace workers in western Europe, those at SEAT fear that their jobs are in jeopardy once the new plant opens. With VW's commitment to cut 36,000 jobs—only 12,500 in Germany—workers in other plants have good reason to be concerned.

Large companies must look beyond growth to examine whether being functionally global is a legitimate objective, as opposed to growth for its own sake. Toyota's new pickup presents a good example of ill-conceived strategy. Normally, Toyota's vehicle strategy has been developed with pinpoint precision. It studies a market, finds the unfulfilled need, and meets it. Simple and effective. But in late 1992 it broke with this tradition when it introduced a full-size pickup truck into the United States. It happens that the best-selling domestic vehicles for many years were pickups—Ford was number one and Chevrolet was number two. There was no unfilled need. For the first time, Toyota was competing head-on with best-selling vehicles in their home markets. It didn't make any sense, and the results were disappointing. Toyota projected it would sell sixty thousand pickups in the United States in 1993, but that appears possible only with heavy discounting.

This is an issue that all Japanese manufacturers must address. As Nobuhiko Kawamoto, president of Honda, recently admitted to this author, "The Japanese made many product mistakes during the 1980s. It was just harder to see them because we introduced so many new models, and some of them were great successes."

During the 1980s, the Japanese launched too many nameplates and variations of vehicles. Such expansion reflected their wealth, but ignored the market trends all around them—the very thing that had long been the key to their success.

In the past, all three companies could afford a bit of adventurism in international investments. Often, new markets weren't thoroughly researched, and investments were made carelessly, causing losses that were obscured by successes elsewhere. GM lost money in Europe for years until GM Europe was organized and restructured. Volkswagen, in partnership with Ford, often loses money in Brazil, Mexico, and elsewhere, and the Westmoreland, Pennsylvania, factory was a disaster. Toyota could afford to absorb losses from transplants well beyond a start-up period. But even it must be mindful of the bottom line. Now none of the companies can afford to pursue growth without regard to profits, and the companies are beginning to see that, instead of solving problems at home, international investments too often bring new ones.

Tokyo—December 1992

KYOSEI—understanding and cooperation among companies for the good of all—is an issue with which Toyota struggles deeply. International development is one thing. Even international joint ventures. But *kyosei* implies a level of cooperation that is foreign to Japanese thinking. It requires mingling with your partner—metaphorically sharing blood. Can a Japanese company do this?

One former insider (who asked to remain nameless) thinks otherwise. He told this author that Toyota has reached its peak of growth and now faces the challenges of international cooperation it is poorly equipped to address. "Toyota has become like a huge tree with great big overhanging limbs," he says. "It overwhelms its foreign operations. But there is a cancer creeping through the limbs of this tree." This observer believes American companies are better able to deal with their problems: "In an American company, if a limb becomes rotten, you can cut it off. In the Toyota system, you can't do this. It is a very conservative company. It resists being multinational. It does not make good use of the people it sends abroad, and it makes no use of them when they come back home. It is not a company that could ever embrace foreigners in its upper management."

According to this source, one of the main flaws in the way Toyota operates overseas is the umbilical link with Toyota City. Unlike some successful international companies, such as IBM and Procter & Gamble, which take pains to establish autonomy in local markets, Toyota pulls all the strings from Japan. All international operations report directly to the management there, even when making minor decisions. "For a long time, this structure was an advantage to Toyota," this insider acknowledges. "One could assume that each market—United States, Europe, and Japan—was essentially the same, so everything could be coordinated out of Japan. But today, the assumption is different. Markets are less predictable, consumers demand different things, and social and political pressures force companies to behave differently as corporate citizens. That is, to embrace more foreigners in their management structure, and to become more local in form and substance. A company like Toyota will have a great deal of difficulty doing this because Toyota does not know how to transfer power in autonomy."

While developing countries are vying for the industrial infusion of global carmakers, no country ultimately wants an industry that is dominated by outsiders. The global carmakers will eventually be forced to confront what it means to be culturally global—citizens, not just guests or Big Brothers, of the world who come and go at will, depending on the inducements offered to lure them elsewhere.

Superficially, it makes some sense that each of the Global Big Three will develop primarily in its own sphere: Toyota in Asia, Volkswagen in Europe, and GM in the Americas. Localizing operations is always easier in places where the culture and customs are similar and the language barriers are fewer. In the short term, this may occur. But during the next century, as the globe continues to shrink, and as companies become more dependent on one another internationally, the winners will be those who are able to make the leap across cultural and language barriers.

One thing is for sure, says GM executive George Eads: "Geography is not destiny. A nation's political and social environment, as well as its attitudes about trade and development, is what constitutes destiny today." Nobuo Tanaka, director general of the Japanese Directorate for Science, Technology and Industry, pushes the envelope even further. "Corporate globalization is taking the trilateral interdependence to unprecedented heights and making it impossible to get an accurate picture of the whole in terms simply of the traditional concepts of competition among nations or blocs." Tanaka wonders what will happen when the interests of a global corporation cease to coincide with those of its home-based citizens. It is one thing to reap the rewards of sales and development abroad. It is another thing to sacrifice one's nationalism for the "third culture" of true internationalism.

Today, the old assumptions behind the desirability of being global have been challenged. In the past, companies like Volkswagen invested in foreign operations such as SEAT and Skoda as a way to offset high costs at home. But cheap labor doesn't stay cheap forever, and the new markets don't sit still. They demand more quality, the infusion of technology, and pay equity.

Frankfurt—September 1991

BACK TO THE FUTURE.

Six weeks before the world's auto industry would be assaulted by glitter in Tokyo, it was assaulted by "green" at Frankfurt's biennual auto show. In the Messegelände, the city's sprawling exhibition center, environmentalism, not horsepower or fancy features, dominated the show—a nod to Germany's thriving Green Movement.

Frankfurt's show was the largest in the world, and the Messegelände was a mammoth site, with nine buildings connected by moving sidewalks. Mercedes and Volkswagen each had their own separate buildings for the show. The event was so huge that it was an exhausting and nearly impossible task for anyone who tried to see everything.

Electric concept cars, somewhat hidden in Tokyo, were a prominent attraction here. Nissan's Future Electric Vehicle was a sleek luxury coupe with a range of 150 miles. Even BMW took the wraps off a luxury electric vehicle.

Volkswagen showed a hybrid car. The Chico, designed for city driving, allowed drivers to switch to gasoline when the battery pack became fully discharged. The car was cute, and the idea addressed the fact that batteries alone had a limited range in powering a commercially acceptable car.

Every company was vying for the title of safest, most environmentally sensitive car producer. Recycling was the big topic of discussion, and virtually every carmaker had a display panel that showed how cars could be taken apart and recycled.

What was said in Frankfurt didn't always reflect what was done back home, however. For example, there were contradictions in Germany's "green" profile, which masked its true love of high speeds and big engines. To this day, the auto industry argues that imposing a speed limit on the Autobahn would threaten jobs and sales. Even though high-speed rides on the Autobahn (during the hours when it is not stopped dead by traffic jams) cause about one thousand deaths a year and are culprits in high pollution, German carmakers fear that if the Autobahn had speed limits, their cars would lose the precious label of having enough muscle for the fastest roadways on earth.

The speed limit is a major topic of debate, with the Greens and Social Democrats favoring it and the conservative government fighting it. Not surprising, polls show a wide gap between men and women on this issue. Seventy percent of women favor an imposed speed limit, compared with 44 percent of men. Regardless, the huge controversy over speed limits shows that German manufacturers are not yet ready to be socially responsible if it is at the cost of engine power. The question in Germany is how to convert good intentions to action in a country of car lovers.

Companies like BMW, whose design and engineering departments have always emphasized high performance over fuel economy, are being pressured to shift their research and development priorities to the critical (albeit less glamorous) issues of environment and safety. They are being forced by consumers who are ever more vocal and who have little patience for the glamour kings of carmaking past.

Germany is often touted as a green country because people are so outspoken on the subject, and a political party has sprung from the movement. But household recycling hasn't even reached the levels found in America.

In some ways, Volkswagen sounds like a green company. Ulrich Seiffert, director of research and development, talks with boyish enthusiasm about the issue. He isn't gloomy about the prospect that the use of cars may decline in the next century. He says he wants VW to be at the forefront of environmental and safety research. However, Seiffert is quick to note that cars must also have power and performance to be acceptable. Ferdinand Piech seems even more committed to traditional German virtues.

To its credit, Volkswagen was the first carmaker to promise to recycle a car, the Golf. The announcement came just before the Frankfurt Show, when the new model would be debuted. VW was amazed when most other companies quickly agreed to do the same. Today, a VW pilot plant in Leer, Germany, dismantles old cars to study ways of assembling them to make recycling viable. Nevertheless, much of VW's environmentalism may be window dressing. And economic reality doesn't always square with environmental goals. In January 1993, burdened by financial problems, Ferdinand Piech abandoned VW's plans to produce the Chico. Piech was not known for his green consciousness. His vision of the future was jokingly dubbed *Sitzverkehr*—translated to mean "sitting in traffic." He proposed that being stuck in traffic jams could be an opportunity for drivers to get some much-needed private time.

In America Chrysler has tapped into the growing awareness of environmental and safety issues—promoting air bag installation and, recently, advertising the Dodge Intrepid as a recyclable car. In truth, the Intrepid may not be any more recyclable than its competitors, but Chrysler is the first American automaker to use the idea in its advertising.

General Motors has a long way to go before it is identified as socially responsible. "After twenty years of fighting CAFE [corporate average fuel economy] and clean air rules, I don't think anyone believes GM is a champion of the environment," says Joel Makower, editor and publisher of *The Green Consumer Letter* and *The Green Business Letter.*

It was General Motors that invented the catalytic converter to clean exhaust emissions, and GM that installed air bags in cars in the 1970s, long before Volvo, Mercedes, or Chrysler. But during the 1980s, GM's initiative declined. The company was criticized for canceling its electric car development program (the Impact) a year after the Frankfurt show. The cancellation itself was not necessarily a bad idea. The real problem was Roger Smith's reckless announcement years earlier that GM had discovered the secret of making a battery-powered car perform like one that ran on gasoline. He launched the Impact program several months before his retirement as chairman, and in typical starry-eyed fashion, promised that GM would assemble fifty thousand of the battery-powered cars by the mid-1990s. Like so many of Roger Smith's publicity gambits, this one faltered.

In many important ways, GM failed to sense emerging interest in environmental and safety issues, especially the latter. In the 1980s, when the government mandated air bags on cars, Roger Smith scoffed at the idea. He didn't believe that air bags would ever actually make it onto cars because of President Reagan's opposition. But he was wrong. He missed the point that consumer demand, not regulations, might drive the change. Chrysler stole the spotlight by quickly installing air bags in all of its cars. Lee Iacocca, who had earlier criticized the devices, cannily sensed that the time was right. Chrysler's television commercials provide a constant reminder of its leadership. The commercials feature ordinary citizens who were in Chrysler cars at the time of collisions, holding air bags and announcing, "I'm alive!" Meanwhile, in delaying air bag installation, GM cars through the 1993 model year were disadvantaged in the market, since most of its rivals offered them.

Under Jack Smith's leadership, GM has started to reevaluate its adversarial approach to issues of social concern. "GM has always been a company reluctant to face up to social issues," admits executive vice-president Harry Pearce. "We need to do a better job of telling customers what we are doing, and we need to be more sensitive to these issues. We usually appear far too defensive.

"You're going to see a different attitude in this company about the environment," he promised. "From now on, the environmental and safety people have to be an integral part of the product development program. You can't impose it. It has to be part of the vehicle design process."

Harry Pearce is a good example of the new breed of GM executive. He received public notice in February 1993 when he played the role of detective in uncovering a fraudulent NBC *Dateline* story on the safety of GM pickup trucks. Pearce's aggressive pursuit of the truth in this incident makes for a telling case of new vs. old at GM. Since the early days of Ralph Nader, General Motors has fought the image of being a huge, irresponsible corporate giant that didn't care whether its cars were safe. The GM full-size pickup truck seemed just another example of the company putting a vehicle into public hands that it knew to be unsafe—in this case, because of the location of the fuel tank on the side of the truck.

The *Dateline* report was spurred by a lawsuit against GM by the parents of an Atlanta teenager who was killed when the pickup truck exploded when it was hit by a speeding drunk driver. *Dateline*'s report featured a test that showed a fire after a side collision. The conclusion was that the fuel tank punctured upon impact, and the gushing fuel ignited and caused an explosion.

When first aired, the report was a severely damaging indictment of GM. But tipped off that NBC might have staged the tests, Harry Pearce led an investigation, employing all the tenacity and thoroughness of TV detective Columbo. His findings were revealed in a dramatic press conference where he showed conclusively that NBC had fitted rockets underneath the pickup truck that were detonated by remote control; that the fuel spillage was caused by a poorly fit gas cap (which was not the truck's original cap) and an overly full gas tank; and that the fuel tank used in the crash showed no sign of having been punctured.

GM threatened to sue. Backed into a corner, *Dateline* issued an unprecedented televised apology, admitting to every one of Harry Pearce's findings. It was a grand victory for General Motors, which for so long had been on the losing side of such disputes. Two weeks later, when Michael G. Gartner, president of NBC News, announced his resignation, the press widely concluded that the GM debacle had brought him down.

Harry Pearce was teaching GM to respond carefully and with the dignity that would be expected of a large public company. He was proud of the success of his investigation and said it had a galvanizing effect on the staff. "It was a vindication," he said. But GM still faced hard questions about the viability of the pickup truck. Later, the government would ask for a voluntary recall after GM lost the suit in Atlanta. But the point was made: Henceforth, GM would address safety issues with a new seriousness, but the press and consumer advocates had to play fair. This event demonstrated GM's new awareness that public perception was based, not only on a company's product quality, but also on the values and honesty of the company itself.

In spite of its often stated environmental and safety goals, Toyota is a follower, not a leader—although it makes up for it with rapid reforms when it is challenged. For example, cars sold in the United States all have air bags, and the Lexus LS 400 is the only luxury car that does not pay a gas-guzzler tax.

A contributing factor to the sluggishness of Toyota's response has been Japan's lack of a consumer movement. This is the way change is often forced in Western countries. As Shigeo Ohki, a rare Japanese activist, puts it, "In American western movies, ordinary citizens sometimes help catch the bad guys, but in Japanese movies, people stay at home and wait for instructions from the authorities."

A 1989 survey conducted by the United Nations Environmental Program ranked Japan last among fourteen nations in environmental concerns and awareness. One need only visit the island's garbage-filled beaches and hiking trails to know that Japan is a long way from cleaning up its act.

Japanese attitudes toward endangered species are symptomatic of its overall lack of interest in global social responsibility. Whale meat, ivory, turtle shell combs, and other products that are illegal in Western countries are freely sold in Japanese stores. But lest the West grow smug and moralistic, a reminder is warranted: Socially responsible companies never become that way because they are more righteous or altruistic than others. Environmental and safety issues in the future will be driven (as they have always been in the past) by financial self-interest. At what point will it be profitable for carmakers to be socially responsible? Maybe the time is here. A recent Gallup poll showed that 87 percent of car purchasers agreed they would be willing to spend more money for cleaner, safer cars. Yet, so far this is the bottom line: Environmentalism will be spurred by consumer demand. And in spite of what people tell pollsters, there is no real evidence that the public, at least in America, is willing to go the distance. Little value is placed on high fuel economy. For example, Americans buy record numbers of low-mileage trucks for personal use. Part of the industry's resistance to taking the leadership on social issues is the valid concern that they not get too far ahead of the public that buys their vehicles.

As these grave matters press in on the world's carmakers, management guru Peter Drucker warns that there is no time to waste. "We are already in the new century," he says, "a century that is fundamentally different from the one we still assume we live in. Almost everyone has a sense of deep unease with prevailing political and economic policies, whether in the United States or Japan or West Germany or England or Eastern Europe. Things somehow don't fit, and there is a clear sign that while we don't yet see the new [era], we know the old one is no longer right, no longer congruent."

Indeed, the pressures of strangled highways, a shrinking globe, and social responsibility are very different from previous imperatives that faced automakers during more innocent times. Sometimes it might seem preferable to the leaders who must cope with these issues to rise above the crunch altogether. Settling into his new president's chair, Tatsuro Toyoda voiced a wistful desire that technology might yet solve the problem. When asked what he dreamed about, he replied (perhaps thinking of the heavily traveled highways of Japan), "I would like to build a vehicle that rides not on the road, but above the road."

TEN

The 21st-Century Car Company

The work of creating goes on.

—Alfred P. Sloan

New York City—February 1993

"WHICH IS THE BEST CAR COMPANY in the world?" People
often ask me this question. Depending on who's asking, they
mean different things by "best"—sheer size, quality of cars, number of different models, financial status, investment potential,
competitive position, and so on. We are conditioned to view corporate competition as a form of war in which there are clear
winners and losers. It's not quite that simple.

Such questions usually get me thinking about how volatile the
car business has been throughout its history, especially during the
last few years, and how rapidly things can change. When I started
writing this book, I couldn't have predicted that Bob Stempel
would resign after receiving a statement of no-confidence from
the GM board of directors, or that the presidency would be
turned over to an unconventional executive like Jack Smith. Nor
could I have predicted that an outside director, John Smale,
would become chairman. Or that Inaki Lopez, GM's maverick
purchasing head, would become a car magazine cover boy and

make the driest division in carmaking a place of high drama. Carl Hahn's forced resignation was equally unexpected. A year and a half ago, Hahn was on top of the world—a highly visible and strong executive, sitting at the head of Europe's largest car company. His contract had been extended through 1993, and he was praised for his managerial daring. He didn't seem like a man about to be toppled from his pedestal. His final months on the job were a virtual repudiation of his tenure, as data spilled out detailing VW's sorry financial condition. Ferdinand Piech did not spare his outgoing predecessor public blame. In Toyota's case, I knew that Shoichiro Toyoda would one day select a new president and move into the chairman's seat, but the change didn't seem imminent—if for no other reason than that there was no ready successor. And in view of Japan's economic turmoil, Shoichiro's leadership seemed a requirement if his company would retain its dominance on the world scene during this rocky period.

Viewed as a whole, it is remarkable that in the space of a single year, there was an upheaval at the top of each company that spread through the ranks. It was the kind of year that could be humbling for us analysts and forecasters—a reminder that assumptions are always subject to challenge, and the business is always full of surprises. It provided a lesson for all leaders of large companies that they could be victims of change as well as architects of change.

"So," people ask me, "which carmaker is the winner of the global showdown? Who's number one?"

I rephrase the question because this really isn't a war in the traditional sense. The real question is: Which company is in the best position to be a leader in the new international age we have already entered? For that, I have an answer.

It doesn't necessarily have to be the largest. Large doesn't automatically equal leader. GM learned that lesson long ago when it was crippled by the slingshot hits of smaller, scrappier companies from Europe and Japan. In terms of innovation and leadership, history shows that the period between 1920 and 1955 belonged to GM. From 1955 to 1970 Volkswagen was the company that took center stage, as the first to challenge the American Big Three on their own turf. And from 1970 to 1990 Toyota led the pack. Since then, the industry has been in a holding pattern as companies grapple with unexpected challenges of size, economic recessions, social imperatives, and competition.

Today, each of these companies is the largest in its home market. For the first time in recent memory all three companies are simultaneously convulsing from self-induced traumas. Each suffers from similar problems related to its sheer size and complexity. And each faces a crisis at the core of its organization that is uniquely defined by its nationality and corporate culture.

History teaches that it often takes a crisis to jolt a company's management into reality and bring about a needed transformation. Chrysler is a good example of this, having twice in one decade nearly gone out of business, only to emerge in 1992 as a solid competitor. Although Chrysler does not have GM's size or international influence, it has taken the leadership in some important areas. In particular, Chrysler has transformed itself completely. It understood that short-term corrective actions (which had rescued it in the past) were not enough. The people at Chrysler made fundamental operational changes. At the same time, Chrysler pulled off a series of market successes with new cars and trucks, which gave consumers the safety features they wanted, as well as the style, performance, and functionality they wouldn't sacrifice. But history has shown even with Chrysler that a company in crisis is actually easier to manage than one in a period of great prosperity.

Each of our Global Big Three is now in crisis, thus opening the way for both the greatest potential for change and the greatest danger of miscalculation.

Looking ahead to the next century, I use four criteria to evaluate the potential of the Global Big Three. These criteria won't be found in the financial statements, but in the underlying cultures of every company. They are:

1. Awareness of Problems
2. Strong Company Vision
3. Adaptability to Circumstances
4. Understanding the Product and the Consumer

Awareness of Problems

Everyone is familiar with the first step in all self-help approaches: Admit you have a problem. This sounds obvious. If your life or your company is falling apart, clearly you have a problem, right? Remarkably, many people deny it even in the face of overwhelming evidence. Recently, I was reading an interview with Roger Smith, and I marveled at how unaware he was of his central role in the near demise of General Motors. He still doesn't understand why the board of directors decided it must take drastic action. Bob Stempel has the same blind spot. He blames the media and meddling outsiders for his ouster, just as he blamed the recession and the Japanese for GM's sinking profits and market share. Bob Stempel is an honorable and direct person, but he is not known for taking decisive action. Perhaps it was these traits that prevented him from fingering the men in his organization who were responsible for the company's decline.

While it is true that companies are affected by external circumstances, managements must look inside to understand how they absorb and respond to the buffeting of economic and competitive challenges they can't control. It is ludicrous to blame the competition for one's own failures. Consider: Was IBM sidetracked by the competition? Of course. Is the reason for IBM's problems the competition? No. The reason IBM is in trouble is that it squandered its leadership position, just as GM did, and stopped paying attention to the market. It rested on its laurels during a time of unprecedented opportunity. In IBM's case, technology advanced to make computers as common as cars, while the company clung to old paradigms that dictated a commitment to mainframe computers. In GM's case, the competition overwhelmed the company with better and cheaper cars, made by organizations that treated time, money, and personnel like the precious commodities that they are.

The notable thing about General Motors (like all companies that survive a crisis) is that it has admitted it has a problem. The action of the board of directors was revolutionary because it went beyond hiring and firing, or merely replacing one failed leader with another. It initiated a process of true change. Making an outside director chairman and choosing a president and CEO who was not a loyalist to the old order sent a clear signal that the board meant business. The activism of GM's board was so exceptional that it has had a domino effect on the behavior of other major companies. In the months that followed, IBM, American Express, Sears, Westinghouse, and others felt the sting of demands for reform.

Although GM admitted that it has a problem, it remains to be seen whether it will rise to the challenge, which is nothing less than the complete remaking of the company. GM has many technical strengths, such as low-cost antilock brakes, good engines, and very good engine management systems and electronics. Among the domestic producers, it currently has the best initial quality rating—from 7.8 defects per car in 1982 to 1.4 defects per car in 1992. It does more safety research than any other auto company and shares its findings with its competitors.

But GM struggles to translate its strengths into a cohesive product program that responds to the market. It has too many car lines with too much overlap, yet in many segments of the market it doesn't even have competitive models—in particular, midsize cars and minivans. It hasn't fully understood how or why trucks appeal to former car owners—in part because, as a senior GM executive said, "The previous management seemed to hate trucks." Furthermore, its position as a high-cost producer will require it to rethink every aspect of how a vehicle is designed, manufactured, assembled, and marketed.

So, while GM has taken a giant step toward facing its problems, it has yet to demonstrate a thorough grasp of their scope.

Toyota's change of leadership was not linked to a change in company direction. Tatsuro Toyoda became president in spite of the company's problems, not because of them.

Toyota's problems are linked to the profound changes taking place in Japan, and they go to the heart of key cultural issues. Japan's economic upheaval is undermining its traditional industrial and economic policies, which depended on a strong group mentality among individual businesses, and assured that the strongest members would not annihilate the weak.

Toyota (and the entire Japanese auto industry, for that matter) succeeded in dominating foreign markets by understanding what Western consumers wanted and giving it to them at lower prices than the Western competition. Administrative guidance from MITI and policies that fostered international expansion enabled the entire industry to grow, although Toyota was superior in every way to its Japanese rivals. While many Japanese auto companies focused on exports, Toyota was satisfied that gradual development of foreign markets, combined with dominance in Japan, suited its risk-adverse temperament and maximized the use of its resources while generating huge amounts of surplus cash. Meanwhile, its dominance of the home market forced other Japanese companies to seek growth opportunities outside of Japan, because they knew there was no way to compete with Toyota at home.

But now the Japanese auto industry faces secular and structural upheaval at home and abroad and can no longer rely on offshore growth in traditional export markets to compensate for lack of growth in Japan. Quotas on more competitive cars in the United States and Europe, along with the postwar high valuation of the yen, has cut off the avenues for profit for several of Japan's weaker manufacturers who lack the resources to shift production overseas.

The crisis in the Japanese auto industry presents Toyota with a unique cultural dilemma: Does it choose to be independent (anathema to the Japanese way) and maximize its opportunities at the expense of others in the Japanese auto industry? Surely, a company with $14 billion or more in cash and a formidable lineup of cars for every buyer could easily take sales away from its less-able rivals. Or does it participate in the traditional Japanese industrial and economic practice whose mandate is group responsibility, with strong companies making a place for the weak?

There is great pressure on Toyota to choose the latter course. Its aggressive pursuit of growth and market share has been publicly criticized by its rivals, especially Nissan, and the Japanese auto industry blames Toyota for the trade friction with the United States and Europe. Although *kyosei* has been portrayed as a policy in which Japanese industry learns to live in harmony with its foreign competitors, its true effect may be to curb strong companies like Toyota so other Japanese automakers can survive. If Toyota pulls back from its goal of Global 10 (10 percent of the world market), the ultimate beneficiaries will be Mazda, Honda, Nissan, and others.

It must be said that Toyota's problems are not of the depth and severity of GM's. Jack Smith would love to have Toyota's problems: two decades of steady growth, high-quality cars, and a foot in important doors around the world. But Toyota is not immune to "big company disease," that creeping ailment that stops winning enterprises in their tracks.

Ironically, if Shoichiro Toyoda becomes head of Keidanren, the powerful policy body of Japanese business, as he might next year, it could make things tougher for Toyota. Always independent from the main forces of Japanese business, it might at last be led into a position of interdependent partnership with other Japanese carmakers. This could further slow the process of growth and change. Even if Shoichiro fails to become chairman of Keidanren, Toyota has already been drawn into a vortex of complaints that have made it the scapegoat for Japan's trade problems with the United States, among other things.

It's no secret that VW is a high-cost, noncompetitive producer of too limited a range of cars to appeal to a diverse international market. In Germany and in several other countries, VW has succeeded with its strategy of infrequent updates of the Golf and a reputation for mechanical excellence that has enabled it to charge more for its cars than the competition.

But the world is changing and VW can no longer ignore the reality that what worked to date no longer works, and it has to change. Its break-even point essentially equals its capacity, costs have soared, and there are limits to how much more consumers are willing to pay for a Golf. The answer is to reduce costs and launch a wider variety of models at more frequent intervals, but this is hardly a simple goal to accomplish—especially since this rigid, bureaucratized company has only begun to digest the fact that it's in trouble.

Any attempt to address VW's core problems will confront the

basic tenets upon which labor and management have coexisted in Germany since the end of World War II. Car production does not require a work force that has gone through three years of apprenticeship and has mastered all aspects of engine technology. While this training has always been cited as one of the German car industry's great strategic advantages, it may now be more of an impediment because of the compensation expectations of such a highly trained work force. After all, high quality cars are being produced in Mexico, Korea, India, and throughout the developing world by competent workers who have learned the production methods developed in the industrialized countries. Superior automotive manufacturing technology is no longer confined to a few companies. The first challenge to VW is to transform its mentality.

VW must also find a way to shed workers as it raises productivity to at least the level of Opel in Germany. Volkswagen's suppliers suffer from similar problems and could be left behind if the company actually seeks less expensive parts and components from suppliers outside of Germany. This will be a painful transition for VW and for all of Germany, for it comes at a time when the nation is already reeling from the costs of reunification. To simultaneously discover that the nation and its premier industrial companies have to go through a major restructuring that overturns the very precepts on which they have built industrial might and a comfortable standard of living is convulsive for the country and its workers.

When I was interviewing Volkswagen executives for this book, I was unable to draw from their remarks any clear, compelling statement of purpose. And I was disturbed by the company's tendency to use an avoidance strategy when asked about its problems. It didn't seem to unnerve Carl Hahn, during the final years of his term, that thousands of unfinished Golfs were piling up on the lawn outside his office and in every other spare corner of the complex. Everyone in the company seems afraid to acknowledge the fact that Halle 54, VW's main assembly plant, is a disaster. Its inflexible (called hard) automation cannot produce anything but a car the size and shape of a Golf. VW is still producing one model while the world turns to more variety, not less.

Furthermore, no one seems willing to topple the sacred cow of Germany's overpaid, underproductive work force. Carl Hahn's failed policy attempted to reduce VW's average wage cost by acquiring companies in nations where labor was cheaper. Each investment was accompanied by a promise that no jobs would be sacrificed in Germany. But Hahn unwittingly nearly sacrificed the entire company because he would not (or could not) force the discipline demanded by reality. On the surface, he perpetuated the myth of German superiority while doing his utmost to diversify away from Germany. Piech's problems are national—and they are faced by every German carmaker, although none with the same urgency. For Piech to succeed, he must convince his work force that they cannot work four or five hundred hours a year less than American workers or seven hundred hours less than the Japanese and expect to survive. The health of the company depends on their cooperation in improving productivity—and that means lower employment. Although Piech is now admitting that his company has a problem, the question remains: Will he be able to convince everyone of its urgency and their role in its solution?

Strong Company Vision

"Visionary" is one of those terms that have been so overused that they have lost any real meaning. "Visionary" has come to be equated with "bold," even though boldness is certainly not always visionary. For example, VW's takeover of Skoda was bold, but was it visionary? GM's decision to close plants was bold, but was it visionary? Being visionary doesn't necessarily mean being different. There are plenty of eccentrics in the world who could hardly be called visionary. Nor does it mean being controversial. To the contrary, it might mean being invisible, as Toyota's management has attempted to be.

A strong company vision implies an understanding of why its organization and products are important and desirable, and an ability to predict how they might have to change in the future.

A visionary leader has many diverse characteristics, but I think the defining ones are: lack of personal fear (the kind of fear that makes keeping your job the number one priority); willingness to seek advice and listen; openness to new approaches; and, finally, the ability to articulate a reasonable long-range plan for the company and operate consistently within that plan. Visionary leaders are not afraid to tackle problems and even implement unpopular decisions at the risk of their personal appeal; they're almost never at the whim of group-think, which has stifled much individuality and creativity in Japanese companies.

Jack Smith is a very down-to-earth guy, a hard worker and a shrewd thinker. Over the years, he has grown into every pair of oversize shoes he put on. He has many of the qualities that make a strong leader, including a practical action plan, an intense interest in getting feedback from a wide range of sources, and a dislike of political game-playing. He would get downright cranky if people wasted his time with issues like who should get which office, or petty internal politics. He is not an elitist. He is a worker who prefers casual clothes to business suits and a spartan office at the center of action to a remote suite on the Fourteenth Floor. Smith can look boyish, with his wide grin and the shock of hair that sometimes falls across his eyes. But although he laughs easily, everyone knows he's bulldog-tough.

He's also very human—as we must remember all leaders are. Not all of his personnel decisions have been praised. Although he wasn't a part of the old-boy network that spawned Stempel and Reuss, he had built a network of his own loyalists, and some critics will say that not all of these men are the best suited for their positions. Nevertheless, Smith's main team has shown itself to be open-minded and impressive. Lou Hughes, who directs GM's international operations, is a remarkable and diverse executive who was always kept in finance positions before Jack Smith gave him the chance to run Opel. Hughes responded to the challenge by learning German and endearing himself to his host country by conducting all of his meetings in the native language. Bill Hoglund, whose reputation of "troublemaker" evolved during the Roger Smith era when that meant occasionally speaking up, quickly became an invaluable jack-of-all-trades for the company. Unconcerned with a title, he has served as Jack Smith's troubleshooter in a wide range of areas. As he demonstrated during the

Dateline fracas, Harry Pearce is an unconventional executive. Smart, dedicated, and media-savvy, Pearce disdains bureaucracy. He refused his title, saying that the last thing GM needed was another layer of management.

But although his personal qualities and the quality of his team are important, what gives Smith his greatest strength is the fact that he is the chosen one. He has been empowered by the board of directors to make fundamental change. GM's board may have no insight about what the future holds, but they have acknowledged that the old ways have failed. Now that they've set a course in motion, General Motors will never return to the way it was.

But the loose mandate to change is not enough. Jack Smith must hold people accountable for their performance in making the needed changes—not so easy given the traditions of General Motors. This can no longer be the old GM, where people were promoted in spite of their failures—or where they quickly moved up the ladder and left the fallout of their mistakes to their unfortunate successors. Managers have to act like managers and expect to be rewarded or penalized based on performance. It is Jack Smith's job to create a company where success or failure can be easily measured against clear goals. He must avoid the paralyzing trap of indecision that has long allowed decision making to get bogged down in a maze of committees and bureaucratic tie-ups.

People have differing opinions about Tatsuro Toyoda, but no one would yet call him a visionary leader. In spite of his denials, everyone believes that Tatsuro was made president because he is Shoichiro's brother. Eiji and Shoichiro were both members of the founding family who happened to be strong leaders in their own right. The same may not be true of Tatsuro, and Toyota could suffer as a result—unless Shoichiro and the executive vice-presidents remain a strong presence, or Tatsuro surprises his critics and grows quickly into his role.

We have to examine whether there is an element of visionary leadership in the company as a whole, however. Eiji was and is a visionary, but he is past eighty years old and his influence is waning. Shoichiro is a pragmatist who has been a strong leader during the past twelve years, although he has been unable to prevent the spread of "big company disease." Indeed, he may have unwittingly fostered it by virtue of the less communal style of his presidency. But Shoichiro's attention may be elsewhere as he involves himself more in Japanese business circles and spends less time in Toyota City. There are certainly other strong executives within the company, but the very system discourages any individual from standing out. Shoichiro was a lone wolf who never served as a mentor to any of Toyota's promising executives.

Toyota is facing an inevitable leadership crisis that will occur when its revered patriarch, Eiji Toyoda, passes away. There is a consistent historical precedent for companies undergoing periods of chaos following the death of their founders. General Motors experienced something like it after Alfred Sloan died. Although he was not, strictly speaking, the founder, he was by every measure GM's first corporate leader. As long as he was alive, all those around him abided by his philosophies. It was only after Sloan's death that the company began to flounder.

Eiji's influence is still very great, and he may live another ten years or more. But his death, when it comes, will signal the end of an era for Toyota. Who will carry the leadership torch? It is doubtful it will be Tatsuro. Eventually, Toyota will turn its management over to non–family members.

Typically, companies experience temporary confusion, internal power struggles, and a loss of momentum as bureaucracies take over to replace the intuitive genius of the men who brought them to prominence. What is extraordinary about Japan is that so many companies now find themselves in this position—as Toyota surely will in the foreseeable future.

A consultant for Volkswagen recently told me, "Everyone always said that Carl Hahn was a visionary because of SEAT and Skoda. But Hahn was not a visionary, he was an opportunist. There's a difference." This man's evaluation cuts to the heart of the problem VW has always had with its leadership. Consider the difference between VW's success in America and Toyota's. When Nordhoff decided to market Beetles in the United States, it was not because he saw a need. He didn't really understand American consumers. Selling overseas suited his simplistic goal of producing more and more Beetles. And selling in the United States signaled international status. The dealers in America initially responded, "You must be kidding!" when they saw the Beetle. Its eventual popularity was the outcome of a serendipitous social shift and an imaginative marketing strategy. But VW never devised a feasible plan beyond selling more and more of a single model, whether it was the Beetle or its successor, the Rabbit. Once the Japanese came along with better and cheaper cars, VW was left holding 100,000 unsold Rabbits, with no idea why it couldn't sell them. On the other hand, Eiji Toyoda had a vision, carefully devised, after long study. Toyota's success in the U.S. market wasn't a fluke, and the company learned from its early mistakes.

In some respects, Ferdinand Piech seemed to be just what Volkswagen needed to shake it out of its lethargy. But he has gotten off to a rocky start. He is not a beloved leader. Unlike Jack Smith, who solicits consensus among a trusted circle and is himself likable and accessible, Piech has a brusque personality and a tendency to micromanage. A company in turmoil is fragile, and leadership is the key to whether the turmoil is used constructively or destructively.

Corporations need to articulate simple, understandable goals and values to their employees. In recent years some companies have been caught up in the touchy-feely wave of corporate vision statements that has ultimately achieved nothing. For example, GM's corporate vision statement, prepared by Lloyd Reuss, consisted of a giant triangle, with more than twenty subgoals leading to the top goal of building better cars and trucks. It was so clumsy and contrived that it served as neither a guide nor a motivation for behavior.

A vision has to be comprehensible to everyone, and it has to be achievable. It also has to stretch the organization toward a long-term goal. The most important part of a vision is not the objective itself, but how the company uses its resources (human and material) to accomplish it. Is there a consistency of purpose in the operations? Are investments directed toward that purpose? A vision loses its meaning when it is not supported by action.

Every company ought to have as its basic purpose to produce great cars and trucks, but the vision should inspire everyone to reach for something that transforms the company—that allows it to reach its goals and see beyond them.

GM's vision should be to strive toward a philosophy of serving the customer. If this is accomplished, all else will follow—lower costs, better quality, and more appealing vehicles.

Toyota's vision should be to become truly international by infusing its organization with the people, thinking, ideas, flexibility, and sensitivity that enable it to be the good citizen it claims it wants to be.

Volkswagen has never learned to develop and use its resources effectively, and that ought to be the foundation for creating a future vision. To achieve this, it will need to open its eyes to the world and begin to learn from other companies and customers in the many markets it serves.

Adaptability to Circumstances

Every great company must first be a student of the successes and failures of others. General Motors never had that chance. It was always the teacher, or at least saw itself in that role. And the stronger it grew, the more resistant it became to listening and learning. In its arrogance, it believed that customers should adapt their needs to the cars it was building, rather than the other way around. Unfortunately, although Roger Smith realized that GM had to adapt to accommodate a changing market, he had no idea how to go about making that change, and his policies made the paralysis worse. Throughout the 1980s he jumped from one false solution to another. First it was automation. Then it was corporate reorganization, which added to the chaos. Then it was diversification into nonautomotive businesses like EDS and Hughes, as well as National Car Rental, which alone cost GM more than $700 million in 1992. Meanwhile, the company became the high-cost producer of vehicles that did not match the style and standards being set by the competition. Ford, Chrysler, Renault, Peugeot, and others demonstrated that companies can be turned around in three to five years once they realize that the alternative is failure. GM-Europe itself had been a candidate for oblivion until the right people turned the company around before it was too late. Although GM was the first international car company, with acquisitions in Germany, Britain, and Australia, and even decent export sales to Japan, in the 1920s, it didn't develop its international operations very effectively. They became a repository for executives who stayed overseas throughout their careers and never passed on their knowledge to the greater company. Many of them abused their positions, pursuing all the opulent trappings that went with belonging to the world's richest automaker. One GM executive even rented a castle as his official residence in Europe! It took a crisis in the late 1970s for GM-Europe to decide what it had to do to be a serious contender there.

The Japanese have always been attentive students. Many of the early industrial advances were based upon improving things they learned from others. Kiichiro Toyoda's first engine design was based on a Chevrolet. His ideas about mass motorization came from Ferdinand Porsche. People in American companies during the 1960s used to laugh when groups of Japanese visitors descended on manufacturing plants with their cameras and notebooks, voraciously absorbing details and taking photographs of everything including the exit signs. The Japanese hardly looked threatening in their polite, attentive little groups. But then they went back home and built better factories, equipment, systems, and cars.

In more recent times it has been fascinating to watch Toyota's transplant operations in America learn to confront challenges that are quite different from the ones they encounter at home. With both NUMMI and Kentucky, they've been successful.

While Toyota has paid lip service to *kyosei,* it is also a product of an ethnocentric culture whose fundamental premise is that its way is the only way. So far, it has not become truly international, in the embracing style of Americans. This is most evident in the executive structures of its transplants in the United States and Great Britain. As long as Toyota is in the position to teach its way to others, it operates well. But it seems unable to accept the idea that Westerners are capable of grasping the subtleties of their management philosophy and organizational philosophies. Toyota's international problems are gravely complicated by the

new choice it faces: international independence or national cooperation. Currently, it is trying to straddle a middle ground. On
one hand, there is evidence that it is striking out on an independent course. It has vastly expanded its network of parts and component plants in the Asia-Pacific region, and seems determined to
maintain or increase its share in those markets where it is established. It has not lost share in Japan or the United States, and has
gained share in Europe. Nor has it yet given in to the demand
among its domestic rivals that it raise prices in Japan and
lengthen product cycles to give others a fighting chance.

On the other hand, Toyota has bowed to pressure to bear the
brunt of Japan's pledge to America to sell more of its cars. It
recently signed a promise with General Motors to begin marketing GM-made passenger cars in Japan under the Toyota name in
1996. In doing so, it bailed out the rest of Japan's auto industry,
which did not have the means to keep the promise. Since this
action does not benefit Toyota, it is clearly a sign that the company is going along with national policies at its own expense.

For most of its history, Volkswagen has spun in its own narrow
orbit. Of the three companies, it may be the least adaptable to
change. The best example is that for twenty-five years it essentially built the same car. And although the Beetle is no longer
manufactured (except in Mexico), VW has replaced it with essentially one other car—the Golf (in its four versions). When its cars
fail to sell, VW doesn't examine the market or the models. It
places blame. Recently, a VW executive rationalized why the
Golf 3 hasn't sold in America. He said it was because it was too
sophisticated for Americans. In effect, he was blaming Americans
for not wanting the car, instead of trying to determine what kind
of car they wanted.

An internationally minded company understands that it is
linked more than peripherally to other corporations around the
world. It has the ability to be multicultural—giving and gaining
strength from its international partners. When it moves into foreign markets, it bends to the social character of those markets,
even as it adds its own uniqueness to the mix. This characteristic
is not company-specific, but nation-specific. In their global atti-

tudes and behaviors, companies are mostly shaped by the underlying attitudes and behaviors of the nations to which they belong.

There is no question that among the three cultures, Americans
are more at ease internationally, because, as a people, they are
fundamentally more flexible. Most Americans have a heritage
from another part of the world. American society is diverse and
its people are therefore more accepting of diversity. The "ugly
American" of the 1950s has been replaced by the student of differences.

Even though we have racial and cultural prejudices in America,
they are not a basic part of our self-understanding—and, by and
large, they are frowned upon. Americans try to take other cultures seriously; even the current wave of Japan-bashing is a sign
of respect for Japanese prowess. With all its problems, America
has demonstrated that it has the potential to be anyone's partner
or investor anywhere in the world.

Japan and Germany both suffer from cultural myopia and an
elitism that often stand in their way when they leave home. Because their national identities are monocultural, they struggle
with being internationally minded. Neither country is tolerant of
foreigners who live in their countries. When the Japanese go elsewhere they remain distant from local cultures and the mainstream of life.

These tendencies may, in part, be generational. As the world
grows smaller and young people have more experience with diverse cultures, acceptance will almost certainly grow. But how
long will it take? In Japan racial superiority is still taught to children in the schools. In Germany the skinhead youth are trying to
revive the ugliest chapter of that nation's history.

Understanding the Product and the Consumer

It is fundamental to understand the function of the product that
the company builds and sells, but it is also in this most basic area
that companies most often stumble. What does it mean to understand the product? It means to know what it does for the person
who purchases it. To understand how it is used by the consumer.
To be aware of the role it plays in society. To see its potential for

fulfilling a variety of needs. To know when it no longer works and has to be changed.

Products don't exist in a vacuum. They only exist in relationship to a perceived need or desire. Alfred Sloan understood this when he created the pyramid of models and defined the market for each one. He realized that while all cars provided transportation, they also fulfilled important secondary functions.

In its lifetime, the automobile has gone through several reincarnations. The first was the invention and development stage when speed, power, style, and size were the focus. The second reincarnation concerned itself with efficiency and quality. And the third, with safety and environmental appropriateness. With each new stage, the old emphasis has either become obsolete (like the lumbering land yachts of the 1950s) or been incorporated into the new wave.

Today, the role of the automobile in society is being challenged. There are too many cars on the roads, the infrastructure of our major cities throughout the world is crumbling, our air quality is declining. In light of these realities, carmakers must once again ask: What is the next reincarnation?

The Global Big Three struggle equally with this next challenge. There is no clear answer. All of them are taking baby steps into a new period, but the road signs are still not visible.

Of the three companies, General Motors is at this point in time best poised to be a strong, dynamic twenty-first-century company. That isn't because it is "better" than the other two. In many ways, it's in worse shape than both Toyota and Volkswagen. But the striking difference, the one thing that makes GM stand out, is that it experienced a near-fatal crisis that shocked every fiber of its corporate being, and it is using that crisis to transform itself. As a result, it is a different company today than it was a year ago.

History demonstrates that every great institution fails—whether it's the Roman Empire or the Communist State or General Motors. It seems to be the human condition that greatness leads to complacency. The early fluidity that accompanies creation and growth solidifies and becomes cemented in place. The passion for change is replaced with an equally fierce passion for the status quo, even when all the evidence is screaming that the world has changed. The examples of this malaise are all around us. Consider: What were the executives at Sears doing while consumers were flocking to malls, or ordering products from dozens of specialty catalogs, or watching the Home Shopping Network? What prevented the creative minds at IBM from imagining a time when computers would be a fact of life in every home, and when consumers would demand that they be portable?

Why didn't someone at American Express figure out that prestige loses its magic when every college kid in America has access to the card?

What happens to successful companies that makes them stop growing?

There are a dozen explanations, but the real answer is, we don't know why. We just know it happens. Big company disease.

I would suggest that if successful companies are doomed to stagnate, it stands to reason that companies in crisis have the best chance of getting better. But they have to know they're in crisis. There has to be urgency and courage to change.

Looking back over the past thirty years of GM's history, it's easy to trace the point when the company stopped adapting. It was around the time when Charlie Wilson was telling the world that what was good for the country was good for General Motors and vice versa. That might have sounded a warning bell if we'd been thinking about it. But how do you tell the greatest, richest, most successful company in the world that it better start changing or it will perish? You'd get laughed right out of the building.

The process of decline at General Motors might have been the precursor to its revival. What else but an indisputable, irreversible calamity could have jolted the board of directors from its long slumber and propelled them to act in such a daring, unprecedented way? Back in the mid-1980s, when Ross Perot was heaving hand grenades into the GM boardroom, everyone thought he was just a crazy troublemaker. They paid him $700 million just to leave them alone. Things hadn't deteriorated to the point where they were worried. It took six more years of declining profits and market share to wake them up. And as a result of this fresh infusion of energy and urgency, General Motors might again turn out to be the leading car company in the world.

Unlike the other two companies, GM is very much in control of its destiny. There is no government control to worry about, and labor in the United States is more malleable to change than in either Germany or Japan. There is an acceptance within the company that times are different. All GM has to do, more complex than it sounds, is to use its resources (people, technology, and factories) to create cars and trucks that customers want to buy. The question is, are there enough leaders down through the ranks of the company to persuade middle managers that they must change? It is easy to improve profits by forcing suppliers to cut prices, as Lopez did. It is harder to alter how people relate to each other within a vast organization to make the entirety function more effectively.

To say that GM is in the best position to succeed is not to say that Toyota and Volkswagen don't have challenges that are capable of transforming them. Toyota has the most complex situation because it is standing in much the same place GM was thirty years ago. It knows how to be successful. The question is: Does it know how to function in a less secure environment? And can it balance the corporate objectives with the social imperatives thrust upon it by a struggling Japanese auto industry?

Toyota has a history of independence and tenacity. When it needed to create something totally different from the Henry Ford system, it did. Can it adapt now? Can it both prosper and cooperate within the Japanese system? Can a company whose culture is grounded in isolation step outside its protected circle and become an equal partner with other international companies?

Volkswagen has the wealth, organization, and stature to be great, but it has a different challenge than the other two companies. Its main problems may not be solvable inside the company; they are endemic to the social structure. I have no doubt that Ferdinand Piech can make some changes and cut some costs. But as he travels down the road to lean manufacturing, he's going to have to confront the very structure of his company's governing body, which represents so many different groups that it seems incapable of reaching a consensus about what is good for the company.

Unless Piech and his governing board begin to address the totality of Volkswagen's problems, and not just the symptoms, the company will continue to limp along until their crisis becomes a matter of life and death.

So when people ask me, "Which is the best car company in the world?" I am compelled to answer, "The one that has most recently overcome great problems." Right now, that company is GM. Beyond that, there is one other fact that has been true of this industry since its beginning. That is, time and again, single individuals have made explosive differences, even when nobody expected it. We might keep in mind as we watch events unfold around Jack Smith, Tatsuro Toyoda, and Ferdinand Piech that in the course of human events, ordinary men always manage to surprise.

AFTERWORD

Suspense in Geneva

The future struggles against being mastered.

—Latin proverb

Geneva—March 1993

GENEVA IN MARCH is usually springlike. Although the surrounding mountains are still rimmed with white, the city nestles in a warmer valley and the blooming flowers add a festive air to the annual Geneva Auto Show. This year, it was still winter, with chilly winds rippling the glasslike surface of Lake Leman, and visitors scurrying to get in out of the cold.

On press day, thousands of people traveled the underground passages that linked the airport to the vast Palexpo Exhibition Center, where the show was being held. Geneva was one of the industry's favorite shows. Here, the elite came to see and be seen, enjoying the elegance of the Swiss event. Café au lait, espresso, and croissants were laid out at every auto company stand, and most had big buckets of champagne, which flowed throughout the day. By midafternoon the air in the hall was thick with cigarette smoke and the din of thousands of voices.

The Geneva show was important for every company, since Switzerland was an open market. Although the Swiss tended to be status conscious and elitist, they were very open in their buying habits. A Swiss family might own both an Opel and a Jeep, as well as a small Japanese car. Japanese vehicles accounted for 25 percent of all sales, and GM and Ford sold briskly. The main criterion in this land of mountains was sturdy construction.

What was clear to me as I walked through the show was that here, in this most international of cities, the high-stakes auto industry was playing out a life-and-death game. I wondered if some of the world's most famous brands would still be around two years from now. Rolls-Royce, Lotus, and Lamborghini were all for sale, but so far there were no serious bidders. Alejandro De Tomaso, the flamboyant owner of Maserati, was gravely ill. At the Geneva show the stands of these venerable makers were noticeably quiet. Normally, the world press would be swarming over the hot red Ferraris. But not now. Perhaps it was the recession that was causing spirits to sag and press attention to turn to more practical modes of transportation. Perhaps it was that no one wanted to ask potentially embarrassing questions about the futures of these and other small specialty cars—especially at a time when world problems seemed so overwhelming and such models seemed a contradiction to the social and economic turmoil.

The activity in Geneva was centered on the mass producers. Ford introduced its new $6-billion world car, Mondeo. The car had already received favorable press, so the management at Ford's stand had the relaxed demeanor of winners.

Perpendicular to Ford on the mezzanine level of the hall were Opel and GM's American cars. At 10:00 A.M. on press day, Lou Hughes presided over the official launch of the Corsa, Opel's new subcompact car. The sturdy, rounded little car could almost be called cute from one angle and tough from another. There had been some discussion among GM and Opel hierarchy before the show about whether they should reveal that the Corsa was designed by twenty-year Opel veteran Hideo Kodama. How would people react to a German Opel designed by a Japanese—even one who had worked for the company so many years? They eventually did decide to give credit to Kodama, who had done a great job.

Opel had reason to be proud of the car and its ability to embrace other nationalities. GM knew it had a winner as journalists crowded the stand, photographing the car from every angle and bombarding the large contingent of GM executives with questions.

Several new models—Corsa, Mondeo, Nissan's Micra, and the Renault Twingo—were proving that designers could have fun with smaller cars. They were a radical departure from the slab-sided cars produced by Volkswagen and its sister models from SEAT and Skoda—which looked decidedly dated against the splashier newcomers.

Volkswagen's stand was crowded, but the press was disappointed that Ferdinand Piech had not made the trip. The official reason was that Piech was nursing the flu. While no one doubted the validity of the excuse, some press members thought it well timed, considering his distaste for public spectacles. Furthermore, by not being there, he could avoid having to comment on the upheaval in his company, and the grim news that was starting to pour out about the company's financial performance. In the first three months of the year, VW would lose an astounding 1.25 billion marks, despite strong production. Costs were simply out of control. Other Volkswagen executives present were circumspect about answering questions. At the stand, VW executives Martin Posth and Ulrich Seiffert responded tentatively to questions by journalists, and were always accompanied by a member of VW's PR department. No one wanted to make a statement that might jeopardize his career.

There was plenty of open speculation among others about the future of Piech's executive team. One name after another was floated as being on the way out. And one notorious name was said to be on the way *in*. In the weeks before the show, there had been a steady stream of rumors that Ferdinand Piech had offered Inaki Lopez a phenomenal sum of money to leave GM and take over VW's purchasing and production. Lopez was being maddeningly coy about the offer, refusing either to confirm or deny rumors that he was leaving General Motors. No one knew what Lopez would do—not even Jack Smith.

Even if Lopez went to Volkswagen, it was questionable how

much he could accomplish in a company that was becoming known as the basket case of Europe, and where his methods would surely slash jobs in Lower Saxony.

Piech's company was in a state of chaos, and he was doing a slash-and-burn on his inherited management. A rumored victim was Goeudevert, who was present in Geneva with the unhappy task of confirming to the press the magnitude of the company's losses. Volkswagen was the talk of the Geneva show among German carmakers. "They are," said one observer, "in a hopeless state of mind, with no clear leadership, no clear goals, no vision or direction."

On March 4 Piech would pull himself out of bed to appear before a meeting of employees. He told them that his goal was to turn a profit in 1993, but to do this would require massive cost cutting and increased productivity. Taking a page out of the Japanese guide for manufacturing success, he said, "Productivity has to be increased with the introduction of leaner and faster production processes." He concluded his speech with these words: "Successful management philosophies are rooted in the idea that employees share common values and cooperate on the grounds of mutual trust and respect." Perhaps Piech knew as he spoke that this mandate was difficult for a company that had been so rigid and indulgent for so long. But the response of the employees was lukewarm. They got nervous whenever anyone started talking about efficiency and cooperation. To them, that meant fewer jobs.

The first sight that greeted the press as they entered the hall in Geneva was the Lexus stand. Toyota had reason to boast about its new luxury car in the heart of luxury car land. Mercedes and BMW were still shaking their corporate heads over the inroads Lexus had made in their traditional markets. All along, they'd said there was no such thing as a prestige Japanese car—certainly not one that could meet their own finely honed standards. Yet there it was, daring them on their own turf.

The success of the Lexus was a perfect example of how complacency inevitably cripples a company—and why the specialty car manufacturers were fighting for their lives. It was once believed that costs determined prices and luxury cars were outrageously expensive to build. But somewhere along the line, Europe's prestigious luxury carmakers were consumed by their own sense of exclusivity. Their cars became so expensive to produce that they no longer conveyed a sense of value. It seemed foolish to pay such high prices when a Lexus could do as much for less money. Luxury car makers have to come to grips with reality or face disaster—as Jaguar learned. When Ford bought the dying company, it took 700 man-hours to assemble a car—as opposed to between 20 and 40 man-hours for most other cars. It occurred to the knighted former chairman of Jaguar, John Egan, that they were on a path to extinction, but he never made any real effort to lower the man-hours per car. Seven hundred man-hours was part of the cachet of hand-sewn seats and laboriously milled and finished walnut trim. Since purchasing Jaguar, Ford has reduced assembly time to 150 man-hours—still high, but a vast improvement.

Lexus proved that a luxury performance car could be produced at mass-production costs. Its success turned the industry upside down.

Alarmed by the enormity and price of transforming their product line and the need to invest in America, Daimler Benz (maker of Mercedes) would opt to comply with American accounting rules so that it could list shares on the New York Stock Exchange. This was a revolutionary action for the German company, since it had to yield on disclosure issues that would provide shareholders with more financial information. Daimler Benz's move jeopardized the old clubbiness that characterized German companies, but it marked a new imperative for companies that sought international status. In Germany, reunification has created such a huge demand for cash that major German companies are expected to follow Daimler's lead in order to raise money in the United States.

But if Toyota's stand was the most threatening at the Geneva show, Nissan's was the most lavish. On a large stage, disco music accompanied six dancing girls, dressed in black with gold bangles, who twirled around rotating platforms featuring Nissan's European star, the Micra. The Micra, assembled in Nissan's new

British plant, had been named European Car of the Year in 1992. The award, which was the result of the votes of journalists from all countries, had never been given to a Japanese carmaker, and Nissan had reason to be proud.

Yet, despite the festive air that surrounded the car, Nissan's executives had to fight to conceal their gloom. A week before the show, Nissan had made what was for a Japanese company an unprecedented announcement: It would reduce its salaried work force by five thousand, close the renowned Zama factory near Tokyo, and shrink its product lines. Normally, Japanese companies did not make such public admissions of failure, preferring to suffer silently and hope for a miracle. Nissan's action was remarkable because it showed just how far the Japanese auto industry had fallen in only two years. No company, not even the rich and powerful Toyota, would be immune from the tough economic realities of recession in all of their major markets.

Japanese automakers had other problems to contemplate, even as they presented a confident face in Geneva. The new American president, Bill Clinton, was taking a tougher stance than Bush had on America's trade deficit, and the Europeans were arguing about the appropriate level of Japanese exports for the year. It was clear that the free-trade era that had given the Japanese auto industry the ability to swarm over Western competitors on their own turf was over.

Even more worrisome was America's desire for a cheaper dollar. Profits on exports to the United States were almost nonexistent, and now the yen was beginning to inch up toward a record high against the greenback. Ford and Chrysler were clamoring for dumping charges to be brought against the Japanese. They were smelling blood as the yen climbed. Despite the glitter in Geneva, 1993 was looking grim for the Japanese automakers.

Jack Smith was one of the few senior executives in attendance at the Geneva show. On the evening of press day, he hosted a dinner for a group of his executives at the Auberge Lion d'Or in Coligny. The executives sat watching the glittering lights on the promenade bouncing off Lake Leman, jet-lagged but happy. The congenial group traded jokes, gossip, and good-natured ribbing about the events of the day. Smith was upbeat about the GM board meeting he'd attended the day before. For the first time, he'd been able to report progress in North America, and this was tremendously gratifying—even though the ever-irritating Roger Smith (who remained on the board until April) tried to take credit for the turnaround by saying it was the result of his grand plan. Most board members considered his ramblings irrelevant. By now everyone knew the truth.

The GM executives had just learned another piece of news worth celebrating: More GM cars were sold in Japan in January and February than in all of 1992.

To some extent, GM's progress in Japan was the result of the import company Yanase's decision in December to pull out of a forty-year agreement with VW. The owner, Jiro Yanase, felt snubbed when VW insisted on expanding to three dealer channels. He began to look at GM's Opel. Yanase was determined to show Volkswagen that it had made a bad decision. Literally overnight, all of Yanase's dealers—numbering in the thousands—pulled down their VW signs. The next day, virtually in unison, they erected the Opel Blitz—the lightning-bolt emblem that was Opel's logo. In January there was a ceremony to officially welcome Opel to the Yanase family, and Jiro Yanase brought out a Daruma doll—a large, fat doll. It is customary at the beginning of ventures in Japan for one eye of the doll to be painted in. The second eye is painted when the venture meets its goal. With Lou Hughes standing next to him, Yanase happily painted in the first eye.

Immediately following the ceremony, Yanase's twelve thousand salesmen flooded Japan's cities selling Opels. In the first two months of the year, GM had the satisfaction of beating VW—long the best-selling foreign brand in Japan.

The Daruma doll was placed in Lou Hughes's office. When sales exceeded eight thousand, Jiro Yanase would join him for a ceremony to paint in the other eye.

At dinner that night in Coligny, Volkswagen was much on the minds of the GM executives. They talked about how aggressive Piech was in pursuing people from GM. It was estimated that between forty and fifty of the company's international staff had been approached with offers of higher compensation, free housing, and other perks. Hughes was on a lean budget and he knew he could not afford to outbid Volkswagen. But he wrote a personal letter to each of his managers expressing his appreciation for their hard work and loyalty, and so far he had lost only two people to VW. The note of appreciation underscored the sense of teamwork and spirit in Opel that had contributed to its success.

Jack Smith said little about Volkwagen's talent grab, although it was known that he had called Piech over Christmas and told him to "lay off my people." No doubt that night he was thinking about Inaki Lopez, his good friend and invaluable colleague. Would the man who had once vowed that he would cut off his right arm for Smith now leave him to join the competition?

Detroit—March 1993

NOTHING in Jack Smith's experience or imagination could have prepared him for the wild ride that Ferdinand Piech and Inaki Lopez were about to take him on. Within days of the Geneva show, word was out that Lopez had chosen to move to Volkswagen. The deciding factor wasn't necessarily the lavish salary (reported at $20 million over five years), the elevated position as one of VW's top three executives, in charge of purchasing and production, or Lopez's supposed desire to return to Europe. Rather, it seemed to be Piech's promise to allow him to build a new factory in Viscaya, Spain, Lopez's birthplace. Lopez was like a man possessed when it came to the longing for such a factory, which he believed would transform a poor region in Spain. The plant of his dreams was to be the most modern and innovative in the world, using his Plateau 6 concept of producing a car in only ten man-hours.

Lopez's nationalistic spirit was renowned. At a meeting of suppliers the weekend before he announced his decision to leave GM, Lopez digressed from his remarks to ask a group of reporters to stand. He then launched into a monologue about the heroes of the press who had stood firm against the Spanish military after the death of Franco.

The timing and nature of the supplier meeting itself was suspect, given the rumors about Lopez. The meeting, along with a special dinner to present the company's Worldwide Suppliers of the Year Awards, was originally scheduled for May. There was some speculation that Lopez pushed to have the event take place earlier, knowing he would be leaving General Motors. Many of the award recipients had no idea why they were chosen, and it may have been meaningful, from Lopez's viewpoint, that the Corporation of the Year award was given to a European, not an American, company. Each company received a small trophy, designed by a Spanish sculptor—of course.

From a corporate standpoint, Piech's promise to build Lopez a factory in Spain seemed crazy. The last thing Volkswagen needed was another assembly plant—especially since workers at SEAT were already facing job reductions and the entire company (as well as the European car industry) was suffering from overcapacity. But Lopez made the Spanish plant his pivotal negotiating point, and Piech was willing to offer him anything he wanted. Whether Piech would ultimately keep his promise once Lopez was on board was another matter.

On Wednesday, March 10, Lopez handed Smith his letter of resignation, and the world began to speculate about the damage his leaving might do to the gradually reviving General Motors.

The day Lopez announced his resignation, the mood in GM's purchasing office was funereal. Many of his staff, who drew their energy and identity from Lopez's messianic personality, were sobbing uncontrollably. They begged Jack Smith to do something to keep Lopez at GM, and Lopez himself was flooded with calls and visits from people asking him to reconsider. When Smith approached him, Lopez made it clear that his decision wasn't a question of title or money. It was about the plant in Viscaya.

In desperation, Smith put in a call to Lou Hughes in Zurich. "Could we possibly justify building a new plant in Viscaya?" he asked.

"No way," Hughes replied. "Volkswagen can't justify it either."

That Smith would even ask such a question was indicative of the manipulative power of Lopez. His star had become so bright that it had effectively blinded two normally savvy men (Piech and

Smith) to common sense. Indeed, Lopez's power play had taken on so much momentum (fed by an avalanche of stories in the media) that the two giant companies were poised to take unsupportable risks to win the prize of his acceptance.

On Friday, Smith, Harry Pearce, and Rick Wagoner, GM's chief financial officer, drove to Lopez's house to try one last time to persuade him to stay. They urged him not to trust Piech, and said that the promise to build a plant in Viscaya was nonsense, possibly a trap. Smith offered him the plum job he had always wanted—executive vice-president and president of North American operations, the second most important job at GM.

Lopez nodded his head. He smiled at Smith, the man he was fond of calling "my leader," and said yes, he would stay, despite the fact that he had apparently signed a contract commiting him to go to VW.

When Piech heard the news, he reacted bitterly. Lopez had come under "persistent interventions" from people at GM, he told the press, making it sound like the worst skullduggery. The pressure, he said, had just been too great.

On Monday morning the relieved GM board agreed unanimously by phone to make Lopez the head of NAOO. Calling to congratulate him after the meeting, Harry Pearce found a jubilant Lopez, who was thrilled to be back on board and couldn't wait to take over his new responsibilities. A press conference was scheduled for 3:00 that afternoon. There was a feeling around the company that it would be in the manner of a public coronation.

But something went wrong.

When Smith walked into the press conference, his face was tight with frustration and barely disguised anger, and his eyes were red. He made no effort to cover up the reason for his dismay. "Today I intended to announce that Inaki Lopez was staying with General Motors and would be given added responsibilities," he said. "Unfortunately, a short time ago, Mr. Lopez sent me a letter saying he was not going to accept the position and is leaving General Motors. It is not clear to me what his intentions are or where he is at this time.

"This morning," he continued, "everything appeared to be on schedule. The GM board of directors endorsed Mr. Lopez's election as a GM executive vice-president and president of NAOO . . . Mr. Lopez was in his office this morning and appeared to be upbeat in his activities. Shortly after 10:00 A.M., Harry Pearce called him and congratulated him on the fact that the board had given his new appointment unanimous support. At approximately 1:00 P.M., a friend of Mr. Lopez delivered a handwritten note from him saying he again was resigning from GM."

Even as Smith was speaking, Lopez was already at Metro Airport preparing to fly to Germany. No one knew precisely what had happened. Had he intended to go to VW all along? Had something happened that morning that made him change his mind again? Was he just crazy—or cruelly manipulative? There were even suggestions that it was Lopez who first approached VW about a job, not the other way around—calling into question the sincerity of Lopez's much-publicized inner struggle.

In the coming days, the focus of conversation in the company was not so much on Lopez's decision to leave, but on the nature of the game he had played. The contents of his final letter to Smith remained a secret, but one person close to Smith said that it was rambling and effusive. Lopez referred to Smith as "my brother" and told him he loved him. But was this any way to treat a brother?

In practical terms, not everyone at GM was so disappointed to see Lopez go. One executive speculated that "if Lopez had stayed and been put in charge of North American operations, Jack Smith would have had a rebellion on his hands. Lopez may have been adored by some, but he preferred to surround himself with second-rate yes-men whom he could manipulate at will. As brilliant and effective as Lopez had been, there was little proof that he could run an entire company. He may have done Smith a very big favor by leaving."

That should have been the end of it. GM would pick up the pieces and move on. Lopez would make a victorious appearance before the *Aufsichtsrat* on March 16 and begin his new job at Volkswagen. But things just got stranger and stranger.

On March 17 Lopez called his old mentor, Hans Huskes, who had first brought him to Smith's attention. Huskes called Lou

Hughes. "Lopez wants to come back," he told him as though this was good news. "We should call Jack."

Hughes said no. "My God, Inaki was elected to the Vorstand last night, this is ridiculous. He has burned his bridges here."

Huskes was determined. He called Smith himself, but was told to his amazement, "It's all over."

Lopez's overture was particularly strange in light of Ferdinand Piech's later claim that Lopez had approached him about a job (not the other way around) as early as November 1992. "He got in touch with me," Piech said in an interview with *Financial Times*. "I did not try to woo him."

Meanwhile, General Motors was taking steps to stop Piech and Lopez in their tracks. As soon as rumors had surfaced that Lopez might be going to VW, Lou Hughes realized that he would try to raid GM-Europe as the easiest way to get a running start. Even before Lopez made an official announcement, GM had determined its strategy, putting together a list of the people Lopez was most likely to call. After Lopez had left GM, Hughes met with these people. He asked them to stick together, and they agreed. Everyone was disgusted by the way Lopez had behaved. His absence of decency had made their former hero untrustworthy. To a person, all of the purchasing staff signed a voluntary contract that locked them into five years with GM plus an additional two-year noncompete clause. Each of them agreed to contact GM if Lopez or VW made any overtures. Then they sat back and waited.

A week went by before the calls came—first from a VW consultant, then from an associate, and finally from Lopez himself. He started with the top layer of purchasing executives and systematically worked his way down the list. The offers were mouth-watering: two to three times the salary they were currently making, a free house, two cars—whatever it took. As they were instructed, everyone who received calls pretended to be interested. Then they reported to Lou Hughes.

Within a week, Lopez had approached twenty-nine people from GM-Europe, and GM was prepared to file a suit against VW. "We can prove that this was systematic raiding, which is illegal in Germany," an executive explained. "We also have concerns that Lopez and his people took proprietary information when they left Detroit." GM said that certain competitively sensitive materials, including documents relating to GM's future products and strategies, could not be found in Lopez's files after he left. Further, GM was looking into Lopez's behavior at the International Strategy Board meeting he attended shortly before he resigned. "We have an excellent case," the GM executive said.

Meanwhile, Lopez was being ridiculed in the German press for his lack of honor and the way he had publicly embarrassed and betrayed Jack Smith. His first months on the job were marked by anger and criticism from VW suppliers, who were suspicious of his intentions. Gerhard Schroeder, minister president of Lower Saxony and member of the *Aufsichtsrat,* pleaded for the media to cease writing negative articles about Lopez. And he called upon GM and VW to stop fighting each other and concentrate on fighting the Japanese. Schroeder also mediated a special meeting between Piech and Lopez and their suppliers, in an attempt to lower the decibel level. But things would not be as easy for Lopez in Wolfsburg as they had been in Detroit.

The story of Inaki Lopez and his impact on the global car companies remains unfinished. But there is something epic about it— like a great morality tale fitting the size of the industry. For as much as we know that one man (or woman) can make a radical impact on a company, we also see in the story of Inaki Lopez how easy it is to give charismatic characters too much power. Charisma can be as dangerous as it is inspiring.

There is another issue, too, regarding loyalty to the company. Lopez always talked big about his life-and-death loyalty to Jack Smith and General Motors, but, in truth, such a concept is quite foreign to Western corporations. For the Japanese, on the other hand, it's very real. Not only is the company committed to be loyal to its employees (witness lifetime employment), but the employees are loyal to the company. Even in the face of humiliation and demotion, it is almost unthinkable for a Japanese executive to forsake his company for another—much less a foreign one.

Today, Ferdinand Piech and Inaki Lopez are joined together in what promises to be a very rocky, and possibly short-lived, marriage. One VW consultant remarked, "We only need Lopez for three years, then we'll do the rest." Who can say what this unpredictable team will do?

I am often struck by the human drama of this industry. It's not surprising that it would be this way when you consider how much is at stake. But the real crux of the industry transcends individuals, who come and go in the predictable course of history. There is a more enduring truth to be examined.

In my twenty years as an auto industry analyst, various theories about the industry have come and gone. It was once believed that auto companies must diversify to survive, since cars alone provided limited opportunity for growth. That theory proved to be folly. Many automakers were certain that luxury cars could only be built by specialty companies. We've seen that idea bite the dust. Most people thought if you were the biggest company in the world, you couldn't go out of business. GM came fearfully close to proving that theory wrong. At various times, the death knell has sounded for companies that later came back to life—Chrysler comes to mind. Few theories about the car industry ever prove enduring.

Yet, I am growing increasingly certain of one simple fact: If a car company, large or small, wants to survive, it has to know who it is and who its customers are. There's an assumption that every car company strives to be the greatest in the world—to be number one. But it is not so important to be number one. Good car companies like Ford and Chrysler will no doubt continue to produce fine vehicles and make money. So will Nissan, if it gets its house in order. Mercedes and BMW will find new ways to produce luxury cars—if they're smart, learning from Toyota. Some smaller specialty companies may not survive, but others will. As long as companies have strong identities and determine to be the best they can be at what they do, they will continue to operate in an industry that makes room for many kinds of companies, and in a world that welcomes many brands of cars.

Selected Bibliography

Abegglen, James C., and Stalk, George, Jr. *Kaisha—The Japanese Corporation: How Marketing, Money and Manpower Strategy, Not Management Style, Make the Japanese World Pacesetters.* New York: Basic Books, 1985.

Altshuler, Alan, et al. *The Future of the Automobile.* Cambridge: MIT Press, 1984.

Anesen, Peter J., ed. *The Japanese Competition—Phase 2.* Ann Arbor: University of Michigan Press, 1987.

Bacarr, Jina. *How to Work for a Japanese Boss.* New York: Birch Lane Books, 1992.

Bailey, L. Scott, et al. *GM: The First 75 Years of Transportation Products.* Detroit: General Motors, 1982.

Ballon, Robert J., and Tomita, Iwao. *The Financial Behavior of Japanese Corporations.* Tokyo: Kodansha International, 1988.

Barnett, Steve, ed. *The Nissan Report: An Inside Look at How a World-Class Japanese Company Makes Products That Make a Difference.* New York: Doubleday, 1992.

Beasley, W. G. *The Rise of Modern Japan.* Tokyo: Charles E. Tuttle Co., 1990.

Befu, Harumi. *Japan: An Anthropological Introduction.* Tokyo: Charles E. Tuttle Co., 1971.

Bergner, Jeffrey T. *The New Superpowers—Germany, Japan, the U.S., and the New World Order.* New York: St. Martin's Press, 1991.

Bhaskar, Krish. *The Future of the World Motor Industry.* London: Kogan Page Ltd., 1980.

Chandler, Alfred D., Jr., and Salsbury, Stephen. *Pierre S. du Pont and the Making of the Modern Corporation.* New York: Harper & Row, 1971.

Chang, C. S. *The Japanese Auto Industry and the U.S. Market.* New York: Praeger Publishers, 1981.

Chapman, William. *Inventing Japan: An Unconventional Account of the Post-War Years.* New York: Prentice-Hall Press, 1991.

Christopher, Robert C. *The Japanese Mind: The Goliah Explained.* Tokyo: Charles E. Tuttle Co., 1983.

Clark, Kim B., and Fujimoto, Takahiro. *Product Development, Performance Strategy, Organization and Management in the World Auto Industry.* Cambridge: Harvard Business School Press, 1991.

Clark, Rodney. *The Japanese Company.* Tokyo: Charles E. Tuttle Co., 1979.

Cole, Robert, et al., eds. *The American and Japanese Auto Industries in Transition.* Ann Arbor: University of Michigan Press, 1984.

Collins, Robert J. *Japan-Think, Ameri-Think: An Irreverent Guide to Understanding the Cultural Differences Between Us.* New York: Penguin Books, 1992.

Cray, Ed. *Chrome Colossus: General Motors and Its Times.* New York: McGraw-Hill, 1980.

Cusumano, Michael A. *The Japanese Automobile Industry: Technology and Management at Nissan and Toyota.* Cambridge: Harvard University Press, 1989.

Dauch, Richard E. *Passion for Manufacturing: Real World Advice from Dick Dauch, the Man Who Engineered the Manufacturing Renaissance at Chrysler.* Dearborn, Mich.: Society of Manufacturing Engineers, 1993.

Deming, W. Edwards. *Out of the Crisis.* Cambridge: MIT Press, 1992.

Dertouzos, Michael L.; Lester, Richard K.; and Solow, Robert M. *Made in America: Regaining the Competitive Edge.* Cambridge: MIT Press, 1989.

Dore, Ronald. *British Factory—Japanese Factory: The Origins of National Diversity in Industrial Relations.* Berkeley: University of California Press, 1973.

Drucker, Peter F. *Managing for the Future: The 1990s and Beyond.* New York: E. P. Dutton, 1992.

———. *Adventures of a Bystander: Memoirs.* HarperCollins, 1978, 1991.

———. *Management: Tasks, Responsibilities, Practices.* New York: Harper & Row, 1973.

Emmott, Bill. *The Sun Also Sets: Why Japan Will Not Be Number One.* New York: Simon & Schuster, 1989.

Encarnation, Dennis J. *Rivals Beyond Trade: America Versus Japan in Global Competition.* Ithaca, N.Y.: Cornell University Press, 1992.

Fallows, James. *More Like Us: Making America Great Again.* Boston: Houghton Mifflin Co., 1989.

Frost, Ellen L. *For Richer, for Poorer: The New U.S.–Japan Relationship.* Washington, D.C.: Council on Foreign Relations, 1987.

Fucini, Joseph J., and Fucini, Suzy. *Working for the Japanese: Inside Mazda's American Auto Plant.* New York: The Free Press/Macmillan, 1990.

Garrahan, Philip, and Steward, Paul. *The Nissan Enigma: Flexibility at Work in a Local Economy.* London: Mansell Publishing Ltd., 1992.

Gelsanliter, David. *Jumpstart: Japan Comes to the Heartland*. New York: Farrar, Straus and Giroux, 1992.

Gercik, Patricia. *On Track with the Japanese*. Tokyo: Kodansha International, 1992.

Gustin, Lawrence R. *Billy Durant—Creator of General Motors*. Flushing, Mich.: Craneshaw Publishers, 1984.

Halberstam, David. *The Reckoning*. New York: William Morrow & Co., 1986.

Hamper, Ben. *Rivethead: Tales from the Assembly Line*. New York: Warner Books, 1986.

Harbour, James E., et al. *The Harbour Report: Competitive Assessment of the North American Automotive Industry, 1989–1992*. Troy, Mich.: Harbour and Associates, Inc., 1992.

Holstein, William J. *The Japanese Power Game: What It Means for America*. New York: Penguin Books, 1990.

Hyoe, Murakami. *Japan: The Years of Trial—1919–52*. Tokyo: Japan Culture Institute, 1982.

Imai, Masaaki. *Kaizen—The Key to Japan's Competitive Success*. New York: McGraw-Hill, 1986.

Ishihara, Shintaro. *The Japan That Can Say No: Why Japan Will Be the First Among Equals*. New York: Simon & Schuster, 1989.

Iyer, Pico. *The Lady and the Monk: Four Seasons in Kyoto*. New York: Alfred A. Knopf, 1991.

Johnson, Chalmers. *MITI and the Japanese Miracle: The Growth of Industrial Policy, 1925–1975*. Stanford, Calif.: Stanford University Press, 1982.

Kato, Seisi. *My Years with Toyota*. Tokyo: Toyota Motor Sales Ltd., 1981.

Kearns, Robert L. *Zaibatsu America: How Japanese Firms Are Colonizing Vital U.S. Industries*. New York: The Free Press/Macmillan, 1992.

Keller, Maryann. *Rude Awakening: The Rise, Fall and Struggle for Recovery of General Motors*. New York: William Morrow & Co., 1989.

Kester, W. Carl. *Japanese Takeovers: The Global Contest for Corporate Control*. Cambridge: Harvard Business School Press, 1991.

Kotter, John P., and Heskett, James L. *Corporate Culture and Performance*. New York: The Free Press/Macmillan, 1992.

Lewis, Flora. *Europe—Road to Unity*. New York: Simon & Schuster, 1987, 1992.

Lewis, Michael. *Pacific Rift: Adventures in the Fault Zone Between the U.S. and Japan*. New York: W. W. Norton & Co., 1991.

Lincoln, Edward J. *Japan's Unequal Trade*. Washington, D.C.: The Brookings Institution, 1990.

———. *Japan: Facing Economic Maturity*. Washington, D.C.: The Brookings Institution, 1988.

Lu, David J. *Inside Corporate Japan: The Art of Fumble-Free Management*. Tokyo: Charles E. Tuttle Co., 1987.

Mason, R. H. P., and Caiger, J. G. *A History of Japan*. Tokyo: Charles E. Tuttle Co., 1972.

McKinsey & Co. *Japan Business—Obstacles and Opportunities*. Tokyo: McKinsey & Co., 1983.

Mitsukini, Yoshida, et al., eds. *The Compact Culture: The Ethos of Japanese Life*. Tokyo: Cosmos Public Relations, 1982.

Monden, Yasuhiro. *Toyota Production System*. Norcross, Ga.: Institute of Industrial Engineers, 1983.

Monnich, Horst. *The BMW Story: A Company in Its Time*. London: Sidgwick & Jackson Ltd., 1991.

Morita, Akio, with Reingold, Edwin M., and Shimomura, Mitsuko. *Made in Japan: Akio Morita and Sony*. New York: E. P. Dutton, 1986.

Nakne, Chie. *Japanese Society*. Tokyo: Charles E. Tuttle Co., 1970.

Nelson, Walter Henry. *Small Wonder: The Amazing Story of the Volkswagen*. Boston: Little, Brown & Co., 1965.

O'Barr, William M., and Conley, John M. *Fortune & Folly: The Wealth and Power of Institutional Investing*. Homewood, Ill.: Business One Irwin, 1992.

Ohno, Taiishi. *Toyota Production System—Beyond Large-Scale Production*. Cambridge, Mass.: Productivity Press, 1978.

Ohno, Taiishi, with Mito, Setsuo. *Just-in-Time for Today and Tomorrow*. Tokyo: Diamond, Inc., 1986.

Okita, Saburo. *Japan in the World Economy of the 1980s*. Tokyo: University of Tokyo Press, 1989.

Oppenheim, Phillip. *Japan Without Blinders: Coming to Terms with Japan's Economic Success*. Tokyo: Kodansha International, 1991.

Porter, Michael E. *The Competitive Advantage of Nations*. New York: The Free Press/Macmillan, 1990.

Reich, Robert B. *The Work of Nations*. New York: Vintage Books, 1991.

———. *The Next American Frontier*. New York: Times Books, 1983.

Reischauer, Edwin O. *The Japanese*. Cambridge: Harvard University Press, 1977.

Richardson, Bradley M., and Ueda, Taizo, eds. *Business and Society in Japan: Fundamentals for Businessmen*. New York: Praeger Publishers, 1981.

Rohlen, Thomas P. *For Harmony & Strength: Japanese White-Collar Organization in Anthropological Perspective*. Berkeley: University of California Press, 1974.

Schneider, Peter. *The German Comedy: Scenes of Life After the Wall*. New York: Farrar, Straus and Giroux, 1991.

Schreiber, J. J. Servan. *The American Challenge*. New York: Atheneum, 1968.

Shibagahi, Kazuo, et al., eds. *Japanese and European Management: Their International Adaptability*. Tokyo: University of Tokyo Press, 1980.

Shirer, William L. *The Rise and Fall of the Third Reich: A History of Nazi Germany*. New York: Simon & Schuster, 1960.

Shuler, Terry, with Borgeson, Griffith, and Sloniger, Jerry. *The Origin and*

Evolution of the VW Beetle. Princeton, N.J.: Princeton Publishing Company, 1985.

Sloan, Alfred P. *My Years with General Motors*. New York: Doubleday, 1963.

Smitka, Michael J. *Competitive Ties: Subcontracting in the Japanese Automotive Industry*. New York: Columbia University Press, 1991.

Speer, Albert. *Inside the Third Reich: Memoirs*. New York: Macmillan Company, 1970.

Stares, Paul B., ed. *The New Germany and the New Europe*. Washington, D.C.: The Brookings Institution, 1992.

Steele, Jonathan. *Inside East Germany: The State That Came in from the Cold*. New York: Urizen Books, 1977.

Taylor, Jared. *Shadows of the Rising Sun: A Critical View of the "Japanese Miracle."* Tokyo: Charles E. Tuttle Co., 1983.

Thurow, Lester. *Head to Head: The Coming Economic Battle Among Japan, Europe and America*. New York: William Morrow & Co., 1992.

Toyoda, Eiji. *Toyota—Fifty Years in Motion*. Tokyo: Kodansha International, 1985.

Toyota: A History of the First 50 Years. Toyota Motor Corporation, 1988.

Tsurumi, Yoshi. *The Japanese Are Coming: A Multinational Interaction of Firms and Politics*. Cambridge, Mass.: Ballinger Publishing Co., 1976.

Turner, Henry Ashby, Jr. *The Two Germanies Since 1945*. New Haven, Conn.: Yale University Press, 1987.

van Wolferen, Karel. *The Enigma of Japanese Power*. London: Macmillan, 1989.

Walton, Mary. *Deming Management at Work: Six Successful Companies That Use the Quality Principles of W. Edwards Deming*. New York: G. P. Putnam's Sons, 1991.

Womack, James P.; Jones, Daniel T.; and Roos, Daniel. *The Machine That Changed the World*. Cambridge: MIT Press, 1990.

Woronoff, Jon. *The Japanese Management Mystique: The Reality Behind the Myth*. Chicago: Probus Publishing Co., 1992.

Wright, J. Patrick. *On a Clear Day You Can See General Motors: John Z. DeLorean's Look Inside the Automotive Giant*. Grosse Pointe, Mich.: Wright Enterprises, 1979.

Yoshino, M. Y., and Lifson, Thomas B. *The Invisible Link: Japan's Sogo Shosha and the Organization of Trade*. Cambridge: MIT Press, 1986.

Index